Intimacy

ALSO AVAILABLE FROM BLOOMSBURY

Desire in Ashes, edited by Simon Morgan Wortham and Chiara Alfano

Dialectic of Enlightenment, Max Horkheimer and Theodor Adorno

Dialectic of Romanticism, Peter Murphy

Negative Dialectics, Theodor W. Adorno

The Suspension of Reason in Hegel and Schelling, Christopher Lauer

Intimacy

A Dialectical Study

CHRISTOPHER LAUER

Bloomsbury Academic
An imprint of Bloomsbury Publishing Plc

B L O O M S B U R Y
LONDON · OXFORD · NEW YORK · NEW DELHI · SYDNEY

Bloomsbury Academic

An imprint of Bloomsbury Publishing Plc

50 Bedford Square	1385 Broadway
London	New York
WC1B 3DP	NY 10018
UK	USA

www.bloomsbury.com

BLOOMSBURY and the Diana logo are trademarks of Bloomsbury Publishing Plc

First published 2016

© Christopher Lauer, 2016

Christopher Lauer has asserted his right under the Copyright, Designs and Patents Act, 1988, to be identified as Author of this work.

British Library Cataloguing-in-Publication Data
A catalogue record for this book is available from the British Library.

ISBN: HB: 9781474226257
PB: 9781474226264
ePDF: 9781474226271
ePub: 9781474226288

Library of Congress Cataloging-in-Publication Data
Lauer, Christopher, author.
Intimacy : a dialectical study / Christopher Lauer.
pages cm
Includes bibliographical references and index.
ISBN 978-1-4742-2625-7 (hardback)– ISBN 978-1-4742-2626-4 (pb)–
ISBN 978-1-4742-2627-1 (epdf) 1. Intimacy (Psychology)–Philosophy. 2. Interpersonal relations–Philosophy. I. Title.
BF575.I5L38 2016
128'.4–dc23
2015019657

Typeset by Fakenham Prepress Solutions, Fakenham, Norfolk NR21 8NN

To Quyen, for showing me the ropes

Contents

Introduction 1

Intimacy and feeling 3

Dialectics 4

Limitations of dialectics 11

Note on terminology 14

1 The Gift 17

Initiation 17

Appeal and delay 21

Absenting 25

A measured gift: Lysias's speech 28

2 Touching 33

Touching as shared experience 34

Proportion 36

The myth of the inmost touch 38

The wound 41

3 The Heartbeat 45

Systole and diastole 47

Indifference and longing 54

4 The Between 57

God and the space between 59

The rupture 67

Accessibility 69

5 The Fetish 71

The interest 72

The fetishized body 75

The promise 80

6 Embedding 83

The secret 84
The third 85
The neutralized third: Gossip 89
The generalized third: Irony 89
Fraudulence 95

7 Conflict 99

The dismissal 102
The dispute 105
Violence 109
Withdrawal 110
Debate 111

8 The *Mêlée* 115

Consumption, destruction and waste 116
Laughter 118
Frenzy 121
Millenarianism 123

9 The Future 125

The test 126
The commitment 127
Planning 129
Identification 132
Anticipatory mourning 135

10 Mourning 139

Gathering and retraction 142
Haunting 145
Singularity 149

Afterword 155

Notes 161
Bibliography 199
Index 207

Introduction

From time to time life conspires to convince us that genuine intimacy is impossible. When a friendship or love affair breaks up, when we lose someone close to us, or even when a closeness we once felt is suddenly transformed into an alienating and insuperable difference, it doesn't feel like sour grapes to say that no one is ever really intimate with anyone else. Instead, it feels like a sudden clearing when we are finally able to reflect that what we previously experienced as genuine closeness was nothing but the dream of some future fulfilment, that despite how much we were able to share with this person, what was shared were merely things and words, and each of us is, our irrational hopes for an ultimate unity notwithstanding, fundamentally alone in the world.[1]

To judge by the most popular books on the subject, contemporary America would seem to have reached a crisis in intimacy. We've been *Bowling Alone* for nigh on two decades now, find ourselves *Alone Together* in the age of portable access to the internet, and if we want to do anything about it we have little recourse but to turn to *The Complete Idiot's Guide to Intimacy*. Yet even a cursory look at the philosophical canon suggests that we've been 'alone together' for a very long time. Kierkegaard bemoaned the incapacity of his contemporaries to see love as anything more than a deception.[2] Montaigne thought the vast majority of human relationships were bleak and meaningless.[3] And Aristotle's paradoxical assertion 'Friends, there are no friends' still packs a wallop that exceeds mere cynicism. The niggling worry that gave this project its impetus is that intimacy itself asks for something impossible, that this generalized anxiety about the decline of our intimate relationships arises not from any structural changes in the modern world, but from the contradictory demands that comprise the very structure of intimacy.

Intimacy, as I take it, is a kind of recognition. In the twenty-odd years since the publication of Charles Taylor's essay 'The Politics of Recognition', philosophers have given renewed attention to Hegel's claim that the drive for recognition is one of the most important forces in public life. With this attention, it has gradually become clearer that recognition is above all something complicated and cannot be coherently conceived as a public good to which all deserve equal access.[4] When I fight for my rights, wheedle my friends to 'like' my latest essay through Facebook, or ask if you'll still respect me in the morning, I am asking for very different things, and this is true even though one of these types of recognition can often placate me as an adequate substitute for another. Recognition is something I feel I need for my own psychic well-being, and yet it is frustratingly manifold.

It is against the backdrop of this reemerging field that I propose to treat intimacy. Axel Honneth made a similar connection when he proposed that affectionate love, especially the love a parent gives a child, is the most basic form of recognition that human beings desire.[5] Honneth's account is thoroughly researched and attentive to both the microscopic and macroscopic in exactly the way that a dialectical treatment of intimacy demands, but I find the term 'love', particularly in its modern senses, intractably messy. Our modern language of love is attended by so many incompletely overlapping ideologies that it is difficult to say even hypothetically what I want when I ask for love. It mixes valuative ('Am I worthy of love?'), affective ('Is what I'm feeling right now truly love?') and intimate senses ('Our love is greater than any other') indiscriminately, and any effort to work through these senses systematically will probably require a prior understanding of personhood,[6] which I contend is best understood as the *result* of various forms of recognition. Various thinkers have responded to this ambiguity by appealing to the more precise Greek terms *eros*, *agape*, *philia* and *aphroditē*, and there is indeed much to be gained from this precision.[7] It is valuable, after all, to be able to distinguish between forms of love that expect something in return from their object and those that do not and again between the various forms of return that may be sought. But for all its benefits, this neoclassical taxonomy of love does not offer much help in explaining why one form of love may transform into another, and it still includes a number of passions that would be out of place in a dialectic of intimacy. To be sure, I will say a great deal about love in the following pages, but I do not want to saddle myself with the responsibility either to speak to every dimension of love or to confine myself to phenomena contemporary English (or any other natural language) designates with the term 'love'.

The frameworks that Honneth and others have built for understanding recognition are, on the other hand, quite relevant to my project. In any field this vibrant, there will of course be fundamental differences over the nature of the object to be studied, and this is particularly true for the contradictions inherent in the study of recognition. Some, like Taylor and Honneth, have argued that recognition is so crucial to a healthy and fulfilling life that we need to take account of these needs in organizing public institutions. Some, like Nancy Fraser and Christopher Zurn, have argued that thinking of recognition as a need risks distracting from real debates over justice. And some, like James Tully and Patchen Markell,[8] have argued that the drive for recognition is itself so problematic that we ought to reserve our focus for its more reasonable cousin acknowledgement. The lesson of this diversity of perspectives is that recognition is a subject that needs to be worked through on many different levels – a project in which this book aims to play a part. While the debate over recognition provides productive lines of inquiry into some of the central political debates of our time, this does not mean that every inquiry into the structures of recognition must orient itself politically. As we will see, such a perspective that denies the separability of the personal and the political can even be an impediment to the development of intimacy. Instead, I propose to investigate not what *good* intimacy can do for a community or by what *right* everyone ought to be able to pursue it, but the instability inherent in the very concept of intimacy. Such a dialectical approach does not assume any particular form of intimacy as paradigmatic, but asks what intimacy would look like if only it could fulfil its own conditions.

Intimacy and feeling

First, it should be clear that by 'intimacy' I do not refer to any objectively present feeling accessible either through phenomenology or neuroscience. The stalker may feel a great deal of affection toward his crush, and yet even if this feeling is neurochemically quite similar to that of someone in a long-term partnership, it would stretch the term past the breaking point to say that he has achieved a high degree of *intimacy* with the crush. Or take the feelings of familiarity that a drug like MDMA ('ecstasy') induces. These feelings may make one more inclined to participate in acts of intimacy like sharing secrets or close touching, but to mistake these feelings for intimacy itself would so subjectivize intimacy as to hollow out everything that can be shared between two partners. Conversely, patients with Capgras syndrome lose the ability to *feel* like they know a family member, even if their recognition is unimpaired and they can still recall their entire histories with these family members.[9] V. S. Ramachandran describes sufferers of the syndrome who are so disoriented by their lack of this feeling of familiarity that they become convinced that their mothers or dogs are impostors.[10] It is easy to imagine how the intimacy of a relationship might break down without the reinforcement of this feeling of familiarity, but a relationship could also suffer by placing too much of an emphasis on this feeling. The moment I say, 'I feel so close to you right now', I have placed a small barrier between us, and if I obsess about my feelings I retreat into the privacy of my own emotions.[11] To identify intimacy with a feeling or set of feelings is thus not only ontologically misleading; it is itself a potential inhibition of intimacy.[12]

When, on the other hand, we attempt to define intimacy not by a particular feeling but by a psychological function, we are drawn into paradox. 'Intimacy' derives from *intimus*, a superlative of *in*, and thus has the sense of 'inmost' or 'most upon'. An intimate is strangely the person whom one is most *in*. To the extent that 'in' means 'inside', the superlative here would seem to be out of place. Either one is inside another person or one is not. Intimacy longs to overcome this binary and to distinguish particular moments of closeness from others. It demands a closeness beyond closeness. This fundamental and inexpugnable ambiguity derives from the fact that intimacy can refer either to what belongs most to oneself or to another. The *OED* offers as one definition of 'intimate' 'that which relates to, or is indicative of, one's deepest nature, that which is very personal or private'. What is most intimate in this sense is what divides one from others. And yet, when we strive for intimacy in a relationship, we strive for a dissolution of this division. What intimacy *wants* is thus contradictory, and it is only by working through the manifold expressions of this contradiction dialectically that we can begin to see what intimacy *means*.

Dialectics

Like all transformative approaches to philosophy, dialectics has had its share of misadventures. Long before Heidegger called it a 'genuine philosophic embarrassment',[13] the term 'dialectics' had been used as a kind of cover for philosophers' inability to explain the rigour of their own thinking to those who had not yet followed the same path. Whereas a student can be led step-by-step to all the insights of Euclid's geometry, Plato found that certain philosophical conclusions could be reached only through the experience of an encounter with another philosopher. In these cases, an argument attempting a shortcut to the conclusion will come off as sophistry and even lose the entire substance of the conclusion. Yet conversations, as Plato understood, are slippery. Interlocutors can forget to define terms, assent too readily to a demonstration when an alternative explanation is available, and give their assent out of exhaustion rather than true enlightenment. The inevitability of such difficulties has thus at times in the history of philosophy made the term 'dialectical' an epithet, as when the early Kant uses the term as a synonym for 'spurious' or 'scholastically dubious'.[14] A dialectical conclusion is in this sense one corrupted by the prejudices of the philosophical tradition, one that has not yet learned to identify a road or *methodos* to knowledge.

Yet if dialectics does not strictly speaking offer a *methodos*, it does nevertheless advance by weighing reasons. In a word, all dialectical accounts are *hypothetical*. One begins with a presumed thought or striving or structure and shows what must be the case *if* it is followed through on its own terms. Thus when Hegel calls the philosophical movement he recounts a 'dialectic', he purports to show how consciousness must come to understand itself *if* it initially takes the contents of its senses as ultimate reality and how thought must form itself into the absolute idea *if* it posits simple being.[15] Likewise, when Marx introduces a dialectical theory of history,[16] he claims to find laws indicating what must happen *if* certain conditions are present. The laws that govern the historical unfolding of feudalism, for instance, will differ from those that govern capitalism, as will the development of capitalism in each country, and it is the job of contemporary economic theory to understand the laws of economics not absolutely, but given the assumptions and social structures of modern capitalism.[17]

But while there is a formal resemblance between these two patterns of thought, there is also a key difference. Whereas Marx claims to begin with hypotheses whose correlates are clearly identifiable in nature, Hegel resists even this attenuated positivism. In the *Republic*'s allegory of the divided line, Plato has Socrates discuss these two approaches, labelling only the latter as properly dialectical (510b–11e). Geometers, Socrates argues, begin with hypotheses they take to be first principles, such as the non-intersection of parallel lines. Dialecticians, in contrast, treat them as true *hupotheseis*, that is, stepping stones.[18] Rather than deducing their reality from their necessity to reach a conclusion, dialecticians accept that their hypotheses can be discarded as the dialectic progresses. Having grasped 'the unhypothetical first principle of everything' (511b), the dialectician can then retrace his steps without relying on anything perceptible (αἰσθητῷ) at all.

As Hegel shows in the *Phenomenology of Spirit*, however, a dialectic that obscures its surpassed moments as mere steps on the way to some greater knowledge is one that fails to appreciate the limitations of human knowledge.[19] Thus in Hegelian dialectic,[20] the stepping stones are only discarded in the way that a numismatist removes a rare coin from circulation. The coin is indeed withdrawn from the activity that gives it its meaning, but it acquires a new meaning, a mnemonic of its former occupation. Karl Popper once said that our hypotheses die in our stead,[21] but for the Hegelian dialectician hypotheses also live in our stead. They are not merely schemata that help us work through varieties of possible outcomes and preserve experimental knowledge, but cross-sections of life.

It is in this sense that I call the project of this book dialectical. It takes intimacy as a hypothesis, but neither of the axiomatic kind on which geometers rely nor of the purely intelligible variety of which Socrates dreamed. Instead, it aims to understand the concept of intimacy by tracing the contradictions that appear in each of the various ways that one may try to achieve a closeness beyond closeness. What makes my work here more modest than the great works of philosophy is that it begins with a thought considerably more contingent and parasitic than any basic concept of philosophy. Whereas Hegel begins the *Science of Logic* with the hypothesis of 'Being' and the *Phenomenology of Spirit* with the hypothesis of a single sensed moment, I begin here with the perhaps intractably messy concept of intimacy.

Such a hypothetical approach yields nothing like an *endorsement* of intimacy, even *ceteris paribus*. There is compelling psychological evidence that the desire for intimacy varies widely from person to person,[22] and it would be philosophically irresponsible to attempt to paper over these differences by positing a universal drive for intimacy in human nature. We thus do not have the luxury to follow Karen Prager, who begins her book on the psychology of intimacy with the claim that 'If any reason needs to be given for devoting an entire book to intimacy, it is that intimacy is good for people'.[23] Since the present account is not guided by any particular assumptions about human nature, but by a hypothetical attempt at intimacy, it is open to the possibility that intimacy is undesirable or harmful on all sorts of occasions.[24] I don't, for instance, particularly want greater intimacy with my state, particularly when I may disagree with its government and the establishment of concord might require the government to make aggressive efforts at reconciliation. And while friendships are often good, this does not imply that more or more intimate friendships are always good. 'To give up on love', as they say, in order either to 'find oneself' or simply because one is tired of others or *an*other cannot always be a bad thing. While we should often be suspicious of those who protest too vehemently that intimacy is of no import to them, since this assertion could itself be a request for intimacy (see Chapter 7), the present book gives no reason to ignore such a suspension of the drive for intimacy outright. Dialectics assumes that every thought or action can be suspended (*aufgehoben* in Hegel's German). But even in suspension, such thoughts and actions are not entirely without force. The Marxist appropriation of the term 'dialectics' has added richly to its sense but has generally obscured what a light touch dialectical thinking can have. When in Chapter 7 I describe the role that conflict can play in intimacy, this does not imply that a couple has to fight in order to be intimate. Rather it shows how fighting can overcome some inhibitions to intimacy even as it shows the instability of a partnership founded on conflict.

In marshalling the monstrous force of the negative, dialectical thought is unsparingly charitable, but charitably unsparing. It traffics in dissolution, but does not therefore assume the impossibility of what dissolves. As provisional manifestations of intimacy, the gift, touching, the heartbeat, and so on are indeed saturated with possibility, but they nonetheless collapse under the weight of their own contradictions. Following this dialectical movement necessarily means exploring the ways that these provisional manifestations wriggle free of their strictures. It is not mere accident when a dysfunctional friendship lasts for years, but a sign that dialectics are pervaded by inertia. While Hegelian methodology assumes that we are free to step away from such snags and traps, it also demands that we take their power into account. We do Hegel and dialectical philosophy in general a disservice when we attempt to simplify the movement of any dialectic. Like the novelist or video game virtuoso, the dialectician should not aim to hurry toward the end of the mission, but should hang back and explore the territory's range of possibilities.

Indeed, this playful approach pervades dialectical thinking more radically than the thought even of those who, like Husserl and Levinas, take play seriously but attempt to delineate the realm of play from a fixed and deter-minate horizon.[25] Since play always depends upon a fixed background, these approaches aim to establish what is constant against what is frivolous and changing. Dialectics, however, suspends itself in the moment of play, working through the rules of the game and gradually learning their incompleteness without attempting to establish the conditions of possibility of the game. This is not to say that it is unserious, as anyone who has made a false move at a five-year-old's tea party knows how dependent play is on certain things being taken with utmost seriousness. But its seriousness is not a desperate search for solid ground but an attempt to engage each moment of intimacy on its own terms.

As such, the dialectical approach of this book is less open, more tempered than Derridean deconstruction. While it would never express anything meaningful without a certain level of hospitable openness to the new and unexpected, it is not the kind of radical openness that awaits and embraces the impossible. It is instead a movement of cultivation, of laying the seeds for future engagement and carefully protecting the other in her approach. It is as such an embracing of *difficulty*, not impossibility. Derridean deconstruction is not the nihilistic attack on meaning that it is sometimes accused of being, but a common approach in Derrida's work after *Glas* is to show that because concepts like friendship, forgiveness, and so on tend to set demands that are impossible in principle, they call for radical reattunement to the sense of the possible. The present project aims to show that attention to the breakdown of the concept of intimacy offers not just a new orientation to the world, but wisdom. It is most interested in those problems that challenge simplistic stratagems and call for ambiguity and ambivalence, not those that leave the thinker so at a loss that answers can only be anticipated, hoped for as a sudden upswell of sense.[26]

Though I do not wish to claim any ultimate priority for my dialectical approach to intimacy over ontological or deconstructive approaches, neither do I believe it is merely a random coupling of philosophical approach and subject matter, as if I could equally have studied the ontology of intimacy or the dialectic of desire. There is indeed *something* special about this connection, something about the 'fallacious frivolity of play'[27] that dialectics tolerates and even endorses that gives intimacy the space to develop. Far from the impetus to withdraw from its object in search for a panoramic vision,[28] dialectics *is* philosophical engagement with intimacy.

Equally, with its tendency to dissolve suddenly or unexpectedly despite or even because of our best interests to maintain it, intimacy is also a felicitous object for dialectical thought. Because intimacy demands a closeness beyond closeness, it is destined to fail by its own standards.[29] But one of the main reasons why I prefer dialectics to deconstruction is that the former is not quite so eager to jump to the end. While deconstruction refuses to accept an analysis of the contradictions of a given position without immediately observing the contradictions inherent in the process of analysis itself, dialectics allows itself to catch its breath at the end of each analysis, knowing in only a vague way that it must eventually turn back on itself. The distinction between deconstruction and dialectics may thus be more a difference in philosophical metabolism than a disagreement about method,[30] but this book contends that it is an important one if we are to allow the movement of intimacy to show itself. I am less concerned with Derridean 'im-possibility' (which of course does not rule out possibility) than I am with possibility itself. Dialectics operates not just at the limits of intelligibility, but endeavours continually to recollect what was once unintelligible. It admits that there is some meaning to speaking of degrees of insideness. If 'intimate' means what is 'most inside', then a full analysis of it calls for a study not only of the various levels of insideness, but of the very striving for *more insideness*.[31]

A chief advantage of this dialectical approach is thus that it neither shies away from nor draws hasty conclusions from the contradictoriness of the concept of intimacy. The cynic will contend that we only have a proper understanding of intimacy when it has run its course – that is, when death or disappointment has brought it to an end. The easy lesson to draw from such an approach is that intimacy is doomed from the beginning – that it is contradictory to want to maintain one's independence and selfhood and at the same time become enmeshed in the life of another. But the end of intimacy no more encapsulates its nature than death encapsulates the nature of life.

But is there not also something profoundly undialectical about focusing so tightly on intimacy? If dialectics gains its philosophical force from its refusal to consider any proposition in isolation, then wouldn't a dialectical account also demand an explanation of how the drive for intimacy emerges and how it transforms into other patterns of thought and action? Insofar as any rigorous dialectical account will point beyond its object, this is indeed a limitation of the present book. But an advantage of this limited focus is that it shows the mechanics of dialectics more clearly than a grand systematic overview can. And since a hypothesis of my approach is that selves do not preexist the drive for intimacy, but are formed in part through it, I do not think my account is vulnerable to the criticism that it presupposes its subject. What I call 'partners' do not begin with any particular ontological status, but become who they are through their failure to become everything they suppose they want to be.[32]

As such, while I take this work to be indebted to the kind of thinking that Hegel pioneered in the *Phenomenology of Spirit*, I am reluctant to recolonize the word 'phenomenology' after Husserl so successfully tied it to the search for essences. If one of the main efforts of recent continental thought has been to formulate 'a nonmetaphysical method of philosophy – phenomenology, but a phenomenology thoroughly secured',[33] then all I have to offer as a counter-proposal is a thoroughly insecure phenomenology.

Yet while my approach is closer to Hegel than to twentieth-century phenomenology, it is not entirely faithful to Hegel. If the hermeneutic tradition has taught the post-Hegelian world anything, it is that philosophy should not be afraid of proper names. Addressing the movement of dialectics through exemplars is a sign of rigour, not parochialism, and to scrub all references to Antigone or Marcus Aurelius as one attempts to follow this movement is to invite unnecessary confusion. While dialectical philosophy does not require us to accept all of the conclusions of twentieth-century hermeneutics, to study dialectics *is* to do hermeneutical philosophy. This does not mean that we have to assume with the deconstructionists that the only things dialectics ever encounters are texts. In hypothesizing motivations for a form of intimacy, a dialectical account does not simply take itself to be 'reading' the contradictions that are already present and self-obscuring in an infinitely analysable text. As hypotheses, the objects of dialectics allow themselves to be stripped down to their constitutive contradictions without insisting on rewriting themselves. Nevertheless, the encounters that dialectics sets up for itself are dependent upon the surprises that encounters with other authors invariably bring, and thus dialectics ought to be receptive to the contingencies that references to paradigmatic texts expose it to.[34] With a perhaps embarrassing earnestness, it closes one eye to the fractal complexity that any text ultimately reveals and attempts to focus on an overriding movement at play. Rather than test every rule for exceptions and unintended consequences, it jumps straightaway into playing the game until it proves unsustainable.

I suspect that much of the allure of Hegel's approach to dialectical thinking comes from the giddy, inchoate intimacy of togetherness forged in poverty. The *Phenomenology of Spirit* is bewitching because it promises so much out of so little exegetical material. Just as a young couple can become enchanted with one another over the course of a date built around a single 60-cent apple, the likes of Lamorisse and Neruda can engage an audience most effectively with a single red balloon or weathered sheep toy. But in the early twenty-first century, what works so beautifully in film and literature seems artificially rustic in a philosophical context. In a world that has learned to support a vast bureaucracy of academics, even the monolingual scholar is gifted with an incomprehensible wealth of insights. I do not want to rule out the possibility of another Descartes or Wittgenstein writing brilliant work from hermeneutical scratch as we speak, but I in any event am not in the position to offer the reader an apple date. Where my analyses are vague and merely evocative, it is because I have failed to be sufficiently clear or rigorous or knowledgeable, not because I have succeeded in emulating Hegel's oracular writing style.

One danger of such a hermeneutical approach is that it risks undue deference to traditional philosophical narratives. When the collapse of a way of life or a form of striving seems inevitable, there is less of an impulse to seek out lines of flight, and the attempt at identifying a pattern comes to appear as a prescription. Dialectical thinking thus must always be tempered by the realization that the patterns it finds are never complete or final. One of the most often overlooked characteristics of Hegelian dialectics is its humility. Hegel's line about the Owl of Minerva[35] applies not just to philosophical knowledge of statecraft, but to philosophical knowledge in general. The task of dialectics is not to predict how the future will or ought to unfold, but to reconstruct the reasons why past stabs at finding a way in the world suddenly worked or gradually failed to work. Dialectics is not so much an attentiveness to phenomena as they appear as an application of the narrative imagination to a specific goal. If it ever encounters saturated phenomena, they are the playthings of the imagination, not proof of the heteronomy of all thought. While Schelling was by this point already seeking to move beyond dialectical philosophy,[36] in the 1811 *Ages of the World* he sums up the humble position of dialectics quite aptly:

This separation, this doubling of ourselves, this secret traffic in which there are two beings – one that questions and one that answers, one that knows or rather *is* knowledge and one that does not know and wrestles for clarity – this inner art of conversation, the authentic mystery of the philosopher, is what from the outside is called the dialectic. When the dialectic becomes a copy, a mere form of this conversation, it is its empty semblance and shadow.[37]

Conversely, we can assume, a dialectical approach that sought to follow this 'secret traffic' carefully would have to preserve its movement as more than mere form.[38] It could not presume to know *a priori* where the inner art of conversation would take it or seek to determine the terms and categories of this conversation in advance. In short, it would have to remain open to being surprised by what it unfolds.

Limitations of dialectics

While I have tried to make a philosophical case for preferring a dialectical approach to deconstructive and ontological approaches to intimacy, it would be irresponsible to ignore its limitations in relation to full-blown developmental theories of intimacy, whether of the psychoanalytic sort that Jessica Benjamin and others have sought to develop or of the philosophical-critical sort that Habermas, Honneth and others have sought to develop. For Benjamin, 'The idea is not to bolster the ideal by proving that we are "born with the ability"; it is to recognize that when we postulate a psychological need (not a social need or a normative ideal) for recognition, we mean that failure to satisfy the need will inevitably result in difficulties or even damages to the psyche'.[39] For the tradition of critical theory as well, it is impossible to study a concept without an empirical investigation of how it came to be operative in a concrete, historical group of individuals. My account offers no empirical claims about the damage that will result from the failure of any particular instantiation of the drive for intimacy or even an empirical claim that such a drive exists in all or most people; it is only an analysis of the structures of these attempts at intimacy and an explanation of why they fail on their own terms. While there is tremendous explanatory value and clinical potential in theories that posit empirically discernible needs for intimacy, my approach offers only the relatively modest promise of showing the structural limitations of various forms of intimacy without offering predictions or prescriptions.

Accordingly, it lacks the statistical and mass-observational tools necessary to make any generalizations about how intimacy has developed (or devolved) in recent times. I do not know whether the conveniences of the modern world are on the whole productive or destructive of intimacy, though I suspect that much of the recent handwringing over the effects of reality TV and social networks on intimacy are confusing profound changes in the media of wish-fulfilment with changes in actual social structures. In any event, the threats to intimacy I focus on are not contingent historical occurrences but contradictions that emerge from the very possibility of striving for intimacy.

They are, to be sure, constructed or shaped by prevailing historical conditions, but they are in this book conceived hypothetically rather than positively.

For this reason, I have given twentieth-century psychoanalysis a lesser role in this project than its accomplishments might otherwise merit. While there have turned out to be many points of convergence (of which I discover more every time I present this material to psychoanalytically informed audiences), the empirical agnosticism of my approach represents a profound challenge to much of the psychoanalytic tradition.[40] By grasping that the ego is historically, contingently, and often incompletely produced, psychoanalysis has managed to explore a great deal about the inhibition and redirection of libidinal energy, which makes it possible not only to identify contradictions in the struggle for intimacy, but to produce plausible narratives regarding their transformation into one another. Insofar as the aim of a dialectical study of intimacy is to trace its continual breakdown and transformation, it might even seem to be repeating the work of psychoanalysis in slightly different language. If both approaches agree that the desire for intimacy tends to be frustrated by its very nature, what difference does it make that one field approaches intimacy positively and the other hypothetically?

Yet the hypothetical structure of dialectics really does make all the difference. Regardless of whether it understands its object as dispersed libidinal energy or a multiplicity of biological drives, psychoanalysis seeks to explain behaviour in terms of the frustration of actually existing drives. Identifying these drives is ultimately an empirical process (whether through clinical sessions, biological investigations, cultural analysis, or other means), with all the epistemological assumptions that empirical investigation entails. This is mostly something to be lauded, since therapeutic interventions ought to respond to real human needs. But the search for a drive for intimacy or a more fundamental drive from which the desire for intimacy arises also fosters clinical assumptions about what constitutes healthy desires that a project like mine simply cannot countenance.[41] It is at least extraordinarily difficult, and might in the end prove impossible, to state with any precision what human beings naturally desire without importing normative assumptions that prejudge the issue. Fortunately, dialectics does not require us to do so and thus leaves us room to follow the concept of intimacy wherever it might lead.[42]

Of course, none of this rules out the possibility of an ultimate convergence of dialectical and empirical accounts of intimacy, and a few times in the book I discuss some exciting possibilities for this convergence. But in pursuing a dialectics of intimacy I have tried wherever possible to avoid getting caught up in the methodological assumptions of other disciplines. One assumption in particular is pervasive enough that it seems worth distancing myself from it explicitly. Psychologists, especially those following the psychiatrist John

Bowlby's *Attachment* trilogy, often explain the need for intimacy as a holdover from the infant's need for attachment.[43] Bowlby makes a compelling case (upon which subsequent studies have expounded) that the social instincts of humans and other animals cannot be explained in terms of our fondness for those who help us survive, but reflect a preference for attachment as such, irrespective of our drives for food, protection, and so on.[44] However, with the exception of the infant's latching onto the breast (an example which Bowlby himself disavows),[45] attachment is an imperfect metaphor for intimacy, since intimacy often has little to do with a literal or metaphorical binding together.[46] Studies of what leads partners to desire and choose to stay together are of unquestionable theoretical and practical value, but such desires and choices are at least conceptually distinct from the dialectic of intimacy itself. To want to be as close as possible to someone does not necessarily entail wanting to remain attached to them, and if my analyses of irony in Chapter 6 and conflict in Chapter 7 are on the right track, even detachment can be constitutive of a kind of intimacy. Moreover, unlike attachment theory, this approach does not assume anything about the nature of the partners seeking intimacy. While it is common for psychologists studying attachment to assume that close relationships are built upon sharing experiences or conversations, either sort of sharing strikes me as philosophically problematic. It is not obvious to me that partners enter relationships with fixed sets of memories or potential experiences just waiting to be shared or even that each party starts off as an ontologically distinct unit.[47] Attachment theory potentially has a great deal to offer in explaining divergences between stated desires for closeness and actual behaviour, but my dialectical approach seeks to show a contradiction in the desire for closeness itself.

Such a dialectical approach must also make an effort to avoid the temptations of typologizing. It is no accident that many of the most profound thinkers of intimacy, notably Kierkegaard, Nietzsche and Beauvoir, were fond of typologies, and occasionally even typologies of typologies. Since intimacy carries contradictory aims and varies vastly with its participants, it might seem that the only ways to speak meaningfully about its manifold varieties would be either to follow monistic thinkers like Augustine in reducing them to a single innate drive or to attempt to systematize the types of intimacy that various types of people pursue. Here we might recall Beauvoir's critiques in *The Ethics of Ambiguity* of the failure of the sub-man, serious man, and so on to appreciate the freedom of others, or Kierkegaard's account in *Works of Love* of the manifold ways people avoid genuine engagement with their neighbours. There is doubtlessly much value in such typologies, particularly when one is choosing friends or attempting to explain why a past friendship never worked out. But such typologies fail to explain the movements among various types of intimacy and do not show why intimacy fails on its own terms.[48] Moreover, any such typology implicitly presupposes some 'true' account of how individuals actually relate to one another. If every type of intimacy is a variation on a theme, then there must be an original theme that is varied.

Dialectics makes no such promises. It does not give us the perfect intimacy against which all others are to be measured[49] or posit an essence of intimacy that may or may not ever be fulfilled in any earthly relationship. And unlike the post-phenomenological approach of a Heidegger[50] or Irigaray,[51] it does not allow itself to indulge in wistful longing that a suitable climate for meaning might one day be secured. It takes only the meaning that history has forged for it and contents itself that even as institutions and arrangements break down we are not left simply with nothing. Intimate engagement is not for it all-or-nothing and thus can persist in less than fully satisfying forms for a great deal of time. From the fact that we never achieve a consummate intimacy and only know ourselves in our various intimacies, we should not conclude that we are left waiting for an intimacy-to-come. The dialectic of intimacy proceeds without prior authorization and requires no future event to be made accessible.

Note on terminology

I use the word 'partner' rather than the too-specific 'friend' or the sterile 'other' primarily for its ambiguity. We use the word for both sexual and business relationships, for both temporary and lifelong associations. Its root is related to senses of both sharing and division, and in my native Texas its pronunciation is almost indistinguishable from that of 'pardoner'. And while 'other' has the advantage of suggesting interchangability among partners and potential partners, its association with Sartre's existentialism and Levinas's search for radical alterity makes it less than ideal for this project. My use of the word 'partner' does not assume that each partner enters the relationship as a pre-formed self. Indeed, it is an assumption of this work that such selves only emerge in concert with mutual recognition, of which intimacy is only one form.

I am considerably less satisfied with my choice of 'relationship' as the term for the context in which intimacy is attempted or sought. In casual usage it tends to imply the existence of some substantial unity between two partners, which is precisely what I argue the dialectic of intimacy continually calls into question. For the same reason, 'partnership' is even worse, since it often indicates a legal or quasi-legal contract that gives the interplay of the partners a normative foundation. The one advantage of the term 'relationship' is that even in its casual use it is so loaded with connotations that it spontaneously calls for its own erasure. Whenever the stakes of intimacy are in doubt, be it in a budding romantic relationship or a long-term friendship that is dependent in part on its conditions not being made explicit, asking about the status of the 'relationship' will provoke immediate backtracking or hedging from one or both partners: 'What do you mean, "Is this a 'relationship'?"' I intend the term to produce a similar unease whenever it appears below.

1

The Gift

•

Suppose it begins with a gift.[1] In cases of intimacy, beginnings are of course artifices, since there is no such thing as an inaugurating moment of a relationship. Even if we privilege sight exclusively (and ignore the ways that we can gradually become aware of another's presence through sounds and subtle shifts in air currents), and even if a meeting of eyes happens to be each partner's very first glimpse of the other, this moment is still founded on a wealth of situational contingencies that have already begun to move the couple toward interaction.[2] In retrospect, a mythology of the relationship's first moment can often play an important role, particularly in romantic relationships where the myth of an inaugural encounter can substitute for any number of missed signals and failed connections.[3] But in this case the initial meeting serves as *archê* to the relationship only by a mutual consent that develops much later.

Initiation

So let us say that it begins with a gift, not with any metaphysical rigour, but because the gift is sufficiently embarrassed of its own prior conditions to put itself forward as a beginning.[4] As Paul Ricoeur explains in *The Course of Recognition*, a gift can often sow the seeds of a relationship even before conventions of gift-giving and -receiving have developed. A gesture of peace, of admiration, of openness, of recognition can make a relationship seem desirable or at least plausible and break the ice, as we say. When I come to you with a gift, you may have doubts about my true intentions. You may wonder if the gift is merely a distraction from the harm I intend to cause you or the intrinsic undesirability of my friendship. But because the gift interrupts the immediacy of our encounter, it at least temporarily stuns you into wondering whether these doubts are really warranted. It shows that even if I have come to take something from you, I am not governed by blind avarice and want the relationship to consist at least in part of my own generosity. The gift carries a promise of openness to future encounters without specifying the conditions under which these encounters are to occur.

Such a gift need not even be particularly heartfelt or spontaneous to invite intimacy. The ritualized gift-giving of an Eastern New Year's Celebration or Western bridal shower can each cultivate tight bonds between donors and recipients despite the fact that not only the act of giving, but the very gift given is prescribed by tradition, a wedding registry, or some other equally constraining institution. In such cases, going through the motions is expected as part of the easygoing, everyday intimacy of the occasion. When, for instance, Vietnamese families celebrate the New Year with lengthy ceremonies in which older generations distribute small amounts of money to progressively younger generations in exchange for formalized well-wishes, it might seem that a mere parody of recognition is occurring. After all, the money to be distributed may have been folded or placed in an envelope without any particular recipient in mind, and the good wishes might be recycled with the same empty cheer one finds in the service industries. But such ceremonies can still be quite meaningful even for the merely formal forms of recognition they provide. What they deliver is not proof that the donor has been thinking about the recipient's needs, but promises of future engagement. While a truly unexpected gift may stun the recipient into an ambivalent 'You shouldn't have', even an expected one can open the gap between individual action and social convention that underlies all intimacy.

But insofar as the gift seeks to fix the meaning of the encounter in an external object, it is at best a solicitation to future intimacy, which can easily be confused with intimacy itself. Witness the teenage boy suddenly exalted from the humdrum sameness of his life by an erotic charge. Convinced that his love could only be desirable as an unconditioned gift, he searches in vain for its consummation, for that ultimate proof that he has given it and it has been received as a pure gift. His gift must be one that expresses unequivocally that he expects nothing in return, for the only proof of his love's absolute difference from all other relationships is that it is withdrawn from every economy of exchange. He schemes to give a gift that meets his beloved's needs or desires perfectly but would place her under no obligation in return. His gift must be different from all the usual kinds of gifts one gives in this situation, but it must also respond to his beloved's desires and not to his own desire to give. It must be given in such a way that she both knows and does not know that it is from him, for his motives are compromised if he gives with the intention of her knowing it, and if he gives without her knowledge then the gift fails to make plain the purity of his intentions. Even an allusion to something he might want in return for his love is likely to annoy him as a misunderstanding of his intentions: 'I don't love you so that you might love me in return; I love you just to love you.' Yet as his insipid love letters invariably attest, nothing he can give his beloved measures up to the very gift of his love. The gift can only serve as a placeholder for his need to give without preconditions or expectations, for as soon as any concrete gift is chosen the expectations attending it become apparent.[5]

When, however, a gift is not taken to be something perfectable, it offers a promise of intimacy without prejudging the intentions of the partners. Thus we often find gifts playing prominent roles in the opening stages of a negotiation. When representatives from two warring communities meet with an exchange of local artefacts, they do not necessarily imply that there is any equivalence between the esteem they hold for the recipients and the value of the gifts, but they do imply that an open-ended discussion is something they are interested in having. Likewise, when two business executives greet each other with high-priced trinkets, they hope to confirm that regardless of whether a satisfactory deal can be reached the other is someone who deserves nice things.

In Fichte's language, the community representatives and business people are offering their gifts in the hopes of establishing a *formally common will*.[6] Before they can begin working out the details of who deserves to own what – in Fichte's language, reaching a *materially common will* – they must first make clear that each believes that the other has the *right* to own certain property and that this right deserves to be protected by others. The gift, we might say, is the symbol of a formally common will in the absence of any assurance that a materially common will will or even can be reached. Such a gift does not bind, but it does announce that some form of binding is at least not out of the question. It thus aims to inaugurate a relationship in a different way than the teenager's perfect gift. In the case of two adversaries seeking to suspend hostilities, the gift object does not need to meet the needs of the recipient or reveal itself as completely disinterested. As long as it does not offend the recipient or impose any obvious obligations for reciprocation, it can still establish an open space for negotiations to be pursued.

But even when given the more limited role of establishing an opening for intimacy, the gift still asks for too much. While the gift is intended to reify the relationship's pure possibility in a formally common will, it finds itself embedded in an economy of exchange. Though the giver may seek clarity by isolating the gift from the events that precede and follow it, the gift still carries with it an impulse toward intimacy. One of our businessmen may indeed be touched by the monogrammed Lucite golfball he receives, but he would be a fool to think that the gift represents the inaugural moment in a pure and unconditioned relationship. For Fichte, this entails the need for an authoritarian state with the power to punish any affront to the formally common will.[7] In this case, what is at stake is no longer intimacy, but a more abstract, legal form of recognition. To protect the gift as the site of intimacy, there cannot be any external restrictions on giving, but the gift must originate in a perfectly pure intention.

In his famous anthropological work on the gift, Marcel Mauss argues that the insistence that gifts be measured by the purity of their intentions is a theological atavism that misunderstands the roles of gifts in actual human economies. Indeed, built into every gift is what he calls the *hau*, the Maori term for what in a gift obligates the recipient to return the favour. In Mauss's account, the Maoris could only explain their need to return gifts even at the risk of financial hardship by positing the existence of a force contained in the gift itself. No gift is purely unidirectional, he concluded, since in any gift a centripetal force pulls the recipient back toward the donor.[8]

But the bond of the gift need not be an obligation to reciprocate for it to bind just as tightly. If in the example of the businessmen the practice of giving initial gifts becomes customary, the need to give may become simply a matter of acknowledgement. A gift would not in this case signal any special openness in the relationship, but would merely indicate that both parties are prepared to follow customary patterns of behaviour. Likewise, gifts can bind by teaching the recipient about the donor or by proving that there is some common cultural thread that pulls the parties together. A gift would in such cases be a gesture not of openness but of interest and commitment. So long as the gift is not taken to be essential to the foundation of the relationship, it can function just as interestedly and impurely as any other gesture.

But for the partner who insists that the relationship be founded on a gift, a gift's social context constitutes a threat. If intimacy requires unconditional giving, then the giver must never expect anything in return. Any gift given in a community where reciprocity is customary would never be able to distinguish itself with any certainty from a trade or investment. Even when the giver has only the vaguest sense that something might be given in return, her gift cannot help but be corrupted by the possibility that it is a strategic move for a potentially greater return. Such a problematic gift thus could not be a foundation for a relationship that hopes to be closer than all others, because it would fail to provide assurance that this relationship is different from any other. This means that the giver should not even wish the recipient know a gift has been given, since the gift would then not be a truly generous act, but a purchase of esteem. As Derrida notes, this suspicion can be extended to the point where the gift is impossible.[9] To the extent that there is any gift present at all, it is bound to incite gratitude or at least some recognition in the recipient. Even a rejection of the gift is a form of recognition of it. And even in the case of a gift the recipient does not even know he has received, the donor still may not give purely, since she gives herself a kind of symbolic recognition for the gift she has given (GT 14).[10]

The problem here is that an attempt to distinguish one relationship from all others by founding it on an act of generosity can only appeal to generosity for generosity's sake. A gift must thus be purified of all economies of exchange to have any hope of grounding an intimate relationship. When in the course of ordinary affairs I give you a compliment or burn you a copy of a great new CD, I probably am not wishing for anything particular in return and indeed would be a little put out if you immediately complimented me in return in the exact same words or burned me a copy of the exact same CD. But I would also be at least a little put out if neither gift was even acknowledged. In such a case, I would suspect that the gift had somehow failed in its intention to bring us slightly closer together. And even if I did not entertain such a suspicion, it would be because your very refusal to acknowledge the gift constituted a kind of acknowledgement. By accepting the gift without a big to-do, you could be gesturing toward an unspoken understanding between us that we are close enough to be able to exchange gifts without any expectations of one another. But this too is an expectation, and even when I give with the intention of bringing us closer together by demonstrating that you and I can give freely and without expectations, I am still giving with the anticipation of some kind of return for my investment. When gifts do succeed in cultivating intimacy, it is not the purity of my intentions that constitutes our bond, but some institution or arrangement prior to the gift. We thus cut intimacy off at the knees when we attempt a gift withdrawn from every prior interest.

Appeal and delay

But if the gift cultivates intimacy not by divesting the giver of self-interested motives but merely by providing an occasion for the giver and recipient to come together, then the giver would not even need to look for such a pure gift. For Fichte in the *Foundations of Natural Right*, the founding moment of any respectful relationship is less the act of generosity itself than the request my partner makes of me. In such an appeal (*Aufforderung*),[11] I become aware of my freedom in a way that escapes me in my normal dealings with nature. While I am free as a rational being to make all sorts of choices – cotton over silk, say, or bourbon over scotch – it is only when I am the object of another's appeal (*Aufforderung*) that I am *recognized* for my freedom. When my neighbour asks me for a jumpstart, I am free to say yes or no, and regardless of my answer my neighbour has made me aware of this freedom.[12] Here a gift given without antecedent would be beside the point, for a gift not motivated by a partner's request would do nothing to secure mutual recognition as free beings. Donor and recipient are bound together not by altruistic intentions but by external gestures of respect: the request and the gift.[13] But because this binding plays a metaphysical role in the very constitution of the soul, it no longer follows merely the hypothetical imperative of a drive for intimacy, but the categorical imperative of the need to express one's freedom.[14] This means that when one party fails to provide the other with the necessary recognition, the second, or indeed the entire society is justified in punishing the offender severely. The violator of the compact has so little standing that neither his wellbeing nor his relations to others in the society can have any bearing on his treatment. Whatever its merits for a theory of statecraft, Fichte's account of the foundational role of the appeal in establishing recognition is thus a poor route to intimacy. In place of a connection, accommodation, or openness between the parties is a mere assertion of the necessity of recognition.

Pierre Bourdieu offers an account of the gift's social adhesiveness that splits the difference between Fichte's necessity and Derrida's impossibility.[15] He is interested in many of the same phenomena as Mauss and Derrida, but for him the lesson of generosity's contradictions is not that gift-giving is im-possible on its own conditions, but that it belongs to a class of actions that only exist because they are unreflective.[16] Every gift does anticipate (or at least hope for) something in return, but both the giver and the recipient use time to obscure this expectation. If I give you a gift and you immediately give me another, then this is a mere trade. If I give you a gift and already know in the instant it is given that you are required to return either it or something of equal or greater value, then it is a loan (Bourdieu, *Logic of Practice*, 105). In either case, the instantaneous nature of the exchange rules out any possibility of slippage or surprise. A gift, on the other hand, does not share this calculation and allows the interaction to maintain a sense of openness. But this openness is entirely dependent on a time lag between the initial gift and the response.[17] For the duration of the interval, the donor is uncertain about what the response will be, and the recipient incurs a deeper obligation to respond, even if her ultimate response is not to respond at all.[18] In such circumstances, time itself comes to have a meaning, and its force is felt all the more strongly when nothing is going on (*Logic of Practice*, 106). By highlighting the gift's ability to escape rulebound calculation, time thus has the curious effect of enhancing the possibility of both deception and intimacy. By introducing slippage into ordinary calculations of what is to be given and received, time shows that no matter how fixed and stable a relationship may seem, it still contains a reserve of indeterminacy that could always well up and overwhelm social conventions.

A quick return to Aristotle might clarify Bourdieu's point. In Books 8 and 9 of the *Nicomachean Ethics*, Aristotle identifies a series of conditions necessary for any fulfilling friendship. Both parties, for instance, must have only the best wishes for the welfare of the other and must periodically work to preserve that welfare. Both must share common interests and work toward common ends. And both must be virtuous people and encourage each other to develop virtuous characters. But even when all these are present, it still may not be enough for two people to be called true friends. No matter how virtuous and committed to each other's welfare the two partners are, their friendship will remain shallow if it is not based on a solid foundation of 'time and familiarity' (χρόνου καὶ συνηθείας).[19] Aristotle's word here for 'familiarity' (συνηθεία) could also be parsed as 'being together'. For a friendship to grow intimate, the two friends need not only to care about one another, but to *be* together for a significant amount of time. In order for interactions between partners to develop a sense of unforced reciprocity, there must be a mutual experience of time's obtrusiveness.

What emerges with such time and familiarity is the possibility of spontaneity, of gifts that are unexpected in their individual occurrences but expected in general. In his fieldwork with the Kabyle, Bourdieu found that gifts were typically divided into three kinds: the completely gratuitous, like the mother's milk; those that were required by social convention; and the so-called 'little gifts', which were occasionally given to mark births, weddings, and so on and typically combined a whimsical arbitrariness with some symbolic value (LP 99). A flower, for instance, might be given at a son's circumcision to convey wishes that he might 'flower into manhood'. What makes these gifts especially intimate is their uncertainty, and 'to reintroduce uncertainty is to reintroduce time' (LP 99). A gift can only be both unexpected and tied to a series of exchanges when it makes use of time's full arbitrariness – its tendency to fill some moments with gifts and leave others empty. The absence of interactions at some times emphasizes the intensity of the relationship not just by providing a contrast to times of intense engagement ('Absence makes the heart grow fonder') but by exposing how even apparent obligations are potential objects of play. Well-received gifts thus stretch time in two complementary ways. They both extend the time that a couple or group spend together (by instilling a sense of security through generosity or ritual) and pull this time to it full extension. And in a society where gifts can be repaid not only by the recipient but by others as well, this extension is magnified by the uncertainty of who exactly will be returning the gift.[20]

Here we can see a convergence in Derrida and Bourdieu's positions. While Derrida frames the hypocrisy of the gift as a failure to meet its own conditions and Bourdieu frames it as a conversion of economic into social capital, both maintain that this hypocrisy is what keeps alive the possibility of spontaneity.[21] For Derrida, every gift requires the coexistence of contradictory impulses: 'There must be chance, encounter, the involuntary, even unconsciousness or disorder, and there must be intentional freedom, and these two conditions must – miraculously, graciously, agree with each other' (123). By forcing partners to deal with each other as both conscientious and contingent beings, gifts open a space for intimacy. The gift promotes intimacy not by buying allegiance – since the obligation to return a gift tends to close off the relationship – but by buying time.

Even if little intimacy inheres in the transfer of an object from one person to another, the gift still buys time by promising a relation. As Derrida also observes, 'When I give something to someone, in the classical semantic of the gift – be it money, a book, or be it simply a promise or a word – I already promise to confirm it, to repeat it, even if I do not repeat it.'[22] To give is not merely to slough off an excess, but to affirm that what is given is *meant* to be given. By opening herself to the time of uncertainty that follows the gift, the donor commits to repeating the gift virtually for an indeterminate amount of time. Giving makes her vulnerable to the whims of the recipient, and her anticipation of this vulnerability allows the gift to carry a promise of intimacy.

Yet such a generous gesture of commitment succeeds in laying the groundwork for intimacy not because it successfully suspends every economy of exchange, but because it works to integrate the lives of the donor and recipient. It is sometimes claimed that bonds are formed only by gifts and not by economies of exchange, since the latter release each party never to think about the other.[23] But this sort of pre-arranged reciprocity need not inhibit the development of intimacy; it can even cultivate it. The cashier at the hardware store and I can take comfort in the circumscription of our roles and enjoy one another's presence all the more for it. To the extent that we share an unspoken appreciation of our encounter, the relationship might even begin to approach intimacy. When, in contrast, I give an interest-free loan to an in-law who has fallen on hard times, the asymmetry of the interaction is far more likely to make each of us want to cut the interaction short and avoid each other for a good deal of time.[24] Whereas the exchange relation creates a circumscribed relationship in which a limited intimacy is free to develop, the unboundedness of the gift relation impedes exactly the sort of indeterminate familiarity on which Aristotle claims friendship is founded. We would thus have to take all hope for intimacy out of the gift if we go along with Derrida in specifying, 'A gift will always be *without* border … A gift that does not run over its borders, a gift that would let itself be contained in a determination and limited by the indivisibility of an identifiable *trait* would not be a gift' (Derrida, *Given Time*, 91). To the extent that a gift is given not-quite-routinely as part of an endless variation on an accepted social practice, it holds the promise of an intimacy yet to develop. But when it attempts to establish a closeness beyond other closenesses, a true connection untainted by expectations, it offers no intimacy at all. It is not even the promise of a dissolution of boundaries because the giving of the unconditional gift denies that there were ever such boundaries at all. The ambiguity and delay upon which Aristotle and Bourdieu think intimacy is founded cannot survive the conscious effort to determine *this* gift as meaningful.

Absenting

Perhaps we ask too much of the gift. While both unreciprocated gifts and gift exchanges fail to tie a knot between donor and recipient, we saw earlier from Ricoeur the suggestion that gift-giving cultivates intimacy not by securing recognition for either party but by opening a space for free interchange. But even this suggestion is dubitable. One of the most striking features of the gift is that while it must at one time be *presented* (and in some cases its presentation is more elaborate than the gift itself), it is generally something enjoyed when the giver is absent. The gift might thus be taken to institute intimacy not by promising the giver's unconditional presence, but by making allowances for her inevitable absence. From this perspective, it is not a problem at all that neither the donor nor the recipient is ever fully present in the gift. Rather, this state of affairs makes plain the nature of the relationship: we are intimates because we recognize each other's inscrutability. A gift would thus leave present with the recipient a totem for the inevitability of the donor's benevolent non-presence.

We find just such a model of the gift in the phenomenological work of Jean-Luc Marion. While Marion has more theological fish to fry than analysing the dialectic of intimacy, his analysis of the role of non-presence in the gift is uniquely helpful to our current project.[25] For Marion, this non-presence is definitive of what is perhaps the most intimate relation of giving we have – God's gift of creation: 'Between the gift given and the giver giving, giving does not open up the (quadri-)dimension of appropriation, but preserves distance … Distance lays out the intimate gap between the giver and the gift so that the self-withdrawal of the giver in the gift may be read on the gift in the very fact that it refers back absolutely to the giver.'[26] According to Marion, an act of giving succeeds if and only if it makes plain the donor's absence. While the given object may remain present, the giving or the givenness of the object withdraws along with the donor. The intimacy of gift-giving consists precisely in this absenting. In its acknowledgement of an intimate space that the recipient will never enter, the gift represents an oblique form of exposure to an area to which most potential partners are never given access.[27]

The easy complaint here is that a revelation of an intimate part of the donor that the recipient can never appreciate is no cultivation of intimacy at all, but rather an excuse for not working to cultivate intimacy.[28] But as Marion takes pains to make clear, a gift is not simply an assertion of my necessary absence, but an effort to make this absence present for both of us. Indeed, for Marion this emphasis on the non-presence of the donor and recipient is a way of rescuing intimacy from an overly strenuous definition of the gift.[29] By searching for a gift absolutely pure in its origins, the donor imposes an absolute boundary between herself and her partner.[30] Only by supposing in advance that she is absolutely independent can she posit a gift removed from all economies of exchange that might ingratiate her with her partner.[31] In contrast, a gift that declines to hide the donor's lack of continuing presence is better able to speak to the actual relationship at hand and thus carries the sense of being let in on a secret.

In a reflection on the gift in a slightly different context, Jean-Luc Nancy attempts to explain the difficulty of this kind of giving withdrawal. In his attempt to think simultaneously the experience of freedom and the *givenness* of the world, Nancy notes that the ambiguity of the gift ultimately stems not from the state of mind of the donor, but from the necessity of interaction that a gift entails: 'It is not a question here of the economy of the gift, where the gift comes back to itself as the benefit and mastery of the giver. On the contrary, it is a question of what makes the gift as such: an offering that may not be returned to anyone, since it remains in itself the free offering that it is … it is presented, made freely available, but is freely held back at the edge of the receiver's free acceptance. The offering is the inestimable price of the gift.'[32] It is the price of this offering, its solicitation of a freedom to respond, that constitutes the force of intimacy. For Nancy, we are able to make an uneasy place for ourselves in the world because of the very inscrutability of its givenness. We do not know precisely why it is here or how it has been given, and this makes feeling at home possible in a way that an explicit gift from God could not. Like houseguests asked to make ourselves at home, we are far more comfortable when an uneven stack of linens has been dumped on the bed than we would be if our host had made meticulous arrangements in a spirit of pure generosity. Even in the former case we will continue to feel like guests and wonder about precisely what codes of conduct apply to us, but this uncertainty indicates less an alienation than an ongoing process of acclimation.

Similarly, when I give you something, it will tend to be more meaningful if I do not make explicit all the conditions under which I give it, and an extreme act of generosity is likely to put a barrier between us. The lover's gift should make clear that it contains a substantial amount of thought, but it is counterproductive to specify the entire thought process, since the vast quantity of pragmatic concerns motivating the selection of any gift ('I chose to search in the mall down the street rather than a market in Mongolia since the latter would have been inexpedient') dissolves the gift's intimacy when made explicit. And even if I did choose to travel to Mongolia for a gift that I thought would be more appealing to the recipient, the gift would still fail to cultivate intimacy, since it would so elevate the recipient that it would ignore the hidden desires of the donor. Perhaps, then, what is given is not a proof of my beneficence so much as a marker of my absence.

But while I think there is something crucial in this realization of the need for withdrawal in intimacy (as we will see especially in Chapter 7), the effort to make this absence present in the figure of the gift relies on a kind of bankshot intimacy. In its desperation[33] to prove that intimacy is even possible, it is suspicious of any direct efforts at intimacy and thus values obliqueness as genuineness. As we will see, this appeal to the oblique is something that appears again and again in the various forms of striving for intimacy, but it is particularly unfulfilling in the form of the gift. For unlike irony or anticipatory mourning, the gift does not offer any means for partners to share their mutual absence. At best the gift is an acknowledgement of the necessity of this absence that retreats from the shared empty space as soon as it enters. The gift is given in a discrete act, and though the given object can stick around as a reminder of this act, it cannot retain the oscillation between presence and absence that marked the initial act of giving.

This is true even of writing (taken in its broadest, Derridean sense to include other artworks and disseminated forms of speech). Though the text continually reminds the reader of its writer's absence, it also constitutes a kind of promise to remain as it is even if subsequent readings radically change its meaning. Unlike a static object, the text begins to fulfil this promise not only by its constant material presence, but by its anticipation of a variety of responses in the reader. The text shows the manifold ways that the writer has already begun to engage the reader's potential responses and thus is never simply disseminated but pulls the reader back toward the writer. But even in the varied form of distancing and presenting that it allows, the written gift still does not respond to the reader as a partner present to her. A good writer can offer a text that engages the reader when approached from a variety of different directions, but a text remains incapable of being surprised by its reader. Nietzsche can draw us in to imagine that he *would* be surprised by the direction we take his thought *if only* he were around today, but he still cannot be drawn up into our own concerns in a way that establishes our connection as intimate, in*most*. While it may be the liveliest form of gift, the text still fails to maintain an intimacy in its distancing. Rather than *holding itself* at a distance, the text announces its distance at the outset and then retreats.[34] Neither a domineering attempt at determining once and for all the grounds of a partnership nor an acknowledgement of eternal mutual intelligibility, the given text allows its acknowledgement of difference to dissipate as the twin scenes of its writing and reading are gradually forgotten.[35] Reading, like religious revelation, might indeed offer something greater or more fulfilling than intimacy, but its drive for intimacy will always remain unfulfilled.

A measured gift: Lysias's speech

Given the instability and uncertainty endemic to the sort of intimacy that the gift brings, a tempting alternative would be to attempt to institutionalize the gift in such a way that all the intimacy is preserved but the frustrating or deadening expectations are removed. After all, we have seen that giving without conditions is no sure path to intimacy; why not then attempt to cleanse the gift of the self-centred generosity of the teenager in love? And if intimacy can be found neither in a Fichtean recognition of the necessity of mutual respect nor in a Bourdieuian need for the unexpected, why not institutionalize the gift such that both parties know exactly what to expect from the exchange and are free to pull out at any time? And finally, if the intimacy of the gift cannot be found in its absenting, why not attempt a gift exchange in which both parties freely contract to be present only when they both agree? This is the proposal made (*in absentia*) by Lysias in Plato's *Phaedrus*. Addressing an imagined potential lover, Lysias argues that instead of yielding his virtue to someone who is in love with him, he should instead give it to someone sober enough to treat the gift dispassionately. Yet despite this promise of intimacy, Lysias's very language suggests a certain standoffishness. Whereas Socrates will later address his imagined paramour in the second person singular and occasionally even in the vocative,[36] Lysias addresses his crush largely in the more indirect second person plural and never in the vocative. He suggests both stylistically and thematically that an intimacy in which both parties give of themselves indiscriminately is bound to lead to suffering. But as Socrates later observes, this effort to fix the logic of the gift eventually collapses into incoherence.

One of the prime advantages of consorting with a non-lover, Lysias notes near the beginning of his speech, is that whereas the lover gives by necessity (ὑπ᾽ ἀνάγκης), the non-lover gives willingly (ἑκόντες) (231a).[37] The non-lover's gifts are not compelled by the weight of his need, but are dispensed freely and without condition. This means that the lover is more likely both to regret the gifts he has given after his passion has dissipated and to keep a tally (σκοποῦσιν) of his gifts in anticipation of their return. This stringent accounting ensures that the beloved is unlikely to receive any great surplus and will be resented for any surplus he does run. In contrast, because the non-lover is released from this economy of necessity, he will have nothing holding him back and will thus tend to give with zeal (προθύμως).

This appeal only works, though, to the extent that the beloved responds to generosity by carefully weighing his in- and outflow of favours. When deciding whether to share one's body, Lysias asks, 'how is it plausible [εἰκός] to hand over something so precious[38] to someone with such an affliction that no experienced person would even try to cure it? For lovers certainly agree that they are sick rather than of sound mind' (231d). The beloved thus needs to meet the madness that Lysias supposes underlies the lover's jealous guarding of his gifts with a clear-headed guarding of his own gifts. But if both madness and clear-headedness inspire stinginess, then where does Lysias suppose the non-lover's generosity comes from? He argues that 'when such ills are cleared out of the way' there is nothing left but for the lover to give openly, but why should the non-lover not engage in exactly the sort of calculation that the beloved does? The indirectness of Lysias's approach suggests that he wants the beloved to treat the relationship with a sense of remove and thus to treat gifts as external goods to be valued for their own worth and not for the (messy) connections they facilitate. But the good that he is asking the beloved to trade is precisely intimacy, and thus in order to make his case he has to transform it into its opposite: an externality. While Lysias would like the beloved to think of sexual favours as surrenderings of what is most proper to him in dealings with a lover, he suggests that they become mere gestures when given to a non-lover. Because non-lovers base their exchanges of favours on a foundation of friendship (φίλοι) rather than desire, 'it is implausible that their engagement in these happy experiences would diminish their friendship; rather such things remain tokens [μνημεῖα] of things to come' (233a). Once love has been excised from a relationship, all gifts can be taken without accruing a sense of debt; they are simply there to be given and taken at one's pleasure. Indeed, Lysias concludes the speech by suggesting that the offer itself be taken simply as a kind of gift, with a promise of more to come if requested: 'My words, are, I trust, sufficient. But if you desire more, thinking that I have left something out, all you need do is ask [εἰ δ' ἔτι <τι> σὺ ποθεῖς, ἡγούμενος παραλελεῖφθαι, ἐρώτα]' (234c). His gift, Lysias wants his listeners to believe, is merely a solicitation to further exchange, not a trap of enforced intimacy.

But as Socrates' counterspeech shows, the gift of oneself cannot be separated from the desire (ἐπιθυμία) and obligations that pervade all intimacy. In his reimagining of Lysias's speech, Socrates gives lip-service to this notion of speech as a gift, invoking the Muses for the only time in all of Plato's dialogues to give him the gift of beautiful speech (237a).[39] Almost immediately, however, he shifts from asking for a unilateral gift from the Muses to suggesting a collaboration with his interlocutor on formulating a definition of love and delineating its powers (237d). For Socrates, the notion of a speech as a gift for the listener to take or leave is repugnant, for speech itself involves a mutual acceptance of necessity (ἀνάγκη).[40]

Accordingly, he concludes that the lover's problem is not that the force of his need is too powerful to give freely, but that he is weakened by his passions and thus cannot stand to be in a relationship with someone more powerful than he. He weakens the beloved not by obliging him to pursue a more intimate relationship, but by severing and forestalling his connections to such other things as friends, family, education, work and property. Here Socrates says nothing about the demands that the lover imposes on the beloved, and indeed the other things that the lover jealously blocks – work, education, family and the lot – all place substantial demands of their own on the beloved. The flaw in the obsessed lover's approach is just that he seeks to dissolve the inclinations toward intimacy that these other demands serve to cultivate in the beloved. In Socrates' reimagining of the speech, it is only when the relationship breaks down that debts become genuine burdens. After the charm of the relationship has worn off, the lover will seek to shirk the promises he has made, and the beloved will become the pursuer, asking for something tangible in return for his past favours (241a–b).

The intimacy the lover desires, however, is in itself something beneficial. Indeed, Socrates goes out of his way to remind the beloved that even the most insufferable lover can be pleasant in some ways. Since love can rejuvenate even the hoariest suitors, there are some pleasures to be found in their company, but the problem is that 'such fellowship reaches a saturation point [ἀλλ' ὅμως κόρονγε καὶ ἡ τοῦ των συνουσία ἔχει]' (240c). The problem, that is, is not that the lover gives, but that some lovers close off the possibility of other gifts whose value they cannot equal. Thus when Socrates reverses course in his second speech and explains why the lover is to be preferred, he has already prepared the way by showing that what the beloved ought to value most is the total quantity of intimacy. While this second speech does not deny the restrictions that love can sometimes place on the beloved, it values the connection inspired by love much more highly. Where the loving relationship offers the divine gift of mutual growth, 'a non-lover's intimacy [οἰκειότης] is diluted by mortal moderation and pays meager mortal benefits' (256e). The fact that the non-lover's gifts are so carefully measured is not a guarantee of rewarding and lifelong intimacy, but rather a throttle that keeps the relationship in first gear.

While this is most obviously a problem when the terms of a gift-exchange are specified in advance, the gift puts a limit on intimacy even for the open-ended and ongoing forms of exchange that Bourdieu and Ricoeur describe. Even when the gift does not close off the relationship through an imperative to give, its openness is merely one-sided. Lysias's measured gift-exchange is only an extreme example of the onesidedness of all forms of giving. The gift does not share in the intimacy of a touch or conversation and in effect states: 'I've done my part. Now it's your move.' Rather than continuously evolving, the interplay it inaugurates is turn-based. The problem (as we saw with Fichte) is not that a gift necessarily imposes an obligation to the donor, since the recipient can choose to accept this obligation and tie himself more closely to the donor. The problem is that the gift always leaves something extant between the partners. No matter how much partners may *enjoy* being tied to one another, the gift holds them apart as much as it pulls them together. The failure of a particular gift is a failure to come to terms, a failure to achieve concord on what property is to be transferred, who shall give, who shall receive, and under what conditions. But the limitation of the gift in general is its appeal to terms in the first place. What it seeks is an endless series of adequate conditions for intimacy rather than intimacy as such. Its unrealized wish is that intimacy might be found in perfect intentions rather than an openness to contradiction.

2

Touching

The failure of the gift, we have just seen, is that even when it goes off without a hitch it leaves something outstanding between donor and recipient. Though it strives to bring donor and recipient as close together as possible, it aims to do so by placing something between them. Touching, on the other hand, seeks intimacy in immediacy. To touch someone, truly to touch them, would seem already to suspend every inhibition of intimacy and achieve it directly. If I am not most inside you, I am at least there with or at you.

The moment before I touch you, when I realize there is nothing to stop me from touching you, the very question of whether we are ever really intimate with one another briefly seems silly. We are, after all, right here together, and we can simply touch. The desire to touch need not be a desire to take hold of or to incorporate one's partner, and the very resistance of the partner provides a certain comfort. When the movie protagonist realizes he is a ghost, he may be excited by the ability to pass unimpeded through walls, but his inability to bring his hands to rest upon another person invariably disturbs him. He longs for that ability to be impeded by another. Such a touching longs for and takes pleasure in borders. If the boundaries of the other were nonexistent or could simply be passed through, then the touch would not be hypersuccessful, but a complete failure.

We thus speak most properly of touching in the progressive aspect. A gift is static, and it is precisely in this stasis that the giver seeks to gain purchase on intimacy. Because it persists in time, the gift would be proof of lasting intimacy. But touching is continuous. The toucher does not hope to establish an enduring connection through a single touch, but to indulge in an ongoing, even if fleeting, intimacy.

But touching is also built on discontinuity. You and I can never occupy the same place, and if we could, we would be in the position of the movie ghost, suddenly frightened that our touch is completely uninhibited. My touch does not wish to displace you, but neither is it a recognition of our respective rights to our places. After tumbling down a hill, I may stand and pat myself all over my body to make sure everything is still in its proper place. But when I seek to touch my partner, I am not just looking for knowledge that she is present and sound. I want to know that we are together, not merely as objects proximal to one another in Newtonian space, but as sharing something through touching. In this way, touching is unique among the senses. As Elaine Scarry has noted, the experience of touching is indexed to a location on my body in a much more obvious way than seeing or hearing.[1] If I see my partner, I do not experience this as seeing her *at* my eyes in the same way that our point of contact is located *at* my hand, my neck, and so on. Touching initially seems to promise a site for partners to be together.

Yet the progressive aspect of touching also allows it to exceed the boundaries of this site. The Greek word ἅπτω, which stands at the origin of so much of the contemporary discussion of touching, meant in Homeric Greek something akin to tying or fixing together. In this archaic sense, a touch is not primarily locative or peripheral; it is a connecting. There is a closeness found in touching that is not reducible to any cognition of my place and yours. As Nancy puts it, 'It is by touching the other that the body is a body, absolutely separated and shared [*partagé*]'.[2]

Touching as shared experience

But what is this something that is shared? As Merleau-Ponty famously showed in *The Visible and the Invisible*, a touch cannot help but divide into an inside and an outside, a subject and an object. When I touch you, when I shake your hand, for instance, we do indeed share a touch, but I do so as one who is touching and you do so as one who is being touched. It matters little for the immediate phenomenon that you are also the touching one and I am also the touched one, since any fixation on the *experience* of touching will reveal my touching and being touched to be separate from your touching and being touched.[3] When, following Merleau-Ponty, I touch my left hand with my right, I find touching and being touched to be separate phenomena even as I can more or less freely switch back and forth between the sensations. My touching is never identical with your being-touched, as I find even my own touching and being-touched to be distinct from one another.[4]

Thus it would seem that an act of touching could never establish a genuine intimacy[5] between two partners. Because my touching and being touched are fundamentally distinct not only from your touching and being touched, but from my own, it would seem that every touch is destined to carve a rift between us. Every time I touched you I could not help but intuit that you and I could never share even the most basic experience. Yet touching *is* satisfying (at least to a degree), which ought to give us pause in applying Merleau-Ponty's phenomenological analysis of touching uncritically. Jean-Luc Nancy offers a powerful critique of this approach: 'The phenomenological analyses of "self-touching" always return to a primary interiority. Which is impossible. To begin with, I have to be in exteriority in order to touch myself. And what I touch remains on the outside' (*Corpus*, 128–9).[6] Nancy here alludes to the dual sense of intimacy as referring both to my closeness to another and to that part of me that is deepest and thus most removed from another. Merleau-Ponty's phenomenological account of touching reaches a dead end in assuming that the first of these senses depends on the second. To say that my touch is distinct from yours because I never feel both at the same time is to assume that what is real about touching is the influence of the exterior on the interior. But this is not at all what touching as a form of intimacy wants. My desire to touch you is not a desire to receive a set of pleasurable stimuli comparable to yours, but a desire to cultivate an intimacy between us. Merleau-Ponty's account of the chiasm of one hand touching the other does not even portray what it means to feel intimate with one's own body. As Nancy writes, to be intimate with one's body is to feel nothing, 'But when I sense my stomach or my ear, or my lung, I sense it, and if I sense it, it's from the outside' (*Corpus*, 129). There is nothing intimate about the way my internal organs touch despite the fact that they are as inside me as anything can get. Wherever touching does begin to approach intimacy, the organ tends to disappear as a phenomenon. The intimacy that touching seeks is not the identity or contiguity of two individuals' sensations, but an intertwining of being. When I hold hands with a partner, I do not need to imagine what it must feel like for him to be holding mine in order to grasp the intimacy of the relation. In a similar observation, Irigaray describes the intimacy of 'the joined hands, not those that take hold one of the other, grasp each other, but the hands that touch without taking hold – like the lips' (ESD 170). Our union need not be a chiasm of two (or four, depending on how one counts) experiences, but can be analysed as a more pervasive feeling of togetherness. This drive for simultaneity grows out of a desire to get a handle on what exactly consti-tutes the relationship, a need to suspend the chiasmatic structure of touching for a simple, undifferentiated unity. As Derrida writes, 'In pleasure, the caress besieges us, it invests us with a nontheoretical and besetting question, with a worry constitutive of pleasure itself: "What is this pleasure? What is that? Where does it come from? From the other or from me? Am I taking it? Am I giving it?"' (Derrida, *On Touching*, 75). Insofar as touching longs for an inter-twining of being, it can be satisfied neither by the differentiation of the two partners nor by their nondifferentiation, for both merely highlight that the intimacy appears somewhere outside of the touch.

Thus it is altogether fitting that we should use the same word, 'intimate', for what is most inside me and my closest connection to another person. For Nancy, it is only natural that intimacy's focus on what is inmost should most commonly be applied to something prevailing among multiple people, since isolated individualism is self-contradictory: 'If intimacy must be defined as the extremity of coincidence with oneself, then what exceeds intimacy in interiority is the distancing of coincidence itself … it is no accident that we use the word "intimacy" to designate a relation between several people more often than a relation to oneself. Our being-with, as a being-many is not at all accidental … *The plurality of beings is at the foundation of Being.*'[7] Here Nancy is making a crucial point about the drive for intimacy's tendency to interpose what is most inside and what is most closely outside, but he also falls into the same trap as Merleau-Ponty or the lover who says, 'I feel so close to you right now' and takes this feeling as intimacy. He is trying to make the *experience* of intimacy central to its very being. But so long as intimacy fixates on a core experience that must somehow be shared with another, it imagines a gap that it does not know how to bridge.[8] While Nancy is right to question the assumption that intimacy consists in the closeness of two self-sufficient beings, his (undialectical) attempt to transform this into a lesson about the 'foundation of Being' fails to establish how touching can be something intimate.

Proportion

But in its escape from the phenomenological trap of prioritizing experience, touching tends to fall into an equally stubborn trap, whose temptations can be seen already in Aristotle's account of touching in *On the Soul*. To Derrida's question of whether a caress is something I give or receive, Aristotle's answer would have to be 'Both'. According to Aristotle, none of our five senses is actually immediate, since even touching gains access to its object through a medium of air or water (*On the Soul*, 423b). Nowadays we might speak of the epidermis in relation to the dermis and various nerves, but the insight would be the same. Aristotle notes that if we were to find that we touched every-thing through a thin cloth membrane, then the toucher's relation to the object of touch would remain essentially unchanged. The skin does not perceive the world in its immediacy, but is rather the medium (μέσος) in which the world appears to us as perceivable.[9] Thus what distinguishes touch from senses like sight and hearing is not its immediacy, but its activity. Like taste (but unlike sight, hearing and smell), touching does not merely receive a sensation from an active medium, but solicits a medium that itself can be affected.[10] To explain this insight, Aristotle gives the example of a shield struck by a spear. When I feel the impact of the spear, I am only able to perceive the impact because the shield is itself affected by the spear (*On the Soul*, 423b). It is built into the very structure of touching that its object provide some resistance but be accessible only on account of a medium that is itself vulnerable. To touch another is not to make her body an immediate object of my sense of touch, but to enter into a relationship in which both my skin and hers are capable of being displaced.

Touching is thus a realm in which excess is reassuringly possible, in which the possibility of failure – of too hard or too light a touch, of too great or too little frequency – makes the contact of surfaces meaningful. Touching both assumes and establishes a proportionality between the toucher and the touched. We share a touch not when it effaces the difference between the inside and outside of an experience, but when it can have an approximately equal effect on both of us. A world in which it is impossible to exceed boundaries, whether of proportion or propriety, is one in which intimacy is impossible. It is no accident that we say someone has *tact* when she grasps that immediacy should sometimes be subordinated to the imperative to back off.[11] Thus the structural limitation of touching is not that it fails to find the immediacy that it is looking for, for immediacy is not requisite for touching in the first place. Touching's structural flaw, rather, is that its sense of proportion is dependent on the possibility of disproportion – signs that the other is not fully contained by his boundaries. When Bart brings his dog to school in an early episode of *The Simpsons*, the bully character Nelson insists, 'You gotta pet him hard so he can *feel* it', and proceeds to stroke the dog so hard that its eyes bulge out. At some level Nelson understands that a touch that fails to affect the partner is no touch at all.

While touching may at first pass itself off as the desire for a fleeting experience of the partner, it always aims for an intimacy beyond mere experience. In order to avoid retreating into a mere phenomenalism that takes the meaning of the touch to be how it feels to me, I need some way of establishing that *this* is a real touch. Boys may shake hands smeared with their own spit or blood to symbolize that the touch is more than a touch, that it actually touches on something inside of each. The pervert (and I use that term in the most loving way possible) wants even more – to be peed on for instance, so as to know that her partner is not limiting access to the mere surface of his body. When the other cannot be held, we seek his detritus – his autograph, his old chewing gum. To touch what has been touched by another is to get a kind of handle on him. When we presuppose a large disproportion-ality between the touched and the one who longs to touch, as for instance in the case of a celebrity, to touch indirectly or to touch only a part of the person can seem more appropriate. I might be so awestruck that shaking hands with the President conveys no intimacy at all, but I could very well feel excited to handle a pen he used to sign important legislation. In touching this pen, I understand implicitly that there is no absolute border separating the President from me, but rather a disproportion that calls for a different sort of touching than the one I typically cultivate with my loved ones. While such an indirect touch is of course no match for the intimacy I feel in stroking the hair of my sick child, it could oddly give me a greater feeling of intimacy than shaking hands with someone so elevated as the President. Likewise, in the book of Mark when the incurably bleeding woman wishes only to touch Jesus' garment, although her healing is a sign that there is a vast disproportion between her and Jesus, Jesus feels enough to know that this is a reciprocal interaction even if a grossly asymmetrical one (Mark 5:25–34). In desiring only the lightest of touches, the woman recognizes the disproportion between herself and the Son of God, but what she wants nevertheless is to touch him, to find some acceptable level of intimacy that can be shared.

The myth of the inmost touch

This need to test and adjust proportions can give rise to some of the most destructive manifestations of touching. The need for a touch to prove its own intimacy leads to the positing of arbitrary boundaries in order to establish, like the two boys shaking blood-smeared hands, that unlike other touches, this is a *real* one. Yet as Simone de Beauvoir has shown, the need to find a touching beyond touching replaces satisfying and open human interactions with ones prestructured and foreclosed by destructive myths. In *The Second Sex*, Beauvoir traces a variety of such myths about sex, many of which are guided by an unhealthy obsession with borders. The globally pervasive fixation on the uncleanliness of menstruation, for instance, can be read as an uncomfortability with women's tendency to exceed their own borders. Even more destructive is the virginity fetish. Since touching in itself does not establish a lasting bond, men have sought ways to establish the permanence or exclusivity of the sexual bond.[12] The fetishization of virginity responds to the ephemerality of the sexual touch by positing that the *first* touch counts more (SS 172). If a man cannot even establish a completely intimate bond with his partner by being *inside* her – which of course quickly shows itself to be a misguided aim since even in sexual intercourse to be 'inside' is still to be outside – then he supposes that what makes a touch the most intimate is not the depth of its penetration but its temporal primacy.[13]

In societies where women are more feared, Beauvoir argues, the same dialectic gives rise to an opposing set of myths. Beauvoir cites various anthropological accounts (of varying reliability, I should note) of indigenous societies in which virginity is so feared that it must be taken by chieftains, outsiders, or inanimate objects before a marriage can be consummated (SS 172–3). Here the same basic assumption is operative as in societies that prize virginity: a touch is just a touch, but a first touch can work wonders. Regardless of whether they take intimacy with a woman as something to be desired or feared, both sets of myths assume that intimacy is not something that can be accomplished through touching. Indeed, the fact that they believe that intimacy is something to be *accomplished* stands at odds with the progressive aspect of touching. This need for a touch to be consummated preordains that no act of touching will ever be adequate. Such myths thus impose on the field of touching an extrinsic fascination with borders that exults only in their overcoming. They thus offer little promise of cultivating lasting intimacy and thus live, as Beauvoir notes, in the mythical realm.

While the persistence of such myths should give us pause in assuming that they are destined to be overcome, what is at issue in them is no longer the intimacy of touch. Such intimacy, whether it is frightening or highly desired, is assumed only to be accessible through some external quality. Indeed, many of these myths are manifestations not of a drive for intimacy, but of the more basic drive of self-consciousness to be master of its universe. In Beauvoir's words, they replace an intimate encounter with a woman with 'the taste for eternity at bargain prices and for a handy, pocket-sized absolute' (SS 272). The virginity fetish reflects not only a desire for intimacy but man's attempt to relate himself to nature or mortality *through* woman (SS 176). Beauvoir even suggests that underlying all of these myths might be a common terror at the impossibility of annexing alterity (SS 187). While it is not in itself conclusive, the alternating fascination, disgust and horror at this possibility of a touch beyond touch points toward a dialectical limitation in all touching. To the extent that I want to instigate intimacy with a partner through touching, I have no way of establishing that my own touch is *intimus*, not just in or upon him but *most* upon him. Such diversions of touching as virginity fetishization thus act as surrogates for a mythical sort of touching that could be consummated. The goal of such intimacy would not be intimacy, but the sort of perfect mirror that gives man a full tangible double of himself rather than a flat image: 'what he wants from her is to be, outside of him, all that he cannot grasp in himself, because the interiority of the existent is only nothingness, and to reach himself, he must project himself onto an object' (SS 203). In this movement, touching becomes a battleground for a war it has no interest in fighting. The recognition needed in order for someone to feel whole is never something that could be accomplished in a stroke, yet when we are starving for it, it sometimes seems that all we need is one final instance of it in order to be complete. Because of its apparent immediacy and because it is by definition fleeting, a touch can act as a surrogate for a more fulfilling and long-lasting form of recognition, but when this occurs it is not intimacy at all that is sought, but something else entirely.

We find a parallel movement in Nancy's analysis of the Catholic Eucharist. In the ritualized statement, *hoc est enim corpus meum*, 'For *this* is my body', the priest says something remarkable. Against all sense of disproportion between the divine and the human, he insists that Christ's body is something here, something *intimate*, something that can be taken up into the body of the worshipper. This promise speaks to a longing for a kind of touching that would be able to cultivate intimacy without worries about the proportionality of the touching. It would be a kind of gift that no longer stands between God and humanity, but in its very giving establishes their unity. But as in the fetishization of virginity that Beauvoir describes, here, too, the possibility of an ongoing intimacy is sacrificed for the dream of a single moment of perfect closeness. The object of the Eucharist is not to prolong the contact with Christ, but to complete a connection, to bring him into oneself and hope that this intimacy might last beyond the immediate touch.[14]

Such a connection can fairly claim to be intimate in the superlative sense, but it has lost the progressive aspect that is constitutive of touching. The Eucharist in effect becomes a gift from God to man, one that stands between the two until it dissolves into a non-entity. To preserve a continuing connection between partners, touching must project itself *into* its partner. What such self-projection wants is to annex the experience of being touched as part of the act of touching and, reciprocally, to make the transfer of the toucher's experience to the touched partner part of this same act. If the toucher feels pleasure, then he longs that the touched partner feel that exact same pleasure, and if he feels pain, then he wants that same pain to appear in his partner as well. Since there is very little intimacy in the privacy of sensation, touching wants confirmation that its is the truest touch, the one that at last brings toucher and touched into perfect concord. But as we have seen, insofar as it is the *experience* that is highlighted, this wish must remain unfulfilled, since the experience of the touch is necessarily something private.[15] The sheer simultaneity and congruence of two sensations, even if we could find sufficient proof that such simultaneity occurs, does not establish their identity.

The wound

It is thus not enough for touching that we be contiguous. I need to establish some greater level of intimacy through the touch. I need to feel your incompleteness, your wounds.[16] For Doubting Thomas, it was impossible to accede to Jesus' injunction to Mary Magdalene not even to think about touching him (John 20:24–9). To know Jesus was real, to establish any kind of meaningful apostolic connection with him, he needed not just to lay his hands on Jesus, but to insert his hand *in him*.[17] Indeed, one finds this emphasis on Christ's vulnerability throughout Christian theology.[18] Christ is not just a God who takes human flesh in order to heal; he also possesses flesh that has been wounded. A God who can be wounded is one whom we can touch not just as a resistant surface, but one on whom our touch can actually have an effect. Touching wants not just to caress[19] the surface of the partner, but to prove that she is accessible, and it takes vulnerability to be the ultimate measure of this accessibility. Such is the lure of stigmata: in someone's sharing of God's wounds, we see the path to a closeness beyond closeness with God.[20]

To be able to inflict a wound on the partner, to be able to penetrate the invisible membrane that shields the partner's face from violence,[21] does in a way demonstrate the possibility of exceeding the caress, but such a violent act is only satisfying in the transgression of boundaries. The intimacy of the blow or cut thus dissipates with the completion of the action and can hardly be renewed even if the wounded party remains present. To touch a preexisting wound, in contrast, is to find the other already accessible to a touch that exceeds touching.

For the child who has learned the impermissibility of hitting, tickling offers a satisfying alternative because it demonstrates her partner's ever-present vulnerability. When I tickle you, my touching does not just give me the immediate sensations of contact, but elicits a response that shows the touching is an arena of mutual participation. As Darwin notes in a charming late essay, an act of tickling will be unsuccessful as long as it fails to find a suitable middle ground between delicacy and malice.[22] And unlike the infliction of pain or injury, tickling encourages ongoing engagement rather than the retreat into private woe. Behavioural and evolutionary psychologists have shown the role of tickling in developing communal bonds among humans and other primates,[23] and Jaak Panksepp has even shown that the same phenomenon can be found in rats.[24] There would seem to be genuine social advantages to being able to show other members of one's species that they can affect you in a powerful but non-threatening way. However, in tickling the response of the partner is still elicited by an action of the tickler, and the giggling of the 'victim' is not the same as their laying themselves bare. The tickling is not itself a wounding, and the giggling is not itself a wound; the giggling only points to a *capacity* to be wounded. The wound would have to be an exposure not solicited by the toucher and thus stands as a vulnerability preceding all openness.

This fascination with wounds is also pervasive in the type of myths of female sexuality that Beauvoir explores.[25] The vagina has been referred to poetically as an 'open' or 'unceasing wound' at least since Lucretius,[26] and it is not difficult to see how this vulnerability can play an erotic role. To the extent that the vagina is a wound, it can be either a site needing the utmost protection from violence (as in Levinas)[27] or the singular location where one can claim complete intimacy with a woman (as in common pornography). In either case, this so-called 'wound' is a sign that the borders of a partner are never absolute, that an open vulnerability always persists.

The exploration of this wound is, however, necessarily one-sided. While my partner appears as open to my touch, I am not open to his. At the site of the wound, there is not mutual touching, but a clear delineation between touching and being touched. And if my partner and I should happen both to be wounded, we are thrown back into the solipsism of phenomenology. Rather than sharing in a common touch, we would each be revelling in each other's discrete wounds. There is, moreover, a disturbing lack of intimacy that arises when the body has been transformed into nothing but a wound. Because the wounded person will often have far more intense a relation to her wound than even the partner given the most intimate access to it,[28] it tends to isolate the wounded person all the more.[29] The wound is initially attractive because it shows that the wounded person is not a closed system, but in all but the rarest cases (as perhaps of the resurrected Jesus with Doubting Thomas) touching it will cause this person to withdraw into herself.[30]

But what of this rare case – when touching the wound makes the wounded party feel not a shock of being violated or a retreat into private pain but an ecstasis into the other induced by the wonder that the partner has finally arrived to touch something no one else has? Here touching is governed not by the desire for an immediate encounter but by what in Chapter 6 I will call embedding – an intimacy developed through the contrast of the relationship at hand with all other relationships. The intimacy of the consensually touched wound is thus an ironic one that lacks the self-sufficiency that touching believes itself to want. Its intimacy would not be found in an immediate encounter or sharing of experiences, but in a contrast of this relation with others. What it wants is not a touching beyond touching, but an enclosure of every other relationship in the relationship at hand. This ironic distance is only magnified when the two partners take on the discrete roles of nurse and patient. While there is undoubtedly an intimacy in this relationship in that the nurse is allowed to touch places to which no one else is permitted access, this intimacy can only be preserved under the stipulation that this relationship is no different from others of the same kind. Even if the newly designated 'nurse' has no other, and has never had any other, patients, the interaction is premised on the assumption that this is just what nurses do, and thus the intimacy of the encounter can only be maintained so long as both partners pretend that there is nothing especially intimate about it.

But insofar as touching seeks to distinguish itself from all other touches primarily through its own character as touching, it will be forced to rely on myths of consanguinal unity, virginal priority, etc., none of which can be established in the act of touching itself. The wound is deeper than the surface-cut through which 'blood brothers' establish their unique connection, but it is precisely this depth that wards off the free approach of the partner. The wound is for the most part too internal to allow for any space of interchange, and even when interchange does emerge, it is on the basis of such an asymmetrical relationship between toucher and touched that the touched can only ever really retreat. Contact with the wound is not a deepening or intensification of the continuity of everyday touching, but a disruption of it.

Thus while touching initially set out to establish intimacy in a manner opposite to that of the gift, namely by removing all intermediaries between the partners rather than by introducing a new and unexpected one, it ultimately succumbs to the same structural failing. Since, as Aristotle had already seen, touching is never simply immediate, the drive for intimacy has led to the positing of a variety of conditions under which its own touch might be more intimate than others. But all along it has assumed that the relationships between partners are structured by their respective borders – that if only these borders could be positioned correctly, one relationship could show itself to be closer than all the others. Since such a border would have to establish a distinction between the inside and the outside of the touched partner, a fixation on touching as a route to intimacy would merely replace the gift one gives the partner with the border the partner gives. While the goal is a touching so perfect that the border disappears, such a disappearance would annul the touch just as a giving in which nothing is ever given would annul the gift. Touching is thus a search for immediacy that cannot help but posit a space of mediation. Yet because it was the very drive for immediacy that drove touching to get bogged down in mediation, its next move is not to eliminate mediation but to seek out something that could be shared perfectly between the partners. Rather than encroaching upon the partner, it wants to find a way of accommodating her so exactly that her very being is shared.

Already in this movement we find an intimation that intimacy cannot just be a matter of letting one's partner be. If intimacy required bringing into accord two preformed subjects who must approach each other in wonder at their differences, then it would always have to stall in the crossing or negotiation of boundaries.[31] For intimacy to emerge, the process must work in the reverse direction: it is not intimacy that is established between subjects, but subjectivity that emerges through intimacy (among other forms of recognition). Here again Beauvoir proves a useful guide in her distinction between revitalizing and damaging forms of touching. For Beauvoir, the fact that touching never completely succeeds in taking hold of the other does not mean that it is doomed to dissatisfaction. She contrasts the incomplete but nevertheless relatively unproblematic striving of healthy adult male sexuality with the conflicting sexuality of a woman resigned to her status as the second sex: 'of course he does not succeed in appropriating them: at least he holds them; the embrace and the kiss imply a partial failure: but this very failure is a stimulant and a joy' (SS 383). If such a man fails to transform his touch into possession, he is unbothered by this fact, pleased with the illusion of intimacy's imminence, if not its immanence. If he accepts it uncritically, this self-satisfaction proves to be a delusion, since it presumes that the self can be made whole and every wound forgotten in the very search for an intimate touch. Worse still, it can deafen him to the complaints that his partners' experiences of touching do not at all coincide with his own. But the restorative aspects of touching nevertheless show that touching is not simply empty of intimacy. Touching cannot lay bare what it means to be oneself or to be intimate with another, but it awakens partners to their non-coincidence with themselves. By engaging in contact irreducible to any private sensation, they begin to experience what it feels like not to be each other.

3

The Heartbeat

The satisfaction of touching is always only provisional. In the undifferentiated, progressive aspect of touching partners can for a time suspend the inevitable non-consummation of the relationship, but this calls for a strict maintenance of each touch's proportionality. Whether very light or very hard, touching must show its adequacy to the relationship, and yet touching cannot help fiddling with this proportionality to establish once and for all that this touch is the *inmost*. The immediacy of touching is thus continually disrupted as new boundaries are introduced, and its closeness remains structurally incomplete.

Touching has thus perhaps gone too far in its rejection of the gift's search for intimacy in discrete encounters. In place of an intimacy that is either achieved or lost in a perfect act of generosity, it posits an ongoing intimacy through contact, then flounders when it fails to distinguish one moment of touching from any other. What seems to be called for is a form of intimacy that operates neither in solely the perfect nor in solely the progressive aspect, but finds intimacy in an ongoing sequence of discrete acts of adjustment to one's partner. What (following Schelling among others) I will call the *heartbeat* strives to split the difference between the gift's discreteness and touching's indeterminacy. Its emphasis on renewing the relationship through constant adjustments escapes the monotony of touching, but where the gift longs for that perfect moment of inauguration, the heartbeat finds itself repeatedly seeing its partner as if for the first time.[1] Here both the repetition of this 'seeing' and the subjunctive form of the 'as if' are crucial to its structure. Such an intimacy does not imagine that its intimacy is *achieved* in a moment of insight, but it does require that these moments be treated *as if* each were the key moment of the relationship. The heartbeat in effect stipulates that these moments of special insight will be *considered* turning points in the relationship.[2]

If I cannot perfectly cancel my partner's otherness, this subjunctive reasoning goes, perhaps I could find myself perfectly in tune with her. I would find our intimacy not by eliminating the distance between us, but by accommodating myself to her.[3] When she contracts into a purely self-seeking kernel I vow to expand to accommodate all her self-seeking needs, and when she expands into beneficence I vow to accept all that she has to offer. At regular or irregular intervals, I find myself suddenly attuned to her anew and seek to calibrate my relation to her such that I am not just sharing a space with her but living *her* world alongside her. While life is apt to distract me from the relationship, unexpected changes in my partner from time to time remind me of her singularity and the necessity of my adjusting to accommodate this singularity. We can turn to Merleau-Ponty's *The Visible and the Invisible* for a particularly vivid account of the phenomenon:

> Here is this well-known countenance, this smile, these modulations of voice, whose style is as familiar to me as myself. Perhaps in many moments of my life the other is for me reduced to this spectacle, which can be a charm. But should the voice alter, should the unwonted appear in the score of the dialogue, or, on the contrary, should a response respond too well to what I thought without really having said it – and suddenly there breaks forth the evidence that yonder also, minute by minute, life is being lived: somewhere behind those eyes, behind those gestures, or rather before them, or again about them, coming from I know not what double ground of space, another private world shows through, through the fabric of my own, and for a moment I live it; I am no more than the respondent for the interpellation that is made to me. To be sure, the least recovery of attention persuades me that this other who invades me is made only of my own substance: how could I conceive, precisely as *his*, *his* colors, *his* pain, *his* world, except as in accordance with the colors I see, the pains I have had, the world wherein I live? But at least my private world has ceased to be mine only; it is now the instrument which another plays, the dimension of a generalized life which is grafted onto my own.[4]

At first glance, the sudden appearance of 'generalized life' at the end of this account seems entirely plausible but not at all necessary. When I suddenly find myself opened up to another's world, I might indeed become aware that my private experience is part of a vast world shared by many others, but I might instead attempt to hold on to this accommodation of my partner's world and go no farther. After all, the possibility of sharing life with someone I know intimately does not imply that all life is essentially shared. We will see later, however, that it is difficult to hold on to this sudden insight without appealing to some common life we both share and thus to some generalized milieu of life. For now, though, it is enough to note the way in which the two senses of 'intimacy', those of connection and depth, merge in Merleau-Ponty's account. I would find myself closest to my partner when I am able to follow him into what is most deeply private in his world. As we saw in the previous chapter, I would not be able to share any actual sensations, but I could at least share his desire to let me in to his world as well as his desire that he be allowed into mine. Intimacy thus would not be conceived as the spatial immediacy of two bodies or the timeless identification of two experiences, but would instead take on the temporal dimension of simultaneity. My partner and I strive for our corresponding impulses of expansion and contraction to occur simultaneously, which would allow us to live alongside one another in harmony. Here Merleau-Ponty appears to get the phenomenology of this striving just right. My partner's look and feel cannot help but become familiar, and this familiarity can itself at times spark a certain fondness. I feel close to him because he is exactly what I expect him to be. Gradually he becomes a brightly growing spectacle and I retreat to being a mere spectator. But when I am struck by something novel about his appearance, I find myself seeking out his inner depths. I no longer reside in a private world, but throw myself out into an expansive and indeterminate one.[5] This oscillation shakes free of the monotony of undifferentiated touching and promises a more vibrant togetherness that does not have to be compressed into an instant.

Systole and diastole

This expansive sense of wonder would be interrupted if I framed it either as my incorporation into my partner or his incorporation into me. If intimacy cannot be found in contact with the surface of the partner, it is still more hopeless to look for it in the incorporation of one partner into the other. The dialectic of touching has shown that if intimacy were nothing but the positing and annulment of boundaries, then intimacy would exist only in its own vanishing. If, on the other hand, intimacy were based on the progressive incorporation of a resistant or recalcitrant partner, then it could be sustained only so long as the progress of this incorporation continues – so long as the shark continues moving forward, as it were.[6] There is no final achievement of the heartbeat, since this could only consist in one partner's slavish (and thus inconsequential) self-subordination to the other. But when I allow my impulse to expand or contract to play off of my partner's symmetrical impulse, our respective expansions and contractions can comprise a stable yet dynamic relationship. This is a relationship in which the partners define their closeness not by who they are or what they share but by their mutual adequation to one another. Though the partners may seek to understand this movement by positing it in some larger medium (a marriage, a friendship, the Holy Spirit, etc.), it is not the medium that structures the intimacy, but the process of expansion and contraction itself. The goal of the heartbeat is not the establishment of some ultimate basis on which the relationship can develop, but a simultaneity whereby one partner expands as the other contracts and vice versa.

To my knowledge, no philosopher has traced this movement as thoroughly as Schelling.[7] (He traces it so thoroughly, in fact, that it will take me a few pages of exegesis before I am able to return to the main thread of the dialectic. To the reader who makes it through this dense section, thank you for your indulgence.) It is a movement that constantly posits distinctions between self and other, spirit and nature, human and God, and reaffirms that these distinctions are after all creations of some greater unity. The differentiation is necessary, but it does not let itself be forgotten, continually reappearing as a pulsing of the boundaries that separate partners. It is no accident, I think, that the metaphor of the expanding and contracting heart appears throughout Schelling's work, describing the functioning of organisms, the relation of the human spirit to its body, and the creation of the universe from out of its dark ground.[8] For Schelling, particularity as such is unintelligible without reference to the unity from which it arises and the pulsing desire each particular feels both to differentiate itself from and reunite it with its opposite. It would thus be a mistake to see Schelling as mapping the alternating fury and languor[9] of human love onto the domains of nature and metaphysics. Just as for the partners sunk in the depths of a pulsing intimacy there is no distinction between the working of the partnership and the workings of the world, for Schelling the movement of lovers *is* the movement of identity.[10] At every level of nature, elements of a broader unity find occasion to divide themselves *as if* they were not always already united.

Since Schelling was a philosopher of unparalleled ambition in the modern era, and since so many of his works aim to touch on the whole of philosophy,[11] his work so vastly outstrips my present concerns that it requires a substantial narrowing of focus simply to justify his inclusion in this project. First, it should be noted that my use of the term 'intimacy' is not a translation of Schelling's *Innigkeit*. The term as Schelling conceives it touches on my project in several places, but when he uses *Innigkeit* he is generally referring only to that which is deepest inside something or someone and not directly to the coming together of two partners (*Werke* 9: 67; WA 30). Second, I do not take intimacy to map easily onto either Schelling's notion of identity or any of the moments in its development. Since so much of Schelling's thinking is concerned with (at varying stages) the necessity, development and contradictoriness of a primordial identity governing and giving birth to the world, it can be difficult to distinguish intimacy's basic drive to be most inside or most with its partner from the dialectics of identity. Nevertheless, it is possible to find in Schelling's various accounts of the expansion and contraction of nature, the soul, and God a dialectic of intimacy that is not dependent on a prior conception of identity.[12] Third, this portion of the dialectic of intimacy can be found in Schelling's work despite the fact that he grew to oppose dialectical thinking as the sole form of philosophy. Indeed, most of his later work was devoted to an attempt to see beyond precisely the sort of Hegelian dialectical, 'negative' philosophy that I am seeking to trace in this book. For the later Schelling, the fault with dialectical philosophy is the very hypothetical structure that I find so useful for describing intimacy: this merely negative approach does not explain why the world is the way that it is; it merely shows how it must be if it were to be at all. But it was the power of Schelling's dialectical thinking that ultimately made this realization possible, in particular the dialectical approach[13] of 'The Past', the first of his three planned books of *The Ages of the World* and the only one that made it past the initial planning stages. The works of this middle period explore the possibility of an intimacy that is neither guaranteed in advance nor lost for good in the tragic history of the human race. Whereas Schelling's early work takes for granted the common origin of everything and everyone in the absolute, the drafts of *The Ages of the World* work to articulate the not-quite-common origin from which finite entities strive to find their bearings in relation to one another.[14] It is this endeavour that I take as my starting point here.

One of the primary tasks of 'The Past' is to discover how to think in what I am calling the 'progressive perfect' – that is, how to think of the past as something living, as a continually *having arrived*. Just as the partner asks, *How is my being-together with my partner neither a dissolution of one of us in the other nor a coming-together of two poles?* Schelling asks, *How is God both one with His creation and distinct from it? How is it that existence is capable of being united with God and yet seeing itself anew at every moment as if for the first time?* Just as in the relationship of two partners, this relationship between God and creation is for Schelling a reciprocal one. The continual novelty of the world is only intelligible to the extent that creation adds something to God, even though God is by definition the creator of every-thing. God and creation each reach out to one another in a spirit of expansive unity and yet contract in assertions of independence. This oscillation occurs because 'All being [*Alles Seyn*] strives for its revelation and accordingly its development; every being [*alles Seyende*] has within it the thorn of progress, of spreading out … for every being longs not to remain merely introverted [*innerlich*], but again to be outwardly what it truly is' (WA 14). The being-together of God and creation would be intolerable if either were unable to express and develop themselves. Such development would be impossible if time were not differentiated – if, for instance, all of reality were bound up in an eternal present. The world does not persist as an undifferentiated unity, but pulses with greater and lesser intimacy. To know the past of the world is to have the capacity to gaze in wonder that so many contrary forces have managed to persist alongside one another and to appreciate the uneven rhythm with which these forces displace one another.

The ability to appreciate these displacements not as threats to intimacy, but as constitutive of it, distinguishes the heartbeat from previous moments of the dialectic. Once intimacy is understood in terms of an interplay of generous and self-seeking tendencies, partners are no longer bound to the pure beneficence of a gift or the immediacy of touching. Intimacy can instead involve a great deal of oscillation in the relations among the partners and even total reversals of their roles. Partners are allowed to be distinct and even wonderful without this implying that they are fundamentally inaccessible.

This assumption that partners' access to each other is possible despite profound shifts in their attitudes to each other is grounded in an account of the past as all-encompassing, of which Schelling again provides the most systematic treatment. The story of this past is the story of the development and interplay of what Schelling calls three potencies (*Potenzen*). The first of these, which he generally labels $A = B$ to indicate that even the most basic identity ($A = A$) is intelligible only as something divided from itself,[15] is the contractive, self-seeking potency. Significantly for Schelling, the verb 'contract' can mean either to condense and concentrate into oneself or to acquire a disease. The identity of this first potency is thus both communicable in the sense that it has been contracted through a swirl of forces beyond its control and incommunicable in that it has no way of being expressed. As Schelling explains in the 1813 *Weltalter*, this potency never appears without an opposing principle of expansion, or A^2:

> If we regard nature in its first beginnings, we find in all corporeal things an attracting, inward returning force, which never shows itself for itself alone, but only ever as the bearer of another essence, fastening it down and holding it together. This other essence is expansive by nature, and it is thus volatilizing and spiritualizing. If there were no negating force, then this other essence would have nothing against which it could externalize itself and through which it could be put into effect. But if there were no overflowing and communicative essence, the attracting force would be empty and genuinely ineffectual, unfulfilled and unbearable to itself. (WA 139)

In Schelling's analysis, to be as such is to reach out to other beings, but only because one pulls them back toward oneself. The most primordial intimacy is neither an original oneness nor a perfect contact with another, but an expansive-contractive heartbeat. This heartbeat is not a timeless oscillation between unity and disunity, but is possible only because of an irregular relationship between the expansive and contractive impulses. As Schelling is careful to note (WA 169), existence is only possible because of the inversion (*Verkehrung*) of the first two potencies. Whereas the expansive urge (A^2) would ordinarily supersede the contractive urge (A^1) to self-sameness (*Selbstheit*), nothing comes into being unless the contractive urge oversteps its bounds. Pure generosity would leave a partner entirely self-contained. It is wanting *for oneself* that allows one to step beyond oneself. Or to put it another way, a beneficent relationship would be incomprehensible without a giving self to anchor the beneficence.

This uneven, unstable, unreconciled pulsing would thus seem to be the *life* of any relationship. In Schelling's analysis, the first two potencies can only be grasped in light of a third, A^3, which symbolizes the living unity of the first two.[16] This third potency reveals that to be oneself is ultimately insepa-rable from being with another because each is informed by expansive and contractive impulses that require an interplay of selfhood and otherness as their foundation. For either of these impulses to win out over the other would be to destroy both, just as allowing an organism to become either completely independent of or dependent on other organisms would mean its death.[17] We might say that organisms are always already intimate with one another because their ceaseless incorporation and expulsion of one another is only intelligible within the general context of life. But Schelling's own reflections on life show that an intimacy consisting in the dynamics of life would have to be incomplete and unstable. For to say that anything is *alive*, be it the God of the *Weltalter*, an organism, or a relationship, is to say that it is essentially incomplete, and the life in which it participates is indifferent to its individuality. As Schelling might put it, the being of any living thing lies outside of the battle between expansion and contraction in a point of indifference.

For this battle to mean anything other than the inevitable non-completion of the relationship, it must be resolved into a kind of beginning. This beginning would not eliminate the rotary conflict of the drives; it would be the meaning of those drives. Intimacy would thus entail seeing one's partner ever anew as if for the first time. I am able to do so because I want both to expand into communion with my partner and to contract into myself. In Schelling's words in the 1813 *Weltalter*, 'Only in this way is a beginning possible, a beginning that does not stop being a beginning, a truly eternal beginning. For here as well, it is true that the beginning cannot know itself. That deed once done, it is done for all eternity' (WA 184). Rather than resolving the conflict between the urges to expansion and contraction, the heartbeat allows this conflict as the condition for ever new beginnings. My partner and I take part in a common course of life, but we avoid simply being washed away by this course by continually renewing our bond.

For Schelling, this creation of time from out of the deadlock of the eternal roiling conflict of expansion and contraction represents a liberation of God's potencies.[18] The rotary motion of the absolute carries the weight of dour necessity before it is released into becoming and the possibility of surprise. In the context of the dialectic of intimacy, what in Chapter 9 I will call 'the future' presents a similar liberation.[19] But at this stage, an intimacy structured entirely by the heartbeat is just as weighty and unsustainable as God's primordial involution. While the capacity to shift between expansive and contractive modes undoubtedly gives a partnership depth and stability that it lacks either in the present perfect of the gift or the present progressive of touching, the heartbeat is still weighed down by the fact that the oscillation between expansion and contraction is all the relationship will ever be. The difficulty of sustaining this attitude toward intimacy is visible in the difficulty of even expressing its modality in grammatical English: We are intimate because *we will be having accommodated*.

Yet if this sentiment is awkward to express, it is easy enough to find in our common narratives about intimacy. It is present whenever we think of intimacy as something that tends to strain under the weight of contrary forces but can nevertheless be renewed at a glance. When the movie hero and heroine discover one another's hidden talents after years together, they instantly realize that the intimacy of accommodation has been there all along even as more immediate concerns threatened to displace it. We see this even more acutely in those writers who, worried that they will never succeed in establishing true intimacy with their readers, allow their hearts to beat faster and faster as they attempt to give everything to the reader and yet pull back with the need to assure a faceless interlocutor that there is really something *there*. In the work of David Foster Wallace we sense this beautiful, painful desperation: *I've got to find some way to tell you everything, which of course also entails everything about me – but it's not really about me, is it?* For the writer who is young, honest, or insecure enough to doubt that synchrony will ever be established but passionate enough to *care* that he makes a connection, the heart tries to beat itself into connection with another.

In these cases, the heartbeat shows that intimacy is not immediacy, but the ceaseless oscillation between going out toward one's partner and returning into oneself. Yet here the term 'ceaseless' gives the lie to the actual temporality of this intimacy. The moments in which we find intimacy with our partners restored, the sudden light in the eyes or the unwonted change in the score of the dialogue, and so on, do not actually indicate any substantial intimacy underlying the relationship. For if our intimacy consists in corresponding expansion and contraction, then aside from these revelatory moments we could just as easily say that everything either of us does is either an expansive or contractive movement as that nothing we do is. What is to distinguish an intimacy in which both partners moderate their expansive and contractive leanings to accommodate one another from an acquaintanceship in which the partners happen from time to time to find one another congenial enough to hang around with? Beneficent actions might be concrete ways in which it is clear that one partner is caring specifically for the other, but in themselves such actions are structurally indistinguishable from gifts and face the same dialectical stasis.

The only way to ascribe life to the intimacy of the heartbeat would seem to be the step Schelling takes in the positing of the A^3: to say that the interplay of the expansive and contractive urges finds its stability in a higher potency. Movements of expansion and contraction would not merely be modifications of a static mutual presence, but would constitute the very *life* of the relationship. We would be intimate neither because some completed action had consummated the relationship nor because of any steady connection we have to one another, but because to alternate between periods of expansion and contraction with one another is *what it means* to be intimate. But the positing of such a 'life' of the relationship gives at once too little and too much determination for what constitutes intimacy in a relationship. It gives too little because it allows for no distinction between greater and lesser levels of intimacy, which is precisely what intimacy as a superlative concept is conditioned to search for. If whatever we do, no matter how much you or I contract or expand, it is all part of the life of the relationship, then intimacy would be there simply by fiat. The intimacy would be even more indeterminate than a bland, continued touching. Yet this notion of life also determines too strictly what should count as intimacy, since to say that a relationship is alive is to say that it is susceptible to sickness and death. To the extent that it means anything to speak of the 'life' of a relationship, one is not just saying that a narrative necessity can be read back into its various twists and turns after the fact. Rather, one is saying that a relationship is defined by the necessity of these twists and turns – that there is a course that the relationship can be expected to take. This expected course can only be something external to the relationship itself. If we take the metaphor of life seriously, then a relationship that lives through its oscillations between expansion and contraction would be opposed to one that is dead. Or, if we look for a more nuanced distinction, a healthy relationship would be opposed to an unhealthy one.

But even this more nuanced approach still imposes a kind of order on the relationship from without. One of the reasons why Schelling broke off each of his three attempts at writing *The Ages of the World* was that each set out to tell the story of the development of freedom but got bogged down in necessity. Because he attempts to narrate the course of life that governs all impulses to expansion and contraction, Schelling cannot help but fall back on phrases like 'the fate [*Verhängnis*] of all life' (WA 34), 'the sequence [*Folge*] of all life's development' (WA 40), and 'the unavoidable way station of freedom' (WA 40).[20] The life that unifies expansion and contraction into a common urge for intimacy can only be grasped as something determinate if it prescribes a *telos* for the relationship.

Indifference and longing

In short, the heartbeat can only succeed in maintaining a genuinely progressive aspect (as opposed to a sequence of discrete acts of accommodation) to the extent that it posits some holistic life beyond this mere sequence. But this positing risks imposing an arbitrary unity on the fundamentally differentiating movements of expansion and contraction and losing the sense of unexpectedness that is crucial to holding the future progressive perfect together. To prevent the intimacy of the heartbeat from dissolving into undifferentiated *life in general*, the last recourse of the heartbeat is to abandon the progressive expanding and contracting and search for intimacy in a future perfect. Such an intimacy would not be defined by the necessity of *continual* adjustment to one's partner, but would instead posit that the very intensity of expanding toward or contracting from a partner constitutes intimacy. Such is an intimacy that is not yet present but promises itself that under some unknowable circumstances it *will have been fulfilled*.

The promise of intimacy can thus lie not only in the life of a relationship, but in the isolated moments of this life. At the moment of greatest contraction, one treats one's partner as a pure simulacrum. Any threat the partner's difference posed would be purely hypothetical. The person I love *must* love me back regardless of any conditions a fair observer might find to impede this love. This attitude posits the consummation of the intimacy in the transparent arrival of the partner. In periods of expansion, on the other hand, everything appears as a saturated phenomenon. I love, and the world is beautiful, and the force of this 'and' is purely truth-functional: it carries no causal or even conditional weight. My love goes out without needing any justification or expecting anything in return. All it needs for its consummation is to be received by someone. In both of these cases, the progressive aspect of the heartbeat's intimacy has been lost, and we are left once again with either the indefiniteness of the gift (pure expansion) or its converse, merely feigned connection (pure contraction).

Yet it is also possible to suspend ourselves between these two moments at a point that is neither expansive nor contractive but has the potential to be either. Merleau-Ponty's description at the beginning of this chapter of seeing one's partner as if for the first time stresses the continuousness of the renewal: the way that experiences of wonder throw us back into the expansion and contraction that constitute the progressivity of a relationship. But one could just as easily stress the wonder itself as what allows for the heartbeat in the first place. Unlike the future progressive perfect of the heartbeat, this wonder is something that can be present and can stay present for quite a while. While the intimacy that wonder gives birth to would still be conditional, the wonder itself can be more or less constantly present as a potential to be either expansive or contractive. Indeed, Descartes describes wonder as the passion that provides precisely this indifference between expansion and contraction.[21] Unlike other passions, wonder does not have an impetus either toward or away from its object, but compels us simply to stand in the middle distance. The feeling of wonder presents itself as an unbounded openness to the world, one in which the kind of reawakening Merleau-Ponty describes seems like a permanent possibility.

A fixation on this permanence of possibility, however, tends to lose track of exactly what gives intimacy its life. Charles Scott opens his book *The Lives of Things* with a reflection on how he is inclined to feel wonder not just in the face of people, places and experiences, but even of *facts*. It is simply astonishing that the very law of gravity emerged over the first few moments after the Big Bang or that the human ear is sensitive enough to detect sound waves that move the ear a mere tenth of the diameter of a molecule (8). Scott tells the story of conveying this sense of wonder to an artist friend, who objected that what Scott was missing in his absorption in the wonder of facts was that true wonder always concerns itself with the *life* of its object (2). Scott takes this challenge seriously and devotes the book to articulating what it would mean to be attentive to the lives of things, but ultimately he arrives at a point of indifference: appreciating the lives of things involves letting them be, even to the point that one holds no necessary preference for their being over their nonbeing. This point of indifference reverses the form of intimacy that has structured the heartbeat to this point. Rather than seeking to accommodate the course of a partner's life, it takes the singularity of the partner's existence as a purely indifferent fact. Indeed, I think Schelling shows us that if life means anything at all, it must be the opposite of indifference.[22] In other words, for Schelling, to consider the life of something is to consider the necessities that drive it. What Scott finds astonishing and wonderful is that we can suspend this form of consideration and still find objects meaningful. When wonder is no longer just one step in a process of renewing inclinations toward expansion and contraction, it steps outside the organic necessity that comprises Schelling's view of life. The wonder we feel toward facts and persons thus always indicates a gap between the life and the non-life of a thing. We can try to cover over this gap by insisting that there *must be* some transition between indifference and natural necessity, some explanation of how meaning arises from the brute physicality of sound, but this would only favour the side of life over the side of indifference and thus blind us to the free appearance of our partners.

The desire to find intimacy in simultaneity with the life of the partner thus becomes a kind of longing: a desire to coexist with another in a recognizable sequence that nevertheless recognizes the infinite otherness of one's partner.[23] As Schelling puts it in the 1811 *Weltalter*, 'This is the fate [*Verhängnis*] of all life, that it first longs for restriction and to move from the open to the closed in order to make itself accessible to itself; afterwards, when it has closed itself off and felt this closure, it longs once again to be in the open and to return into the still nothingness in which it previously was, but it cannot because it must suspend its own self-given life' (WA 34). To live with another requires restriction, but for them to be other requires freedom. To simply accept this contradiction as the necessary structure of all intimacy is to treat intimacy as part of the order of nature and thus to ignore the experience of wonder that allows this contradiction to be renewed. Scott's astonishment thus pauses the movement of the heartbeat and propels it on to the next stage of the dialectic. In order to connect the wonder that inaugurates openness to one's partner with the actual life of being together with them (Aristotle's συνηθεία), intimacy must be not merely temporal, but spatial.

While the dual sentiments of reaching out toward the partner and expecting him to reach back capture well the *feeling* of intimacy, they are merely the obsessions of an individual without the simultaneous and corresponding movements of one's partner. Longing can offer depth of feeling, but nothing further. So long as it fixates on the establishment of some future connection, the heartbeat loses the progressive-perfect temporality that gives a relationship life. Yet as we have seen, this life is not in itself an achievement of intimacy. When one partner expands as the other contracts and when the other later reciprocates, each movement is something discrete: the bare desire to be oneself or be outside oneself. It is only the continuity of time that allows the partners to treat the relationship as something real, but in this reification nothing is shared beside that time. The Aristotelian appreciation for the unexpectedness of familiar συνηθεία is lost in the brutal necessity of each partner's expansion and contraction. The reciprocal acts of accommodation have not yet found what makes them part of an intimate whole. There is, in short, not yet a common space in which the partners can come together as intimates.

4

The Between

We have already observed that the literal meaning of intimacy is spatial, deriving as it does from the Latin for 'most in' or 'most upon'. Still, it is not obvious how to interpret this spatial meaning in even a naïve sense. The gift tried to interpret it as a passage, and touching saw it as immediacy, but neither interpretation proved to be intelligible, so the heartbeat eschewed spatiality altogether in favour of a temporal understanding of intimacy. Though this approach enabled the heartbeat to appreciate the dynamism of relationships, it left no space to understand the *place* where the intimacy appears. Might intimacy consist in the open space that allows partners to encounter one another? To be sure, the dialectic of touching has shown that partners are never simply present before one another. Intimacy requires that partners remain distinct, and there can be no such thing as an immediate encounter. But the hypothesis of what Kierkegaard and Irigaray (among many others) have called the 'between' is that intimacy can be found in the very space where partners come to meet and engage one another. They need not make themselves perfectly present in this space, since withdrawing can contribute to intimacy as well as presence. But when we ask for the location of intimacy, we cannot help but assume there must be some arena in which the partners can appear to and withdraw from each other. There is intimacy not just between us, but *in* this between. We thus begin to speak of intimacy inhering not in our contiguity but in our co-presence. Jean-Luc Nancy takes this movement to its natural conclusion:

> In order to say 'we', one must present the 'here and now' of this 'we'. Or rather, saying 'we' brings about the presentation of a 'here and now', however it is determined: as a room, a region, a group of friends, an association, a 'people'.[1]

For Nancy, we will see, this 'between' can only ever exist as a rupture, but Kierkegaard and Irigaray at least agree that a thinking of intimacy without reference to its 'here and now' would be incomplete.

The challenge of thinking this between is to allow it to be the place of intimacy without demarcating it from the partners themselves. If intimacy only appears when two partners leave their private worlds and enter a common one, then they are forced to sacrifice precisely that innermost part of themselves that gives intimacy its name. Conversely, it would only impede our understanding to attempt to naturalize this space between as existing in the mind of each partner along the lines of Jessica Benjamin:

> Intersubjective space may be thought of practically as mental activity occurring in or between persons that, like our well-loved metaphor, the container, expands and collapses, depending on the quality of the destruction and of our practice in sustaining our capacities in the face of it.[2]

Here Benjamin gives careful attention to the plasticity of the between, but in positing it as a space constructed in the mind of each partner she closes it off as a private cognition. In order to constitute the place of intimacy, the between cannot be a public realm that private parties come to share, but can only be the very happening of their encounter.

Yet if it is misleading to suggest that intimacy occurs in the space where two subjectivities come together, it is insufficient to treat intimacy as an *event*, as Jean-Luc Marion has attempted. For Marion, friendship reveals itself as *an event*, and thus as *given* to each friend. When Montaigne states of La Boétie, 'If one presses me to say why I loved him, I sense that this can only be expressed in replying: because it was him; because it was me', he notes a fact common to every friendship: that it arrives for no reason other than 'the pure energy of its unquestionable happening'.[3] Montaigne and Boétie's friendship can be considered an *event* in three senses. First, Montaigne could not have anticipated this friendship simply by understanding his own character and that of Boétie; rather, the friendship in part revealed to Montaigne who he was. Second, the friendship did not appear in stages or according to any 'rhythm', but arrived all at once. And third, the friendship appears not as part of some greater truth, but as meaningful in its own right; he does not have to appeal to any external conditions to make sense of the friendship, and indeed, such an appeal would only be a distraction from the immediacy of the encounter (*In Excess*, 37). Marion thus presents a vocabulary by which we can avoid the temporal distension of the heartbeat without collapsing it into a simple present. Intimacy does not consist in any number of steps by which one accommodates one partners or even the totality of this sequence of steps. Nor does it consist in the simple presence of each partner before the other. Marion's rigorous analysis thus allows us to strip away everything that interrupts or delays intimacy. But for all this, it does not yield (or even attempt to develop) a concept of intimacy, and thus Marion's work can at most offer a useful corrective to unfounded assumptions about the ontology of intimacy. To show dialectically what intimacy entails, we must go beyond the claim that friendship only ever appears unbidden.

To take this next step, Nancy has argued, we need to work through the contradictory and problematic ontology of the between: 'This "between", as its name implies, has neither a consistency nor a continuity of its own. It does not lead from one to the other; it constitutes no connective tissue, no cement, no bridge' (BSP 5). Likewise, 'Contact is beyond fullness and emptiness, beyond connection and disconnection. If "to come into contact" is to begin to make sense of one another, then this "coming" penetrates nothing; there is no intermediate and mediating "milieu"' (BSP 5). We need, in short, an account not merely of the temporal happening of intimacy, but of the *there* where the intimacy appears. We will return to Nancy briefly at the end of this chapter to check on our progress (in anticipation of a longer discussion in Chapter 8), but our study will be more profitable if we first turn to Kierkegaard and Irigaray, each of whom treats the between as the key to understanding love. In the introduction to this book I registered my unease with the term 'love' as a substitute for intimacy, but so long our focus remains on this limited stage of the dialectic and the circumscribed way in which these two philosophers speak of 'love', not very much will be lost with this shift in vocabulary. For each, love is something manifold that follows no single paradigm[4] and is properly investigated not in the soul of either party, but in the space between them.

God and the space between

The language of God, however, presents a trickier challenge to our tracing of this dialectic than the language of love. In the Western tradition, 'God' has at times served as another name for the between. According to Paul, for instance, God, especially when conceived as the Holy Spirit, is a kind of miasma that makes all communication and sharing of the world possible.[5] But because this God as Spirit is simultaneously the Law,[6] the question of the nature of the between is obscured. We are intimate with one another in precisely the way we must be, and it is this 'must' that constitutes our intimacy. On the other hand, Christian Wiman has elegantly argued that it is precisely the openness and contingency of loving God with another that gives a space for true intimacy between lovers to develop:

When my wife and I fell in love eight years ago, both of us – spontaneously, though we'd been away from any sort of organized religion for years – began praying together. The prayers were at once formal and improvisational, clear spirited but tentative, absolute but open-ended ... I don't think the human love preceded the divine love, exactly; as I have already said, I never experienced a conversion so much as an assent to a faith that had long been latent within me. But it was human love that reawakened divine love. Put another way, it was pure contingency that caught fire in our lives. (Wiman, 22)

For Wiman and his wife, there could be no Law that would bind their love, since the very contingency of this love is what opens the path to God. This raises the uncomfortable metaphysical question of the etiology of divine love, but the more relevant question for the dialectic of the between is whether contingency establishes a more suitable site for intimacy to grow than divine command. To push past the tangle of assumptions involved in this question, we should neither take this language of God as Holy Spirit as a 'close enough' approximation of the between nor excise this tradition completely. Rather than asking whether 'God' is the proper name for the between, we should instead ask what the between would have to be like in order to allow intimacy (or love) to flourish and thus allow Kierkegaard and Irigaray to speak to one another from across their terminological divisions.

For two texts that differ so radically on the role of God in human relationships, Kierkegaard's *Works of Love* and Irigaray's *An Ethics of Sexual Difference*[7] start from remarkably similar assumptions about the nature of love. For both, love is only meaningful when it manages to sustain a tension between recognizing the complete self-sufficiency of the relationship at hand and pointing beyond it to something that exceeds its scope. A relationship that derives its excitement primarily from closeness and commonality is liable to stifle independent growth, and one that searches for consummation in an infinitely deferred beyond is liable to waste away in misdirected longing. Yet whereas for Kierkegaard this tension is only manageable to the extent that both parties in the relationship maintain a faith in God, for Irigaray such faith is a fetishization of the relationship's interplay that succeeds only in covering over the irreducible interval between the parties. In *Sharing the World*,[8] Irigaray will later complicate this picture by observing that not every such fetishization is a dangerous thing, but she will remain committed to the proposition that loving one another through God is the death-knell of intimacy. In this section I will show that there is indeed something right about Irigaray's critique of the invocation of the divine in love, but the problem does not lie in Kierkegaard's postulation of a neuter divine beyond the relationship. Instead, Kierkegaard's real mistake is that he misunderstands the nature of dialectics and thus fails to grasp the role of the infinite beyond in intimate relationships.

In *An Ethics of Sexual Difference*, Irigaray proposes that philosophy be recentred on the passion of wonder. Descartes, like the Stoics before him, observed that philosophical judgements are just as susceptible to the influences of the passions as everyday prudential judgements. While we strive in our scientific judgements to be as free of contaminating influences as possible, the simple fact that we as human beings are never free of our bodies implies that our passions will always incline us in a particular direction. Wonder, however, is unique among the passions in that it inclines us neither toward its object (as desire does) nor away from it (as fear does), but inspires us to suspend our self-seeking drives and stand at a respectful distance.[9] When wonder holds sway over desire, fear, and the others, the mind is still influenced by bodily passions, but it is not inclined to dominate, ignore or evade its object.

Irigaray contends that any satisfying and sustainable encounter between the sexes must be founded on a healthy dose of such wonder. Intimacy does not require that we know everything about our partner or find foolproof ways of avoiding conflict, but instead calls for a continually self-renewing wonder at sexual difference.[10] This wonder in turn entails what Irigaray describes as a four-term dialectic (ESD 20). In addition to the two parties, there is also what lies beyond them and what lies here between them. Whenever wonder weakens, the temptation can arise either to absolutize the between and insist on the couple's unity in a common field or to absolutize the beyond and resign oneself to the fundamental unknowability of the other.

When wonder persists, there is always an outstanding and unsettling remainder between the partners, such that neither partner can be wholly incorporated into the other or into some greater whole. To reduce (or at least manage) this remainder without absolutizing the beyond and conceding that there is no fundamental unity between the parties, a common inclination is to posit a *neuter* in which the nonunity of the partners acquires its meaning. In Hegel's *Philosophy of Right* this unity is the child, in whom the differences of the mother and father come together in a common product.[11] For much of the Christian tradition, this unity is God, in whom the nonidentity of the married couple finds its higher meaning. The problem with such a move, Irigaray argues, is that it concedes the impossibility of unity too easily and places it in an infinitely deferred neuter term: 'It always stays at an insurmountable distance, a respectful or deadly sort of no-man's-land: no alliance is forged; nothing is celebrated. The immediacy of the encounter is annihilated or deferred to a future that never comes' (ESD 14). When partners find their intimacy solely in caring for a child, they lose the sense that one-to-one interaction can be invigorating and continually new.[12] And when they posit the meaning of their intimacy in God's eternal love, they likewise assume that there is something insufficient in the nonconsummation of direct interaction.

In her recent works, especially *Sharing the World*, Irigaray has begun to tell a more complicated story. In the case of a biological child in particular, she notes, the very fact that the child is clearly an independent person and not merely the consummation of a sexual relationship can reawaken wonder at the difference between the sexes (SW 40). And yet the unfathomable neediness of the child can just as easily spur the parents to abandon themselves completely to the child as Other:

> Such an abandon seems to be an end, beyond which it is not possible to go and from which it is not possible to come back. It has thus been extrapolated into God: a dark end towards which we move as towards the Absolute, beyond which is nothing, and into which each loses oneself for ever [*sic*]. (SW 40–1)

While the child occupies a more ambiguous place in Irigaray's later thought, here we see that her earlier critique of the distractions of monotheism stands largely intact.

In both the earlier and the later work she asks us to view intimacy as inhering neither in physical contiguity nor in the sharing of objects, but in a fluid *between*. To the extent that intimacy is found in touching, we run into the insuperable problem of how two people can ever be intimate if they are defined by their respective boundaries. And to the extent that it is defined by reference to some shared object, the uniqueness of each party is overshadowed by the pull of the object. The between, however, is fluid enough that it posits a connection that can be observed without overwhelming the partners. Intimacy is made possible not by the ontological structure of either partner, but by the indistinctness of their boundaries and their cultivation of a space between them in which wonder can survive and flourish.

At first glance, Kierkegaard's account of loving through God seems to fall into exactly the sort of dissolution of intimacy that Irigaray warns us about. 'In love and friendship', he writes in *Works of Love*, 'preference is the middle term; in love to one's neighbor God is the middle term' (WL 70). Does God here not take the place of that preference or desire that pulls a couple together? But here Kierkegaard is not saying that when genuine intimacy falters we always have God to pick up the slack, but rather that love does not have to be tied to the preferences or advantages of the lover, but can grow out of a genuine openness to the other's difference, which God's own love for us both establishes and names.

While daily life provides plenty of examples that make Irigaray's depiction of a cold and indifferent neuter term intuitively appealing, we should not let the image of an icy, passionless married couple prejudice us against the satisfactions of finding intimacy in a neuter third term. In *Works of Love*, Kierkegaard presents a compelling defence of the Christian marriage rite, noting that it is precisely through the enforced separation of their two consciences that the bride and groom achieve the more meaningful bond of Christian marriage (WL 138).[13] The pastor does not ask for an expression of unanimity, but rather asks the bride and groom each if they have deliberated on the marriage with God and with their consciences. The marriage is a matter of finding unanimity with God in one's conscience, and outward expressions of love are secondary. The wedding, Kierkegaard notes, makes no pretentions to undermine its embeddedness in patriarchal traditions, and even emphasizes the woman's submissive role, but in this acknowledgement that the inner conscience is what matters most, it places the man and woman on exactly equal footing at least on the level of intimate connection, if not of social reality (WL 138). To this extent at least, it falls into exactly the trap Irigaray identifies: by preserving an external difference between the sexes within an ideology of inner sameness, it seeks to mask all sexual difference with an otherworldly assertion of sameness. But under Kierkegaard's account, the bride and groom do not run away from their differences, but commit conscientiously to a unity regardless of these differences. To take God as a third party or intruder into a loving relationship is to misunderstand what Christian love is (WL 143). Intimacy in a Christian sense lets what is inmost – one's relationship with God – come to the surface and hold sway over one's actions.

God is therefore far from being a neuter surrogate for the between in the sense that a child is. Though he is the common end toward which both partners aim, he does not demand feeding or changing and continually reawakens each party's love for the other rather than redirecting it to an extrinsic end. Kierkegaard is after all the philosopher of the *Øieblikket* (moment of vision) and thus is as allergic as Irigaray is to any conception of God that disparages the present in comparison to an infinitely deferred beyond. To express one's love for God is simply to bring one's conscience to bear on the world and in particular on those who are closest. Kierkegaard's image of the loving relationship is thus one of both openness to sacrifice and cozy togetherness: 'When we see a large family cramped into close quarters and at the same time see that they inhabit a cozy, friendly, spacious [*hyggelig, venlig – rummelig*] place, then we say it is up-building to see', since such a scene shows how greatly interpersonal space can expand and contract (WL 203). The between promises intimacy because it does not separate what is most inside one partner from the other. The space of the encounter itself expands and contracts, such that a tiny hovel might leave plenty of room for a close family but a large mansion might be cramped for a distant one.

To a certain extent, Kierkegaard's position is of a piece with Irigaray's. Just as she claims that wonder does not let itself get lost in the beyond, he claims, 'The most dangerous of all escapes as far as love is concerned is wanting to love only the unseen or that which one has not seen' (WL 159). The love of God, and consequently the love of another through God, ought not to be based on a retreat from worldly presence and limitation, but ought to consist in an excessive welling up of divine love.[14] If this love lets itself get distracted by fixating on its own character as love or comparing itself to other loves, it loses sight of the *moment* [Øieblikket] in which it could express its love for the other. Such a love that has lost the sense of the moment, of the availability of the other even in her absencing, becomes merely 'episodic and momentary' (WL 178). It breaks love apart into a series of nows. For Kierkegaard as for Irigaray, the problem with claiming that God cements my love for my partner even as we fight or get lost in our petty concerns is that it seeks to step back and take a surveying view of the relationship rather than remaining in the difficult and complex between (WL 177). For Kierkegaard as well, the problem with such a relationship is that it takes a neutral, neuter stand and thus pretends to annihilate the sexual difference that subtends the relationship.

Works of Love is thus not merely an exploration of the ways that love breaks down; it is a series of definitions of *what is to count as love*. The various chapter titles, 'Love is the Fulfilling of the Law', 'Love Builds Up', 'Love Seeks Not Its Own', and so on, show the essentially didactic structure of the work. It is not just a series of investigations into the nature and possibility of love, but a manual explaining how one *ought to love*. By the end of the book, Kierkegaard (who does not here write pseudonymously) has extended this position so hyperbolically that one expects that some form of irony lurks under the surface. 'If one wants to make sure that love is completely unselfish,' he writes in the book's penultimate chapter, 'he eliminates every possibility of repayment. But precisely this is eliminated in the relationship to one who is dead' (WL 320). The fulfilment of love is thus found in the elimination of the beloved, a paradoxical conclusion that gives the lie to his earlier emphasis on the importance of presence and the between in a loving relationship. This elimination of the partner seems to share the form of those 'requirements, a prioris, laws, ideals, which paralyze the becoming of a different human reality' that Irigaray inveighs against in *Sharing the World* (xi). How has this celebration of love's cozy togetherness become such a dour and rulebound dissertation on how to use others to develop your ability to love?

Contrary to Irigaray's complaints about the invocation of a neuter God into whom all of love's remainder is poured, Kierkegaard's appeal to God does not by itself doom him to such a set of 'requirements, a prioris, etc.'. God for Kierkegaard is nothing like a consummation of love, but rather provides a space in which two lovers come together and recognize each other's differences. Kierkegaard repeatedly emphasizes that God's command to love one another is not a cudgel to fend off threats of infidelity, but rather a solicitation always to remain open to whatever one's partner has to offer. Nor is the problem that Kierkegaard appeals to a single transcendent God rather than the multiple divinities and angelic intermediaries that Irigaray likes to reference. Though Kierkegaard's God is indeed beyond the world in a way that prevents easy intermingling, this God is still a figure that asks us to live in the contradiction between closeness and reverential difference from one another. The problem, I think, is that Kierkegaard's God gives his directive to find unity and yet respect differences in the form of a command, which calcifies the dialectical structure of the encounter. Though Kierkegaard displays an acute sensitivity to the interplay of presence and absence in any loving encounter, in *Works of Love* he presents this interplay as a truth that can be passed down from above rather than one that can only be reached through dialectical encounters with another. But to assume that we can convey how to be with another through a few choice anecdotes and metaphors is to assume the existence of a common vocabulary between potential lovers.

It is exactly the existence of such a vocabulary that Irigaray calls into question in *Sharing the World*. When I assume that 'the other is the bearer of a speech which is dependent on the already existing world and not a speech of their own' (125), I must assume that I already know what my partner and I share in common. But this assumption cuts off the experience of wonder. It seeks to enforce exactly the kind of commonality with one's partner that Kierkegaard insists it is the lover's duty to strive to avoid. The entire project of *Works of Love*[15] is structured by a demand to cut off all possible escape routes for the non-lover and show the utter necessity of love for any Christian. By presenting love as something that is impossible to escape, Kierkegaard ignores the experience of a genuine encounter with one's partner and thus conceals how the love he describes could possibly arise.

In the concluding pages of the work, Kierkegaard seems to recognize the incongruity between the form of the treatise and the content of loving openness. Like Paul's invocation, 'Beloved, let us love each other', he realizes, *Works of Love* is not merely a series of commands, for 'These words, which consequently have apostolic authority, also have, if you will consider them, a middle tone or a middle mood with respect to the contrasts in love itself, which has its basis in that they are said by one who was perfected in love. You do not hear in these words the rigors of duty' (WL 344). Instead, Kierkegaard wants his words to be taken in the form, 'Let us love' or even 'May we love'. He asks us to take loving as something we learn to do together rather than something whose task can be encapsulated by a series of commands: 'You should love your neighbor', 'You should be in debt to the one you love', and so on. Here Kierkegaard seems to backtrack on his earlier insistence that love is founded on a command (WL 54) and to anticipate Irigaray's own suggestion in *Sharing the World*. For her, a philosophical treatment of love's openness to intimate encounters can only be spoken in the middle voice. Our task, both as lovers and as philosophers, is to explore our own boundaries alongside others so that we may learn together to learn to speak of intimacy in a way that is neither active nor passive, a form of speech that we are only ever on the way to learning.

While this appeal to the middle voice responds to the fact that intimacy can be generated neither wholly by either partner nor without some sort of expansive effort, it covers over an important gap in the capacity of the beyond to express intimacy. If only we had the right grammar, Irigaray and Kierkegaard would like their readers to believe, then we could express what it means to love. But the expressions 'May we love' and 'Let us love' are not in the middle voice but the optative mood, which modern European languages have no trouble expressing. Their emphasis is less on the fact that love comes to presence without an agent than on the unknowable and unforeseeable beyond to which all intimacy points. This beyond is problematic because it is never clear whether it belongs to the partners alone or some more generalized interruption of mutual presence. As both Kierkegaard and Irigaray emphasize, we cannot expect our partners ever to be completely present to us, since this would annul the very space in which we appear to each other. We encounter one another and reveal ourselves to a greater or lesser extent but never reach a consummation of the relationship. Kierkegaard is at times tempted to combat this uncertainty by appealing to a command, but he, too, ultimately sees that a command would close off the freedom that makes the between a space of encounter and withdrawal and thus agrees with Irigaray that the foundation of intimacy can only be expressed as a wish. But again, whose wish is this? Are both parties expressing an optative of desire and thus allowing the beyond to appear along with the between? For Irigaray it is the passion of wonder that holds me in thrall to the between and leaves me respectful of the beyond. Wonder, to be sure, comes neither completely as a result of my own volitions nor completely passively. And yet, if I am not merely to be thrown about from wondrous encounter to wondrous encounter, it seems that it must be *I* who wish for this wonder to hold me in thrall and *I* who work to remain open to what is knowable and unknowable about my partner so that wonder can again appear.

Here my success is by no means guaranteed. Since it is so difficult to maintain openness to the between and an awareness of the uniqueness of *this* between, this openness can be slowly and almost unnoticeably replaced by a *command* to respect the between. Since my partner, no matter how unique and interesting he is, will fall into consistent patterns of behaviour and responses to me, it can easily appear that I am working only to be open to a fixed and closed world of two people. To maintain wonder at the between will thus begin to seem naïve, as an illusion discontented people cultivate in order to avoid confronting the fact that this is just one contingent relationship among all possible relationships and the so-called wonder that initiates it merely a veil for a conservative desire for the comfortable.[16] But even when I succeed in holding on to this wonder, the work I undertake to do so would be fundamentally private. Irigaray confesses as much when she treats what is intimate in the between as something that must *correspond* to what is intimate in a partner: 'Welcoming will first take place outside of us, even if this outside has a corresponding place within us and belongs to the most intimate part of ourselves' (*Sharing the World*, 19). This welcoming that wonder makes possible would, like the gift, be a mere invitation to intimacy. Without a way to identify *this* relationship as more intimate than the others, wonder will remain locked up in a private consciousness and merely gesture toward a shared world that *must* be out there somewhere. What is missing in the very structure of the between is a way to conceive the work of maintaining it as something shared.

The rupture

This gap leaves us with two alternatives: either we can attempt to find intimacy in the very lack or impossibility of such sharing, or we can take it upon ourselves to create something that can be shared. The first of these I will call 'the rupture', in honour of (if not entirely in fidelity to) Jean-Luc Nancy,[17] and the second will initiate a series of movements beginning with the 'interesting' in this chapter and moving on into fetishes in the next.

Given the centrality of difference and alterity in continental philosophy over the last seventy years, it is probably worth it to stop and recall that we are still following the development of the dialectic of intimacy rather that attempting to articulate what genuine otherness would entail. When Nancy speaks in *Being Singular Plural* of the 'rupture' of the between, he does not mean what Levinas means by the chasm or abyss between the self and Other. The latter is an unbridgeable gap that opens up the possibility of desire[18] but warns in advance of the impossibility of intimacy in the superlative sense.[19] Because it comes from beyond us, our desire for the Other not only fails to find any consummation but does not even grasp the conditions under which it *might* be consummated. The rupture, on the other hand, is an acknowledgement that the fact that partners come from distinct origins, have conflicting interests, and understand the world through irreconcilable terms not only does not attenuate their intimacy, but lies at its very ground.[20] For Nancy, the reason why we use the word 'intimacy' to refer to both what is deepest inside someone and the deepest connection one may have to another is that the latter is an intensification of the former: 'If intimacy must be defined as the extremity of coincidence with oneself, then what exceeds intimacy in interiority is the distancing of coincidence itself. It is a coexistence of the origin 'in' itself, a coexistence of origins' (BSP 12). To be intimate with someone is not to be arrested in wonder at our differences, but to be drawn so deep into ourselves that we find there a fundamental disunity. This disunity, in turn, is not what allows us to go back out into a world shared with others; this rupture *is* our being with others. When we receive (Nancy is careful to avoid the term 'perceive'[21]) our partner in her singularity, we open ourselves to other origins of the world (BSP 9). While it can be disorienting to be suddenly confronted with the utter strangeness of one's partner, this is not always an inhibition of intimacy. Because it calls us back to our own strangeness, the rupture makes us realize that we, too, are strange and thus that intimacy is not the coming-together of two self-identical beings, but the being-together and being-different of two self-differing beings.

Yet in investigating so carefully the conditions for the possibility of intimacy, the rupture can stand in the way of it actually developing. Nancy may indeed have discovered the basis for the possibility of intimacy – on such ontological questions our dialectical account has to remain agnostic – but the recognition of a plural coexistence of origins cannot be enough to constitute intimacy itself. The rupture explains how Nancy and I, should we ever meet, could share a common community despite the fact that there is so much that we do not share in common, but it does not bridge the 8,000 miles between us or establish any actual intimacy. Here we are reminded that built into the concept of intimacy is not just a superlative (in*most*), but a comparative (clos*er*). To be sure, I would say that I am more intimate with Nancy than many other writers I have never met because I have read his affecting account of his heart transplant and any number of charming asides about passing cats and transubstantiation. And the fact that these actions have not been reciprocal – that Nancy has in all likelihood never even heard of me – cannot be read a priori to preclude any intimacy between us at all. But it does show that Nancy's conception of rupture does not take us all the way to intimacy or give an account of what would constitute its fulfilment.[22]

Instead, it explains what Nancy calls our *access* to one another, our openness to the coming of potential partners (BSP 14). This access, however, was already seen (albeit in a different light) in the dialectic of the gift. While our suspicions that we all come from fundamentally irreconcilable places, interests and desires can never be eliminated without ruling out in advance the possibility of learning about our partners, we can at least suspend these suspicions. Regardless of whether we do so in means that initially appear external (the gift) or internal (the rupture), this suspension challenges the very basis of such an internal/external distinction.[23] We know that we have access to one another because the initial assumption that we are separate individuals has shown itself to be unsustainable. We have, then, a dialectical collapse of the notion that we are each individual selves who occasionally find points of intimacy with one another. Such a notion of an independent self coming into contact with other selves and cancelling their differences shows itself to be incoherent because the self would then have to create the very possibility of the others it encounters.[24]

Yet intimacy does not just pop out of the collapse of this particular inhibition of intimacy any more than friendship arises from the realization that a childhood acquaintance has moved into one's new hometown. Nor does it appear in the realization that we are never wholly self-identical and thus 'originally plunged into mourning'.[25] It can be a profound therapeutic insight (in the way that only ontological insights can be) to know that loneliness does not belong to human beings by some metaphysical necessity, but this is still only an insight. For the between to be a place of intimacy, it would have to be filled not just with our having-been-ruptured from ourselves, but with a common project.

Accessibility

Because wonder will appear to be heteronomous to partners at this stage of the dialectic, one (or both) of the partners may attempt to construct the between as something over which they have more control. The true source of wonder, the disaffected partner postulates, is not the structure of the between itself, but the uniqueness of each individual that makes its appearance in the between. At some point partners learn all they can from each other, and the vocation of each is to continue to grow as wondrous as possible in her own light, filling up new betweens as she goes. The task of intimacy is thus taken to be the continuous preparation to encounter others in a mutual spirit of wonder. Intimacy would in this case be those points of access that we cultivate and carry about with us, offering them up whenever the occasion calls.

When it becomes an end in itself, such preparation for the establishment of a between becomes an infinite deferral of intimacy. To cultivate one's capacity to receive the other is a matter of becoming *interesting*.[26] By reading well, travelling, and so on, one makes oneself into a vast network of possibilities, able to engage any number of individuals on their own terms. Most of all, one develops a rich and varied conception of oneself, one not derivable from any single concept but also not overly attached to one's own uniqueness. Because particular individuals can tie one down to fixed patterns of interaction, one seeks a diversity of encounters and experiences in the interest of personal growth. 'Intimacy' thus again refers to allowing others access to what is deepest inside oneself, but now with the caveat that what constitutes this 'inside' is nothing but the possibility of relating to many others in many ways.[27] The between is in effect a commodity that one treats as having value regardless of whom one shares it with.

While such commoditization might initially seem the antithesis of intimacy, it helps correct a very real tendency to build a moat around the between. Though one-to-one friendships can bring fulfilment to a sometimes astonishing degree, to see the relationship as a complete dissolution of respective wills into a single overarching unity is to miss the importance of a fetishized between. For Montaigne, in a 'noble relationship, services and benefits, on which other friendships feed, do not even deserve to be taken into account: the reason for this is the complete fusion of our wills' ('On Friendship', 194). Leaving to the side the question of whether such a 'fusion' of wills is ever really possible, such a union would constitute an annihilation of the between in which Irigaray's disinterested wonder appears. By attending to the areas where one might find common ground with others rather than the ultimate unity that would result, one opens oneself to those partial intimacies from which deeper connections can develop. They can be a solicitation to future engagement that does not assume in advance what the relationship would need to be.

Yet becoming interesting is never an achievement of intimacy itself. The ability to discuss philosophy *and* scuba dive *and* appreciate wine *and* play the fiddle *and* … might make one an attractive partner, but even when one finds a suitable partner to feel this attraction (the odds of which decrease the more one cares about being interesting), this attraction is a poor substitute for intimacy. So long as the partners are only relating through this interest, the interesting partner must continually work to stay interesting in new ways, and the interested partner must treat the interest as purely heteronomous. The between would no longer be an indeterminate site of optative wonder, but the concrete interest that one partner draws out of another. In order that both partners might share it, the between thus becomes something concrete: a fetish.

5

The Fetish

This they would never do unless they experienced mutual joys,
which can trap them and hold them bound. Wherefore again and
again, I say, pleasure is shared.

– LUCRETIUS[1]

With the fetish, we return to the gift's preoccupation with locating intimacy in something *present*. Yet as something in which both partners take an *interest*, the fetish shifts its focus from the temporality of the gift's *having been given* to the fact that there is something *there* for both partners to cultivate an interest in together. The interest they share can take many forms, but what unites such forms of fetish as fandom, body worship, promising, and so on is an assumption that partners can find intimacy in the relation to an inanimate third term.

'Fetish' is, of course, far from a neutral term. It suggests at once an unreality, since religious fetishes are supposed to be mere inventions in contrast with revealed religions,[2] and a hyperreality, since in contemporary American English 'fetish' carries an aura of transgressive self-creation. Despite its ugly racist history with figures like Charles de Brosses, who believed that fetishes are the means of 'primitive' peoples to get a handle on the divine, I use the term 'fetish' to refer to a broad range of phenomena that is neither necessarily religious nor sexual in nature. A fetish lifts a thing out of its sphere and takes it to be more important than one ordinarily would. Without this elevation, the fetish object would be merely one object among many others in a shared world and thus would give no site in which the between could be intensified. Thus my use of the term agrees with Freud's in that it treats the creation of a fetish as a *process* by which an object is given a significance far greater than utilitarian aims would justify, but it differs both in referring to objects outside of the sexual sphere and insofar as it does not assume a perversion of a more fundamental drive.[3] The question of how this factically plays out, namely what kinds of things can be fetish objects and under what circumstances, is too bound up in the vagaries of cultures and history to be addressed dialectically, but from a structural standpoint a fetish must in some way set partners apart from the general course of life.[4] In a society in which every waking hour was devoted to cultivating potatoes, for instance, we could not say that a couple who spent their days weeding and talking about nothing but potatoes thereby had developed a potato fetish. If, however, they chose one patch of land to cultivate together to the exclusion of all others, then they might indeed be said to be developing a kind of fetish for this plot of land. The fetish is defined not by its agreement with or opposition to anything we might call 'nature', but by its shared elevation above other aspects of life.[5]

The interest

Jessica Benjamin gives an evocative picture of the magical moment when a mother and infant are no longer merely oscillating between responding to each other's needs and expressing their own, but begin to *share* a particular moment. When a nine-month-old boy reaches for a toy and checks his mother's response, her excitement is a mirror of his own and he feels his own desire both recognized and reinforced. Later, 'When mother and child play "peekaboo" (a game based on the tension between shared expectancy and surprise), the mother takes similar pleasure in contacting her child's mind. The conscious pleasure in sharing a feeling introduces a new level of mutuality – a sense that inner experience can be joined, that two minds can cooperate in one intention' (*Bonds of Love*, 30). This mutual recognition that an experience can be shared with another does not just find intimacy in a common field of interaction or a corresponding of expansion and contraction but identifies an arena in which both partners are engaged in the same enterprise. In Chapter 7 I will present a somewhat different reading of the structure of 'peekaboo' than Benjamin, but her account of sharing an interest in an object is instructive. When the mother shows that she is responding to the same object as the child, she both mirrors the child's own reaction and transforms his interest from something private to something sharable.

Typically when we speak of an interest, we mean something that regularly draws our attention, something that we tend to fall back into thinking about when our minds are insufficiently occupied and with which we will seek to have new experiences when convenient. While interest would seem in this case to be necessarily private and even in many cases solipsistic, interests even in this general sense can be meaningfully shared. Think, for instance, of two partners who become friends through their love of the same musician. While this enthusiasm may have alienated them from most of their peers, their shared commitment to the musician constitutes a kind of intimacy. They are not merely two anions who happen to be drawn to the same cathode; their interest involves some shared activity. They listen to the musician's songs, talk about the meaning of lyrics and novelty of chord progressions, and speculate about what the musician might produce next. Far from isolation, their fetish involves active mutual engagement.

An interest also makes access to a partner much more obvious than that achieved through the rupture of the between. Since we generally encounter people in the absence of an appeal, wound, rupture, or otherwise apparent sign of openness to intimacy, it can be difficult to know how to begin a relationship. To the extent that one's partner appears wholly intact, she gives no indication of her willingness to step out into a space of intimacy. The fetish can thus operate as a kind of reassurance, isolating a particular domain in which both the partner's incompleteness and openness to engaging this incompleteness is assured in advance. Socially adept teenagers (or ones, in any event, who are more socially adept than I was) learn to ask new acquaintances about what kind of music they listen to, since almost any answer will signify a break in their solipsism and potential ground for engagement. The fetish can also be productive of intimacy when the inhibition is not a generalized anxiety but a more localized one that takes on an outsized importance and overwhelms free interrelation with another. Thus Jerome Braun analyses a number of sexual fetishes as specialized interventions in response to a particular repeated failure (Braun, 257). If, for instance, I have been unable to cope with the indifference of a series of women in whom I have been interested, I might seek out scenarios of ritualized subordination to women. If I am despised, then this was only what I was expecting. But though the fetish in this case is a way of fleeing the indeterminacy of more intimate relationships, it constitutes a kind of intimacy in its own right. The two partners agree to parameters and open a space of play whose topography and boundaries can then be explored.

However, while this isolation of the domain of play makes the fetish comfortable and even welcoming, it also circumscribes it. A ritualized practice (such as sexual bondage) or a focus of attention (such as an obsession with the New York Giants) can help partners to conceal or bracket many common obstacles to intimacy, such as insecurity, differences in class, and so on, but such rituals and obsessions can also become ends in themselves and stifling in their lack of variation. To the extent that the pleasure of sexualized bondage or the success of the Giants matters more than any other way one's partner might be revealed, the promise of intimacy is exchanged for a mere comfort. When this happens, the fetishized interest falls prey to the same dialectic that Marx identified in the fetishized commodity. For Marx, modern capitalism has obscured the network of social relations by which objects acquire value, and the value is taken to be something natural or inherent in the objects. This prevents us from interacting with one another as free agents and restricts us to a narrow range of possible responses to one another.[6] The interest tends to do precisely the same thing. While it initially appears as a form of access to a potentially reserved or standoffish partner, it prescribes such a determinate range of relations that the delay, contingency and surprise that comprise Aristotelian συνηθεία become impossible.

Usually, of course, the stakes of the interest are not so extreme, both because the partners do not take any particular fetish object to encompass the meaning of their relationship and because subtle divergences in attitude toward the object are not taken to annul the commonality of the interest. If two partners bond over their mutual love for the songs of Lady Gaga, for instance, it might not be fatal to the relationship if one favours 'Bad Romance' to 'Paparazzi' and the other takes the opposite position. The disagreement might even deepen their appreciation of Lady Gaga and one another, as each is forced to articulate the artistic merits of her preferred song and thus cultivate deeper understandings of each other's aesthetic sensibility.[7] While the growth opportunities from this dispute would likely be exhausted in short order, there is no structural necessity that this is the case. I can imagine spending the remaining fifty or so years of my life having ever new and invigorating conversations with a fellow lover of Shakespeare or Hegel, and I would not want to deny in principle that the same could be the case for two lovers of Lady Gaga.

Thus the fetish should not be taken to constitute the entirety of the relationship's intimacy or even to underlie the very possibility of the between. Instead, the fetish acts as a fixed centre point that allows both partners to orient themselves to one another. It transforms the between from a pulsing, indeterminate space in which new dimensions of the beyond pop into and out of existence unexpectedly into a navigable Newtonian grid whose single centre of gravity allows the partners to orbit and come into contact in predictable ways. Such predictability is not absolute, however, and allows the same sort of interplay and variation on themes as the Kabyle gift-giving described by Bourdieu. By fixing the centre of the between, the fetish manages neither to keep the partners at an infinite distance from one another nor to collapse this distance into an infinitesimal differential.

Nevertheless, the space established by the fetish confines the partners to a limited range of intercourse. One of the reasons why discussions of Shakespeare really can go on forever is that his works involve and implicate each of us in idiosyncratic ways. If you see yourself in Cordelia and I see myself in Kent, we will develop different interpretations of Lear's downfall. We can grow a great deal from our discussions and learn to appreciate each other's interpretation, but no matter how thoroughly we understand each other, at the end of the discussion we will not have shared any particular fetish object, be it *King Lear*, Shakespeare, or even the conversation itself. The fetish object remains an independent thing to which we each have personal relations. We can see this still more strongly in the instance of two fans of the New York Giants. Though they may earnestly enjoy each other's stories of how they reacted to Mario Manningham's catch in Super Bowl XLVI, these reactions remain private, and this would be the case even if they had watched the game together. Though the interest helps define the centre point of the partners' relationship, it does so by placing this centre outside of either partner and thus limiting the content of the relationship to a dead externality.

The fetishized body

The stakes are slightly different when the fetish object is not an independent thing, but a partner's body. While fetishizing a body (or body part) ultimately risks the same alienation and stultifying sameness as an interest, it requires the partners to take an asymmetric relation to their fetish object, which prevents expectations of homogeneous attitudes to the object. I can become disenchanted if I discover that you've loved the Beatles for all the wrong reasons (whatever the 'right' ones may be), but if you fetishize my hair I know from the start that your attitude to it cannot be the same as mine.[8] I can love my hair and love your love of my hair, but I am not likely to be misled into thinking that my love and your love of my hair are the same. Or, to take a less fanciful example, if one partner is attracted to another because of her race, there is no assumption that they share the fetish in common, regardless of whether they share related external interests, such as a commitment to racial justice. It would sound odd to say, 'We'll always have your blackness' in the way another couple might say, 'We'll always have Paris', but the very asymmetry in the former statement suggests a commitment to an attempt at sharing without the possibility of consummation – an attitude that, at the very least, deserves an analysis distinct from that of the interest.

The problems that attend fetishizing a partner's body are so widely observed that I would like to attend for a little while to the positive contributions body fetishization can make toward intimacy. While we encourage friends and lovers to develop common interests as if it were simply common sense that interests enhance intimacy, we all *know* that loving someone for their body is a pale substitute for intimacy. To counteract the obviousness of this claim, I would like to look at Mario Perniola's 2000 treatise *The Sex Appeal of the Organic*.[9] Taking his title from an autobiographical reflection of Walter Benjamin,[10] the Italian philosopher traces the emergence over the past several decades of a new[11] form of sexual experience that allows its participants to relate not mutually as desiring subjects, but as 'things that feel'. As things that feel, we eschew the satisfaction of organic needs for the sheer materiality of the relations between bodies, as if we were sets of clothing interwoven with one another:

> To give oneself as a thing that feels means asking that the clothes that make up the body of the partner are mixed with one's own, thus creating a single extension in which one can travel for hours or for days. To take a thing that feels means asking that one's own clothing be welcomed everywhere and for always, to the point of no longer being recognized either by oneself or by one's partner as belonging to someone. Thus the difference between giving and taking disappears and an extraneous body or, better, extraneous clothing appears that does not belong to anyone. (Perniola, 10)

When the body is treated as clothing, it can no longer be said simply to belong to somebody. It is instead a piece of material belonging to the general circulation of commodities. Bodies are in this sense not even shared with partners, since this would imply an initial ownership that gets suspended. Such deorganicized bodies can be 'welcomed everywhere' because there are no grounds for distinguishing propriety from impropriety.

Despite Perniola's insistence that this represents a 'new' form of sexuality, this fetishization of bodies is not a reorganization or repurposing of a 'natural' or 'pure' encounter between subjects. To assume that a fetish is a derivative phenomenon is to take independent subjectivity itself as a given, which we have already seen to be problematic in the dialectics of touching and the between. Treating the body as wearable sensibility is a distinct way of conceiving intimacy whose dialectic should be evaluated on its own terms. Between two bodies that feel, the between grows so great that the two poles dissolve into insignificance. While this means that there is no one left to give or receive a gift, this does not leave the relationship unproductive. Rather, a new between, new clothing emerges that does not demand unity. But though such becoming-clothing is a becoming-exterior, it is by no means a dissimulation.

> In fact in this process there is no longer room for the crafty individual who plots his own advancement, who makes plans and dreams up intrigues, who hides in the caves of his secret intentions. (Perniola, 12)

The self-exteriorization of becoming a body that feels is not a self-renunciation, nor does it deny the partner access to one's true self. Rather, it allows what is denied the other in the presumption that each of us has something private to give and take to dissolve into a moment of pure sharing.

Ultimately, however, this faith in such a moment of 'pure sharing' can only be sustained on the basis of a fantasy in which feeling is immediate and sexual pleasure can be called forth at will:

> When your partner sinks his fingers in your vagina or when the lips of your mistress bare the penis, don't be excited by the old-fashioned idea that your body is reanimating and coming to life again, but by the more actual idea that you are sentient clothing! This way, there is no longer any interruption, any hiatus between you and the feeling. (Perniola, 48)

Here Perniola's claim is different from the claim (criticized by Aristotle and Merleau-Ponty) that touching is immediate. Perniola is not claiming that one can through a fetishized body come into immediate contact with one's partner, but that in such a body there is no ground for distinguishing feeler and feeling. It is the sensation, not the contact, that is immediate. Thus this absence of hiatus is not between one partner and the other, for such a distinction loses its meaning when each partner is mere sentient clothing. Rather, it is feeling that becomes the sole reality. But such a feeling is neither something shared nor a meeting ground for two partners. Perniola's 'neutral sexuality' leaves no room for 'partners' at all, since there is neither division nor totality. The body as clothing may have set out to so externalize the body that it is always already intimate with others, but this attempted shortcut turns out to be an abandonment of the project of intimacy entirely.[12]

To maintain itself as a fetish, the body as clothing has to push itself to ever more extreme self-abnegations to suspend the subjectivity that it takes to be the primary inhibition of intimacy. Perniola explains:

> To be sure, in order to access the anonymous and impersonal territory of things that feel, one must be able to say 'do with me what you wish' and be transported by an irresistible excitement in assisting the transformation of the person who burns and throbs in your arms into an inert and opaque entity which, nonetheless, is so receptive and sensitive to feeling the most tenuous caress, the most imperceptible kiss, the slightest touch. (Perniola, 21)

Just as touching required proof that its caress was in*most* in order to overcome the monotony of the progressive aspect, the thing that feels cannot confirm its intimacy without proof of the partner's infinite sensitivity. Without such proof, we once again become aware that the partner and her feelings are distinct and thus that the body is a fetish object like any other on which the partners must come to an accord. A thing that feels can only deliver comparative intimacy that is dependent on the alienating subjectivity that it opposes.

If, however, the elimination of every hiatus in sentient clothing is treated not as a terminus, but as a restorative moment in an ongoing relationship, then it is possible to fetishize not the body, but the feeling of pleasure.[13] The restorative and self-constituting force of pleasure is sometimes so great that a self can reappear unbidden. It would be a shame to let all this pleasure go to waste without someone there to feel it! With so much pleasure sloshing around, I cannot help but feel that it is *I* who am enjoying it and even *I* who deserve it. 'How could this not be intimacy,' the partners might ask, 'when I feel so *free*?' But this freedom is the opposite of the dissolution of self that Perniola means to investigate. Allowing my partner to enjoy my body and being allowed to enjoy hers would reaffirm to each of us who we are and allow us to retreat to opposite poles. With this renewed polarization, it is easy for the fetish to revert to an instrument. Such is the direction of Kant's assertion that marriage is a contract for the mutual use of one another's sexual attributes.[14] So long as I treat sex merely as the experience of pleasure in *my* body in its interrelations with external bodies, I remain trapped in the solipsism of touching. The most extreme form of this fetishization of the partner's body involves the elimination of the partner entirely. The lover who runs away with only a lock of his partner's hair or the one who fantasizes about her partner vanishing into thin air once he has impregnated her uses the fetish as a more easily manageable substitute for intimacy. While for each the action might initially seem to be an attempt at intimacy through other means, for each the original connection will wither. But when other bodies are treated as things that can be used rather than routes to the intimate being of one's partner, this retreat into one's own interiority is interrupted and my engagement with them is not limited to their brute existence. My partner and I are not trapped in separate bodies because our very being is there on the surface ready to be incorporated into the general usefulness of bodies to each other. Yet in place of retreat into solipsism is a new form of division that subordinates intimacy to the achievement of some goal. When bodies can be used, they are once again composed of organs, tools that can be loaned and borrowed. It is easy to see how empowering this could seem for an impaired subjectivity, since it allows the subject to feel not only effective, but recognized in her right to effectuality ('At least I'm good for something'). But it is nothing like intimacy and even impedes it, since it tends to shrink the range of possible interplay.[15] So long as I share my body with you as something that you have the *right* to enjoy (regardless whether this right is conceived narrowly or as broadly as Kant intends), recognizing this right affirms our separation rather than securing our intimacy.[16]

Only when such instrumentalization is ironic does it open new possibilities for mutual play. The partner who insists on being loved only for her body already establishes a relationship beyond mere fetishization because her partner's acquiescence to these conditions itself constitutes an agreement of a higher order. When a partner instrumentalizes herself with the full knowledge that such instrumentalization is a gift and that the other partner understands this, then the sharing is once again a gift, with all of the benefits and inhibitions of intimacy that this implies. And when the partner gives herself with the mutual understanding that the instrumentalization is a game, then a beyond is maintained in the relation and a sense of wonder is left free to develop. Such irony, however, requires the dialectical structure of embedding and thus cannot be addressed until the next chapter.

While my concerns thus far in this subsection have been mostly sexual, the fetishization of the body does not take place exclusively in the sexual realm. The titters from cultural critics about repressed homosexuality notwithstanding, the undergraduate men I see spending hours together at the gym assisting each other's workouts seem to be developing a form of intimacy in which sexuality plays a relatively minor part. The same can be said of the adult who allows a small child to inspect and prod his nose or artificial knee. Dieters often bond over fetishizing their own and each other's bodies, though this bond can sometimes grow into the type of mutual and future-directed relationship I discuss in Chapter 9. In all these cases, the body gives an occasion for intimacy without purporting (as in touching) to be a site of immediate connection. The body acts instead as a common object of attention in which each partner takes a somewhat different interest.[17]

Though this difference in interest is what makes body fetishism differ from such shared interests as collecting and fandom, it also opens it to a unique set of structural flaws. While body fetishism does not risk the same disappointment as the interest because it does not carry the expectation that the partners' attitudes toward the fetish object could potentially correspond, it replaces this disappointment with the potential for jealousy. Because the partners' attitudes to the body or body part will always be separated as if by a thin membrane, the fetish object becomes the site of their separation rather than of their connection. If you and I both love my hair, it cannot help but divide us. You will realize that you'll likely never know what it's like to have such sparse, oily hair that seems to vanish perceptibly by the day, and I will recognize that I'll never know what it's like to see this hair as something purely objective, whose vanishing indicates not my personal senescence but the passage of time itself. Even if you happen to be balding in the exact same revelatory pattern (God help you), the chiasm of our hair fetishes will not establish a shared fetish but the impossibility of their being shared. (Loving you loving my thinning hair, which happens to resemble your thinning hair, does not constitute a shared loving of anybody's hair.)

Even in the case of the two cooperating bodybuilders, their interests in each other's bodies will never fully coincide. While their interest in bodybuilding in general (including reading magazines, admiring heroes, etc.) can be more or less shared and thus will face all the advantages and problems of interests in general, the interest of each in his own physical development will differ from that of his partner. If, say, they decide to devote a workout to chest muscles, they will spot each other on the bench press and give encouragement to push harder, and they will likely even care whether their partner is maximizing his bodybuilding potential, but their attitude to the exercise at hand will always be different depending on whether they are lifting or spotting. We can say, rather, that their relationship is symbiotic, with one partner's interests and actions *fitting* the other's. The intimacy of this fitting does not lie in the fetish itself, but in their commitment to a common project (or two common projects, depending on how you count), whose dialectical structure we will only be able to explore in Chapter 9.

The promise

Where body fetishization required a (lukewarm) defence to show that what we commonly call objectification has a positive (though flawed) role to play in the dialectic of intimacy, the opposite is true of promising.[18] It is often taken on faith that trust is such an unalloyed good in a relationship that promises are not only productive of intimacy, but necessary for it.[19] Yet every promise is its own sort of fetish and thus carries the baggage of an artificial external limit.[20] While Kant analysed the making and keeping of promises as matters of pure practical reason and thus ultimately as relations of the self to itself,[21] we should not let this important insight obscure the fact that promises present themselves not as tests of individual moral worth but as means of cementing social bonds. The promise takes an object in the present that may or may not persist in the future (a written, spoken, or symbolic expression of intention) as standing in for the entire future of the partners' dealings with one another. Regardless of whether we follow Nietzsche in tracing the advent of the *capacity* to make such commitments back to the *menemotechnics* of cruelty[22] or agree with Kant that it arises from reason's constitutive compulsion to self-identity, any particular promise will arise not solely from the conscience of an individual but in relation to some concrete social situation in which intimacy might be one of the things at stake.[23]

The promise is a gift, but it also demands more of a reception than the gift. One cannot leave a promise at one's partner's doorstep or humbly offer it up as something the recipient may or may not want. The promise instead demands a two-sided relation to a single proposition. The promiser takes this proposition as determining her future actions and the promisee agrees to hold the promiser to this commitment. Without this implicit agreement on the part of the promisee, the promise is a mere suggestion of a possible meeting point, like an ignored dare or opening offer in a business negotiation. The very externality of the promise – the fact that it appears in words heard or read by both partners – gives it an external sign of intimacy that is no longer merely private. The promise acts as a fetish that guarantees at least one route of access to the partner. Of course, the promise does not ensure that any particular state of affairs will obtain in the future between the partners since the promiser can always renege, but this very possibility maintains a line of access between the partners. A broken promise provides grounds for a confrontation,[24] and even an as yet unfulfilled promise calls for reaffirmation whenever either party should request it. The child who reminds her father every day for a week that he has promised they would go to the zoo on Sunday may be irksome, but she is well within her rights to ask for his reassurance.

This access, however, does not extend (or contract) all the way to intimacy. To take one of the strongest examples of a promise, a wedding vow can not only do a great deal to lessen suspicions between partners, but also serves as a legally (or religiously) sanctioned entry point for intimate discussion.[25] Because the partner has *vowed* to remain faithful, she has permitted in advance sincere inquiries when it appears she has been unfaithful. The vow is not just an acknowledgement of some previously existing commitment, but a public promise of open-ended accountability. But it is precisely the sanctioning of this discussion, whether legal, religious, or just conscientious, that closes off intimacy by forcing its access point to remain open. Even if one has oneself made a promise, it can still appear to impose an alien injunction. When I attempt to account for my actions in light of what I have previously promised, I am not necessarily sharing what is inmost in me, but may simply be accommodating myself to the external measure provided by the words in the promise. The promise in this case is not bringing us closer together, but is standing as a *tertium quid* outside of the relationship. If I have not lived up to my wedding vows to you, the mere fact that I have made them does not draw us any closer. Demanding that one's partner adhere to a promise she has made may be both just and prudent, but it does not help restore the original intimacy ostensibly fostered by the promise. It shows instead that insofar as we are partners seeking intimacy we are never exactly equal to our promises.

The promise is thus a fetish that cancels one of the main dialectical reasons why one might pursue a fetish together with a partner. In its opposition to a perfectly transparent between, the fetish can be productive of intimacy precisely in its admission of the impossibility of two partners coming perfectly to terms with one another. As we saw in the previous chapter, the assumption that one's partner is a complete and independent subject denies in advance the possibility of access to one another. To say 'I love you for who you are' is to risk reifying the other as a fixed and knowable self-identity. An intimacy that announces its openness to redirection toward external interests or ancillary products of the relationship is one that leaves one's partner space to develop. By stipulating only that their intimacy extends at least as far as their common interest in Shakespeare or *Star Trek* or sex, partners decline to specify the precise connection between the between and the beyond in the relationship and yet still give themselves something real to hold onto. In contrast, treating a promise as determining the intimacy of a relationship assumes a knowable connection between a person's inner essence and her external expression. The proposition is taken to be something that can and must be shared, such that every truth can be exchanged and preserved. I trust you when there are no ontological barriers to your beliefs and intentions becoming my own. This refusal of barriers would deny in advance the possibility of a beyond that calls the partners' relation into question.

But perhaps we have been considering the matter slightly askew, and it is not the promise that structures intimacy, but trust. Trust, after all, is not reducible to a set of promises.[26] No matter how explicit two partners have made the condition of their arrangement, there will always be ways to violate the trust they have developed without breaking any explicit agreements. If relationship advice books are at all on the right track, then trust would be the fertile medium in which intimacy grows.[27] Yet though it is common to think of it as a kind of soft and spongy between, trust remains isolated within each partner's private consciousness. There is my trust of you and your trust of me, but not a generalized trust. Regardless of whether we analyse it as a feeling of comfort (as its etymology suggests) or as a more cognitive judgement of a partner's disposition to act with constancy, trust is an attitude one takes toward one's partner and thus is not shared. While it is conceivable that both partners could *distrust* one of the partners in the same way, as when an alcoholic and his partner have each learned not to trust him to take home a paycheck without wasting it on liquor, the trust one has for oneself will always be different from the trust one has for one's partner.

The lesson here is that the 'between' of intimacy cannot be furnished either by a single specific object of interest or by a vaguely defined collection of common commitments. The fetish fails as a site or vehicle of intimacy because it asks a determinate, present thing to stand in for an indeterminate future. At its best, it promises the partners continued access to one another on the basis of a shared object, but this very promise submits intimacy to an exterior qualification that stands permanently between them.

6

Embedding

Unlike the between, the fetish was attractive because it aimed to fill the indeterminacy of shared possibilities with something concrete. It is of course unavoidable that an extended relationship will exceed the confines of the world of bodybuilding or *Star Trek*, but the fetish assures the partners that it does not *infinitely* exceed this world, and even if it did, this world would still have a centre. This centring fetish gives partners the boldness to explore strange new worlds without fear of losing track of one another. As we have just seen, however, this effort to furnish the space of the between requires them each to take up determinate relations to the furniture, which cannot help dividing them. The more fixed their agreed definitions of the fetish object, the less available it is for genuinely raucous play. We have, in effect, only partially unfolded the meaning of intimacy. While we have suspended touching's longing to be most inside the other, it is now no longer clear what constitutes the inside and the outside.

In the moment of embedding, the etymological priority of the inside in intimacy is reversed. The most intimate relationship is not the innermost, but the outermost, the relationship in which all other relationships are embedded. What distinguishes a more intimate relationship from a less intimate one is not that it is grounded in a broader, richer, or more stable 'between', but that it encompasses more of our relationships to the rest of the world. For Montaigne, this prioritization of one relationship over all others is the hallmark of true friendship:

this friendship that possesses the soul and rules it with absolute sovereignty cannot possibly be double. If two called for help at the same time, which one would you run to? If they demanded conflicting services of you, how would you arrange it? If one confided to your silence a thing that would be useful for the other to know, how would you extricate yourself? A single dominant friendship dissolves all other obligations. ('On Friendship', 195)

While a complete dissolution of other obligations depends on a consummation of intimacy that is likely untenable, Montaigne makes an important point about the spatiality of intense friendships. We give weight to a relationship simply by bringing other relationships inside of it. Rather than threatening the original relationships, these new ones prove both that and why the original one matters. Embedding is structurally unidirectional. In the same way that Montaigne must at some point choose between Boétie and all other men, A cannot find intimacy in her relationship to B by incorporating C and simultaneously find intimacy in her relationship to C by incorporating B.[1] To the extent that A subjugates other relationships to any given relationship, she recognizes it as paramount.

But if the greatest or most extensive friendship cannot be doubled, this does not mean that its intimacy consists in its singularity. On the contrary, it is the folding of other relationships into it that makes it so rich. In *The Fold*, Deleuze imagines a house divided into upper and lower sections. The upper level is the more 'intimate' one and is ornamented with the folds of draperies, dividing and multiplying itself in its windowless removal from the lower section.[2] Here the separation of the upper from the lower level is important, but what gives it its livability is the draping. In an embedding relationship, we do not treat any particular dyad as exclusive and accept intimacy as open to various levels or gradients. Higher levels of intimacy are not demarcated by any sharp separations but fold other intimacies inside themselves.

The secret

While the secret is one of the most common forms of embedding, the intimacy it solicits is already quite complex. By making it explicit that I am sharing knowledge with you and no one else, I make the content of our relationship not only the secret itself but the fact that this sharing is exclusive. Here my presumption that you and I share an interior space from which everyone else is excluded inverts the space of intimacy and brings everyone not party to the secret *into* our relationship. In the words of the sociologist Anthony Giddens, secrets function as 'markers of intimacy, information that is special to them alone'.[3] If he is right that secrets are valuable primarily for their ability to distinguish an in group from an out group, then they are a special form of fetish based on the outside world's non-relation to the fetish object.[4] As external, relatively unchanging entities, secrets bind the couple to something solid in the midst of the fluidity of the relationship. But because secrets are by definition exclusive, they give rise to what I am here calling embedding. If the secret is not simply a fetish, but a unique mark of intimacy founded on exclusivity, then its intimacy consists in my decision to subordinate every other relationship to this one and register the nonfulfilment of these relationships as the fulfilment of our own. In a relationship founded on a secret, what matters is not the content of what is inmost to each partner, but the exclusion of others from this field of interaction. It is not the content of my admission of my childhood crush on Paula Abdul that establishes our intimacy – since by itself this is just a fact about me that, if anything, is likely to lower the average person's esteem for me – but the fact that so many others are excluded from this admission.

Yet few relationships beyond eighth grade can survive on secrets alone, for the secret takes a purely negative relation to the outside world. All I share with you in a secret is the bare fact that others don't share a particular piece of knowledge. If my ten-year-old nephew were to share with me an intensely private fact, I would likely be touched at his gesture and might even reciprocate, but I would not judge our relationship to be especially intimate. On the other hand, I do think that my relationship with my wife is more intimate because of our relationship to our son, and my relationship to my mother is more intimate because of our relationship to my sister. In each case, there is something positive about the embedded relationships that allows for a richer range of reciprocal behaviour than the mere negativity of the secret could ever allow.

The third[5]

I have found no better exploration of the dialectic of such positive embedding than Beauvoir's novel *L'Invitée*, translated into English as *She Came to Stay*. The central drama of the novel is built on the assumption that intimacy need not entail being close *apart* from others; one can equally become close *through* others. Early in the novel, the protagonist Françoise has gotten to know her friend Pierre so closely as to match the rough conditions for what I called the heartbeat in Chapter 3. Though he alternates between such extremes of selfishness and humility that no one else has grown especially close to him, Françoise has learned to anticipate his mood swings and even appreciate through them his depth and unpredictability. Like Montaigne with Boétie, she considers their unity in organic terms, musing that 'there was but one life between them and at its core one entity, which could be termed neither he nor she nor they' (51). Their unity is not exclusive of others, but pulses with the vitality and disappointments of city theatre life.

When the two meet Xavière, the titular guest of the novel, they are equally attracted to her youth and beauty and resolve both to help integrate her into the world of Paris theatre and to share her charms equally. Xavière is an impetuous and self-absorbed[6] young woman who frames her reluctance to assume any responsibility to others as a rejection of bourgeois complaisance: '"One should never be bound to a country or a profession; or ... to anybody or anything", she pouts' (235).[7] Yet far from disdaining her for this refusal to commit to anything beyond herself, Françoise and Pierre find common cause in the project of shaping the future of someone so completely uninterested in anything beyond the present. She thus initially holds for them the place of Irigaray's neuter: an external expression or condensation of their love, more a fetish than a companion. But her beauty and self-absorption soon turn her into an object of desire for both Françoise and Pierre. Indeed, Pierre answers her indifference primarily with amusement but grows distressed when contemplating the possibility that she might act out her own desires, particularly in regard to the handsome young Gerbert. So long as Xavière flits from whim to whim without worrying about establishing anything like a life-project, Pierre is not overly concerned that she may never love him. But once he senses that she might develop long-lasting desires, he senses a threat to the trio. To allow a third full-blown subjectivity into the relationship is to expand it unsustainably.

For Françoise, on the other hand, the triad grows unpleasant not because it lets too much in, but because it offers no way out. She finds herself longing for time alone with Pierre because she feels 'stifled ... hermetically sealed' in the relationship (237). Xavière's jealousy prevents all manner of adult conversation and forestalls the free play of two adults running with one another's ideas. Within the context of a dyad, on the other hand, Françoise is attracted to Xavière's stubborn standoffishness. The younger woman's insistence that the opinions of others do not concern her enhances Françoise's feelings of their intimacy. When the two walk arm in arm to a restaurant, failing to disabuse the other patrons of the presumption that they are lesbians, 'Françoise experienced real pleasure at feeling herself included in the stupid spite of this bunch of gossips; she felt as if she and Xavière were being cut away from the rest of the world and imprisoned in an impassioned intimacy' (246). Released by the patrons' bigotry of any obligation to attempt to win their recognition, Françoise experiences the same enclosure of the triad as liberating in the dyad.

Yet even as she comes to appreciate how pleasant the otherwise frustrating Xavière can be one-on-one, Françoise realizes the tenuousness and even falseness of dyadic intimacy in general. Dismissing the synchronized heartbeat she had shared with Pierre before Xavière as a 'convenient fallacy' (135), Françoise decides that she cannot judge Pierre for the dissolution of their friendship; after all, he had remained the same person throughout. Her mistake had been simply to forget their separateness, which led her to the rash conclusion that because he could still surprise, frustrate and baffle her, he must be a stranger. It is preferable, she decides, not to assume any original or destined unity between them and simply to let their lives pulse at different rhythms.

Xavière, in contrast, rejects dyadic intimacy in principle and even goes so far as to mock Gerbert for his seeming desire for a bourgeois one-to-one relationship. Speaking to Pierre and Françoise, she exclaims: '"Ah! It would be so nice if we three were alone in the world!"' (287). Even in her fantasies, intimacy requires the unstable variation of a triad. It is only in the dissolution of the triad that Pierre can articulate what was so appealing about this dream: '"We wanted to build a real trio, a well-balanced life for three, in which no one was sacrificed. Perhaps it was taking a risk, but at least it was worth trying! But if Xavière wants to behave like a jealous little bitch, and you have to be the unfortunate victim, while I play the gallant lover, it becomes nothing but a dirty business"' (295).

For Merleau-Ponty, the trio's dissolution into such 'dirty business' shows the tendency of trios in general to decompose into three dyads. Because intimacy is always the closeness of one person to another, a trio really consists in three relations rather than one. But this very dissolution, Merleau-Ponty continues, shows the incompleteness of the dyad itself. A dyad never accomplishes all the work it aims or needs to, because the other is never the absolute other, but at most a paradigm of otherness, of all the people the self cannot be. Indeed, since 'the most strict couple always has its witnesses in third parties',[8] the supposition that the relation to the other in general can play out through any relationship with *an* other is bound to prove illusory.

Xavière's primary fault is that she treats her relationships with Françoise, Pierre and Gerbert each as ultimate expressions of her identity and thus collapses in despair every time each relationship carries her in an unexpected direction. To invert Merleau-Ponty's formulation, her desire for an exclusively triadic relationship with Françoise and Pierre shows her appreciation for the fact that every dyad is in fact a triad, even as she remains blind to the tendency of triads to become dyads. While she refuses to engage with broader political concerns that she has no chance of controlling, she rightly criticizes the 'bourgeois' illusion that two people can form a nation unto themselves. While Merleau-Ponty is probably right in an anthropological sense that there are 'successful couples' and that 'there can be no trio that would be successful in the same sense, since it adds to the difficulties of the couple those of the concord between the three possible couples of which it is composed',[9] it would be a mere abstraction to assume that such couples are absent in even the closest of dyads. Indeed, at the end of the novel Françoise finds her fulfilment (such as it is) not in any reduction of the relationship into an uncorrupted pair, but in her withdrawal from all relationships and decision to act solely for herself. The dyad may be more easily manageable than the trio, but this does not imply an ontological difference between the two.

Since it cannot assume an ontological difference between the dyad and triad, embedding gives itself no lasting reason why the third should not transform itself from the content of the relationship into part of the relationship itself. To attempt to manufacture a partnership without another person standing between the two partners would be even more futile than attempting to form one in which no gift ever stood between them. While incorporating a third party into a partnership will almost always introduce more complications and frustrations than a fetish will, Pierre and Françoise grasp from the very beginning of their dalliance with Xavière that frustrations and complications are not incompatible with intimacy. Indeed, embedding avoids the stifling directionlessness of fetishism because the third always invites additional opportunities for intimacy. Whereas partners' relationship to a fetish object is confined to a narrow range of envious alternatives, their relationship to the third provides opportunity for the play and unexpectedness that Aristotle calls συνηθεία.[10]

But this very surfeit of opportunities for intimacy can itself be a bar to intimacy. When intimacy can be achieved among multiple partners along multiple dimensions, the embarrassment of choices can inhibit the συνηθεία on which any relationship depends. We might call this the summer camp phenomenon: when novel encounters can be found in any direction, there is no reason to wait for the unexpected responses that intimacy demands. In this space of infinite playfulness, there ceases to be a distinction between the most exterior and the embedded relationship, and the very efforts that might bring another into the relationship and thus make it more inclusive become potential betrayals. Insofar as it has overcome fetishism (with all the stifling impulses that it brings), the problem of embedding is its lack of demarcation. Whereas touching at least provides easily observable instances of greater proximity – this touch is closer, deeper, or prior to all others, even though these turn out to be meaningless distinctions – it will be difficult for embedding to discern which partners are doing the embedding and which is the third in the absence of some external marker of priority.

The neutralized third: Gossip

What intimacy thus demands is that the most exterior relationship find a way to insulate itself from the embedded relationships. The threat of betrayal opened by the inclusion of the third can be significantly reduced if the insignificance of the third is made plain. Gossip, for instance, takes as its starting point the assumption that regardless of how positively or negatively the person being gossiped about is received, the gossipers' respective relationships to her are subordinate to their relationship to each other. The object of gossip is thus interchangeable with any other person in whom the partners might take a fleeting interest. While the partners' indifference to this revolving circuit of third parties makes them something like fetish objects, they are different in that an important part of the bond stems from the shared knowledge that the conversation is a minor betrayal of the third. Their gossip is thrilling because its inclusion of the other is a kind of exclusion.

This exclusion, though, is a one-note tune that quickly becomes more boring than all but the simplest fetishes. Because they have nothing to say about themselves or each other that could cement the embedded bond, gossips require an endless sequence of suitable objects. While critical gossip can survive for a time on implicit contrasts that allow the gossips to praise one another indirectly – Frank is unkind (but we are kind); Sandy is unattractive (but we are attractive) – there is little ground here for variety or playfulness beyond experimentation with language and perspective. The gossips' attitudes toward one another are fixed by what they exclude.

The generalized third: Irony

Irony, on the other hand, is also built on the embedding of excluded parties, but it does not treat this exclusion as its primary content, but as an assumption for the cultivation of more complex relations. While rhetoricians have long categorized irony as one of the four tropes, its placement among them has always been awkward since even simple irony requires a reflection on the intention of the speaker that even the most complex metaphors do not demand. Kierkegaard gives an acute analysis of this complexity in *The Concept of Irony*, where he finds that irony is not merely a figure of speech, but a way of life. His primary emphasis is on Socrates' use of irony to begin to develop a private self independent of the strictures of his community, but in the book's most careful analyses he shows how deeply embedded this development of self is in the cultivation of intimacy. Since the work is, as a whole, critical of irony, we might expect Kierkegaard to conclude that just as there is no honour among thieves, there is no intimacy among ironists. True irony, after all, 'is directed not against this or that particular existing entity but against the entire given actuality at a certain time and under certain conditions ... It is not this or that phenomenon but the totality of existence that it contemplates *sub specie ironiae*' (CI 254).[11] Like Socrates, the ironist defines herself by the independence of her judgements and thus resists any permanent relationship that could stifle her efforts at self-definition. Also like Socrates, she can expect to alienate much of her community and reject as constraining any bonds that her generous compatriots try to establish.

But of course, Socrates was not alone, even on his deathbed. His rejection of his community was attractive not just in a superficial way that could draw in the likes of an Aristodemus, but in a way that seems to have grounded friendships as rich as anyone can expect to find.[12] Moreover, his friends seem to have loved him precisely because of his rejection of every doctrine, including the very ones they cherished. Kierkegaard goes a long way toward explaining why the rejection of her community gives the ironist a sense of individuality and power and thus how Socrates was so happy even up to the moment of his death, but he stops only at the vestibule of intimacy. To fully understand what Kierkegaard calls the *personality* of Socrates, we need to understand not only how setting himself apart from others brought him a sense of individuality, but how this individuality could not have been cultivated without the concrete instances of intimacy that Socrates' very rejections of his peers helped to cultivate. I take this to be a two-step process, involving both irony and what, in the next chapter, I will call the dismissal.

For Kierkegaard, irony gains its power to individualize from its negativity. By denying that the conventions of her community have any power over her, the ironist frees herself to take any position she might wish (though she cannot actually take any such position without affirming something about the community and thus cancelling her infinite negativity). If someone attempts such negativity in the privacy of her own conscience, then it is mere agnosticism. In order to be ironic, it must be announced to a community. This involvement of the community makes the irony a form of embedding. Just as in gossip I attempt to cultivate an intimacy with my fellow gossipers by excluding others through their very inclusion in our conversation, in irony I exclude the entire community by embedding it in a conversation with a member of that community. Here there is even less threat of this third party meaning more to me than my partner than in gossip because this third party is merely a generalized other. When my partner *gets* my irony, I am emboldened by the possibility that what distinguishes me from the rest of the community can be shared with another. Irony thus looks quite similar to a secret in that my intimacy with my partner depends on the fact that everyone else fails to share in what we share. Yet irony does not simply take a negative position toward those who are not in on it. If my ironic statement were simply inaccessible or incomprehensible to others, then I would gain only a mild pleasure from being able to share it with my partner. Irony only gains its richness from the manifoldness of interpretations that my speech allows. The most intimate irony is one in which I share one meaning with most people and another with my partner. The latter meaning is significant not for its truth but for its limited accessibility.[13]

Given this structure, irony is necessarily dismissive of a great many potential relationships. According to Kierkegaard's account, Plato's love for Socrates is founded on a mutual rejection of the ways of Athenian society. They are not just excluding Athens from their dyad, but are agreeing on a both explicit and implicit critique of it. In this critique, they free themselves to establish their own sort of relationship, but they also find a continual source of reinvigoration in their professions of disdain for the community. Like Pierre and Françoise with Xavière, they are titillated by a living object of conspiracy.

This sort of relationship appears wherever irony is used to establish even a fleeting intimacy. To borrow an example from one of my students, I – or a hip-looking twenty-year-old, at least – could wear a home-knitted sweater with a cat on it on the streets of an urban centre and exchange appreciative glances with a similarly hip-looking twenty-year-old who acknowledges wordlessly our mutual understanding of my effort to escape the doomed dialectic of the consumerist fantasy that we all can achieve a perfect concord between external appearance and internal essence if we just found the perfect outfit. If, later in the day, an old, blue-haired cat-lover should compliment the sweater, I would only be excited by her misunderstanding, since it would show that the earlier shared moment really did constitute a dyad from which others were excluded. It would secure the content of the embedded relationship.

While the relationship between Socrates and Plato seems far richer than my relationship with the twenty-year-old sweater-appreciator, they suffer from the same basic flaw: their content consists in a dismissal of others from the relationship and yet relies on their presence in order to secure the continuing possibility of this dismissal. The partners have to find ways to keep the others they profess to despise around to keep the intimacy from dissolving. Ordinarily, this is not much of a problem because ironic statements are rarely comprehensible by only two people. Though Socrates (if Kierkegaard is to be believed) inaugurated an entirely new form of relation to his community, a variety of close associates seemed to be in on the joke. Ironic statements can *feel* especially intimate when only two people are present to understand them, but irony works as a way of life because the interlocutors are still reasonably understandable to outsiders.

The most complete ironic relationship is thus not one in which a message is shared privately, but one in which the privacy is made to be a message to *others*. Public displays of affection (such as a couple kissing in a public park) are met with such hostility because (unlike inside jokes) they are explicit rejections of bystanders. The inside joke assumes that bystanders simply happen not to understand the joke, but a public display of affection asserts that others *cannot* share the couple's moment. This rejection of others can make the couple giddy in their mutual rejection of the outside world, for in closing out this world so completely they completely enclose it *within* their relationship.

But because it gets its power from irony, even this seemingly completely insulated relationship cannot escape Beauvoir's problem of the third. During the riots following Vancouver's loss in the 2011 Stanley Cup, a widely circulated photo was taken of a young man who had bent down to comfort and then kiss his fallen girlfriend. It was beautiful as a gesture of the couple's perfect isolation from the surrounding chaos, but, of course, events showed them not actually to be so isolated. The young man's mother was interviewed on national television to discuss what a romantic fellow he was, and the event doubtlessly became cause for all sorts of conversations with the couple's respective friends. The kiss could not seal in the external world, but was itself embedded in any number of growing and decaying intimacies. Like Beauvoir's protagonists, the two young lovers could not help but find themselves pulled out into the community they had held within.

The perfect instance of irony would thus be a message perfectly transparent to one's partner and perfectly opaque to everyone else. Moreover, the irony would not succeed if the community were perfectly indifferent to it, so both partners would also have to know that the message is incomprehensible to the community and that the community nevertheless strives to understand it truly. For obvious reasons, empirical examples of successful irony are impossible for outsiders to confirm, but even a possible attempt at irony could be instructive here. June 16, 1904, the day on which James Joyce set *Ulysses*, was also the day of his first date with his future wife Nora Barnacle. Joyce considered the events of that day a triumph of intimacy and later mentioned in a letter to Nora that on that night she 'made me a man'.[14] Thus the fact that Joyce chose that date for Bloomsday can be read as an ironic gesture to Barnacle dependent on her recognition that the book's readers would fail to understand the private significance of that date. What better way to show the singularity of their relationship than to force generations of scholars to pore over the intricate details of a day whose true significance, known only to Joyce and a single reader, is an unexpected sex act? Yet the success of this ironic gesture was always in doubt. Barnacle was far from an avid reader of Joyce's writings, and he could not have been sure she would even notice the reference.[15] On the other hand, less than a century after its composition scholars have managed to piece together the ostensibly private significance of that date. Does this mean the irony has failed? It seems just as odd to say that an ironic message can fail to be intimate because of events after the author's death as it is to say that a man is made unhappy because of events after his death.[16] But if our conclusion instead is that the irony never succeeded in the first place, then it is difficult to discern what could make any irony successful. Rather than situating a couple in relation to an actual community, ironic embedding seems here to rely on a mere projection or simulation of this outside community.

Here irony threatens to rip the dialectic of intimacy open. If my tie to you depends on embedding the rest of the world in our relationship by announcing its exclusion from what we have, but this announcement by its very expression places itself in doubt as something distinct from that inmost place to which I grant access only to you, then it is not only you who must doubt the sincerity of this connection, but I as well. I cannot even ask whether this inmost place exists, since this would be precisely the sort of solipsism that cancels all intimacy. In the introduction I stressed that the dialectic of intimacy as a whole should be understood in a hypothetical or conditional mood: for instance, *if* I mean to establish intimacy through a gift, *then* I will place something between us. This is problematic only because gift-giving seeks an impossible intimacy, not because it seeks to make this impossibility itself the condition of the possibility of intimacy.

But if the desire for intimacy is itself explicitly understood as conditional, then it will forever be stalled upon the hypothesis of the conditional. Like the absolute of Schelling's identity philosophy, it would remain poised at the precise point of indifference, with no reason either to bring itself into being or to remain in itself. If the only way for me to be intimate with you is to share the fact that there are conditions in which I might not want to be intimate with you, then these alternative worlds cannot help but overwhelm the structure of embedding. As Kierkegaard puts it in his reading of Aristophanes' *Clouds*, the ironist 'hovers' (*svaeven*) over his contemporaries like Socrates in a basket, claiming to have a superior view but failing to come into genuine contact with them.[17] The ironic approach to intimacy will refuse to accept this impossibility of connection and chase it as far as it can, determined that everything that belongs to either partner's innermost self be included in the embedded content of the relationship. For instance, I may acknowledge that my previous assertion that intimacy is impossible is just my way of avoiding intimacy with someone I genuinely care about, and that this results from my parents' divorce when I was younger, which I wanted to share with you because I don't want us to keep anything from one another. But this obser-vation, I cannot help noting, is an appeal to pop psychology that pretends to reveal my deepest self but really only offers you a pat explanation that allows me to hide my true feelings. But shouldn't the very fact that I am revealing this (now tripled) deception count as true intimacy? But maybe I am only sharing the triple deception because I don't even know what I *could* share with you.

In a familiar dialectical reversal, this 'everything' that is embedded in the relationship turns out to be nothing at all. By insisting that a relationship is real if it can accommodate the sharing of every feeling and every feeling about these feelings, the ironist rejects the external world that can never be fully embedded in the relationship and replaces it with an entirely simulated world that can. Let us return to the example of the public display of affection. By the very structure of embedding, the isolation of the lovers necessarily depends on the public from which they are isolated. While they pretend to be indifferent to the world, the couple needs the public's recognition of the couple's non-recognition of them. The public sees through this ruse, however, and grows tired of its alarm and offense. Soon the public display of affection becomes just another fact of life or part of the scenery. In the face of this indifference the couple cannot last long in their impression that their own union is extraordinary. Against this background, Barthes bases an entire book on the presumption 'that the lover's discourse is today *of an extreme solitude.* This discourse is spoken, perhaps, by thousands of subjects (who knows?), but is warranted by no one.'[18] The world around the lovers loses its solidity as something against which to push off and thus the content of the embedding relationship vanishes. The lover who wishes to announce his love in public finds himself just as alone as the partner who sought communion in touch. In both cases, it is not that there is nothing to share, but that there is no meaningful way in which it might be shared.

What Barthes thus offers is the impossible flipside of a dialectic of intimacy: a 'simulation' of a discourse that has withdrawn itself from every possibility of meeting the partner, one that occurs in 'the site of someone speaking within himself, *amorously,* confronting the other (the loved object), who does not speak' (LD 3). The discourse is affecting and personal, but it is intimate only to the extent that Barthes seeks to seduce his reader into a shared contemplation of an impossible desire. The lover through whom Barthes speaks is resigned to an impossibility of intimacy and thus is less embedded in the reader's relationship with Barthes than fetishized. While irony is continually repelled from professions of sharing, it cannot survive without alluding to them. Thus the impossibility of intimacy could never be a suitable object of irony. Just as verbal irony could not occur in a language in which all statements were ironic (Colebrook, 30), relational irony could not exist without the promise of something inmost from which the rest of the community is excluded. Barthes means the discourse he presents to be an 'affirmation' of love, but without the stretched, syn-ethetic sharing at which fetishism and embedding aim it is a mere negation of intimacy without any ironic recapturing.

Fraudulence

Even if both partners recognize this emptiness, however, this is no sure route to intimacy. The mere understanding that a shared withdrawal from intimacy is not itself intimacy does not force partners to embrace each other in their immediacy. If anything, it heightens embedding's sense of the meaninglessness of immediacy. The only route for the ironist is to plunge even deeper into irony. In a desperate move to hold on to a deep interiority that might be shared, one partner can confide about her inability to be anything but fraudulent. Thus it is not human nature or even anything about the character of either partner that prevents them from sharing anything from compatible perspectives, but the ironist's own inability to attempt to present a genuine account of herself, even in this very moment. The profession of fraudulence is thus a doubled irony that seeks to reach a common understanding that it is solely the ironist's fault for entering the dialectic of irony.

And if the simpler variety of irony threatens to suspend the momentum of the dialectic, fraudulence aims to accelerate it by embedding the dialectic as the very content of the relationship. David Foster Wallace gives a memorable account of this process of embedding in his short story 'Good Old Neon'. The story's protagonist (unnamed because he is apparently modelled on a high school acquaintance of Wallace) enters psychoanalysis for his inability to engage in even the simplest interactions with others without trying to influence their opinions and thus thinking himself a fraud. Smugly thinking he has cracked the case and might force the protagonist to acknowledge his capacity for sincerity, the analyst points out that the very fact that he is expressing these feelings in analysis proves that he is in fact able to make a connection on a non-fraudulent basis. The protagonist, however, has already anticipated this entire line of thinking and acts out traditional expressions of enlightenment to make the genial enough analyst think he has identified a profound insight. This charade makes the protagonist feel even more alone because it shows the analysis was destined to fail from the beginning because the analyst simply lacks the 'intellectual firepower' even to attempt to follow the dialectic that pulls the protagonist away from intimacy even as he attempts to establish it.

The protagonist contends that this is a two-part dialectic, the first of which he calls the 'fraudulence paradox':

The fraudulence paradox was that the more time and effort you put into trying to appear impressive or attractive to other people, the less impressive or attractive you felt inside – you were a fraud. And the more of a fraud you felt like, the harder you tried to convey an impressive and likable image of yourself so that other people wouldn't find out what a hollow, fraudulent person you were. (147)

While this is exactly the sort of dialectical collapse that would generally force the move to a higher stage, in the protagonist's case it is attended by a second dialectical movement that neutralizes its effect:

> Discovering the first paradox at age nineteen just brought home to me in spades what an empty, fraudulent person I'd basically been ever since at least the time I was four and lied to my stepdad because I'd realized somehow right in the middle of his asking me if I'd broken the bowl that if I said I did it but 'confessed' in a sort of clumsy, implausible way, then he wouldn't believe me and would instead believe that my sister Fern ... was the one who'd actually broken the antique Moser glass bowl ... plus it would lead or induce him to see me as a kind, good stepbrother who was so anxious to keep Fern (whom I really did like) from getting in trouble that I'd be willing to lie and take the punishment for it for her. (147–8)

Whereas the simpler form of irony we saw above pushes itself to such a complete rejection of oneself and others that it rejects the very impulse toward intimacy, fraudulence loses itself in the dual paradox that one can neither achieve the recognition that one is bound to seek nor fail to achieve it through exactly the activities that ought to doom it to failure. The result of these dual paradoxes is a seemingly intractable stasis: because fraudulence attempts to make the dialectic of irony the embedded object that the fraudster shares with his partner, he both cannot authentically share it with her and cannot fail to share it in a way that nevertheless must remain insincere. The very act of admitting he is a fraud, though done for fraudulent purposes, comes off as a deeper sincerity, which accomplishes the ironic goal of moving through dissembling to sincerity in a way that at last does not appear to be dissembling (even though it is).

Yet this stasis is not as stable as it appears. For while fraudulence was taken to be a path to intimacy as a hypertrophied form of irony, fraudulence could not maintain its goal of intimacy and at the same time attempt to achieve the appearance of intimacy. The protagonist of Wallace's story thinks he has no way to establish any kind of intimacy with the analyst because the latter thinks that the admission of fraud is already an intimate gesture, but this misunderstanding is by no means necessary, the analyst's lack of 'intellectual firepower' notwithstanding. The protagonist feels trapped in the cycle of fraudulence because any effort to express the extent of this fraudulence will be met with too facile an acceptance. But the simple act of expressing how undesirable this facile acceptance is ought to be enough to dislodge both partners from the dialectics of irony and fraudulence. If the protagonist were simply to tell the analyst that he had already thought of his simplistic solution and that it does not apply in his case, then the analyst would be forced either to defend his interpretation or agree that he understands the dual paradoxes and pursue the philosophical puzzle further. Either way, the protagonist and analyst would have begun to engage in a new sort of interaction that (the institutional strictures of psychoanalysis not withstanding) is no longer simply about the protagonist's retreat into interiority.[19] What emerges is the possibility of *conflict*: no longer seeking intimacy down the rabbit hole of private interiority, the partners seek it in their very rejection of (some aspect of) one another.

7

Conflict

Irony rejects the earnest drive for intimacy as clumsy and obtrusive, but its own indirect route fails as a path to intimacy by relinquishing responsibility for the divisions between the partners. For the ironist, the future of intimacy is always grounded in some fact about the world, and thus there is nothing to be done about it besides make it explicit. Yet if union can be frustratingly elusive, either partner can create causes for disunion quite directly. The ironist may pretend that his rejection of his partner comes from a necessity independent of his private desires, but it is a rejection all the same that can be made intentional. By making our relationship the frame for the inability of anyone else to appreciate my interiority, I cannot help implicating you in this failure. This reversal of embedding can carry a giddy freedom in that neither of us is responsible for bridging what is in principle an unbridgeable gap between us, but it does so in removing the very possibility of adequate responses to one another. I admit that you cannot know me, but offer that only you know the extent to which you cannot know me. Our only recourse at this point is an infinite series of variations on the theme of our nonadequation. But when I make it clear that it is my *choice* to reject our union, a route back to intimacy suddenly appears. If you could somehow only cancel the force of this choice by changing my mind, outfighting me, or some other means, then intimacy would once again be possible. We need not even wait for a full reconciliation, for intimacy might be found in the activity of conflict itself.

Pulling out of this cycle requires efforts by each partner to suspend this nonadequation. When the TV characters align their hands on either side of the glass of the prison visitation room, they are not really attempting to touch one another, but communicating that the failure of their intimacy is exogenous.[1] Conflict responds to exogenous failure not by seeking out something the partners might share (which would ultimately be a search for a between or fetish), but by establishing a mutual willingness to tear apart the indifference that irony leaves behind. Here it is crucial to recall the limits imposed by the hypothetical structure of this dialectic of intimacy. An anthropological account of the origins of conflict would have to explore a vast range of biological, psychological, economic and cultural reasons for conflicts among human beings, and even then there would have to remain a great deal of confusion over the priority of these respective explanations. The psychological literature in particular has tended to treat conflict as an unfortunate byproduct of close relationships. Various psychologists have lamented that the very factors that encourage intimacy (living together, working toward common goals, and so on) also tend to encourage more frequent and serious conflict.[2] Conflict, from this perspective, is perhaps inevitable in general but avoidable in particular instances if partners make a concerted effort to build healthy communication skills.

Yet what most of these approaches fail to consider is the way that conflict itself serves as a vehicle for intimacy – though, to be sure, a particularly fraught one. It is this latter course that I will pursue in this chapter, a luxury made possible because I am not considering either the anthropological causes of conflicts or their empirical effects.[3] When tracing the emergence of conflict in the dialectic of intimacy, we can confine our inquiry to how conflict will appear *if* it emerges between two partners striving for intimacy who recoil from irony's indifference. In Hegel's master–slave dialectic, conflict emerges from a desire for recognition that does not yet recognize itself as such. A self-consciousness fights to have itself mirrored in another self-consciousness without yet having realized what such a process of mirroring would entail.[4] In intimate conflict this indeterminate longing also plays a key role, but intimacy is far from the only form of recognition. Fights *can* start because the partners long for a closeness whose consummation they cannot conceive, but they can also start because the partners want to be *valued* or for their opponents to share their values. And we cannot rule out in advance the possibility that some fights break out for no purpose at all. I plan to discuss the place of such conflicts in a dialectic of value in future works, but I suspect that even a full dialectical study of value will not be enough to catalogue the various forms that conflict can take.

For now, I would simply like to pick up where the dialectic of embedding left off. Secrets and gossip pull partners together because they make everyone who is not party to the sharing constituents of the shared relationship. In sharing something that no one else has, you and I are tied together in something private. But the ironic relationship realizes that this privacy is dependent on much that is not private and thus throws itself into a fury trying to find content that could be shared completely by only the partners. Partners thus seek proximity by embedding their very relationship in the context of a higher-order conversation, embedding this conversation in the context of a higher-order one, and so on. Take this imagined example:

A: 'I'm starting to think that human beings are biologically maladapted for lifelong relationships.'
B: 'I knew I should have dated that ring-tailed lemur when I had the chance.'
A: 'I'm pretty sure you're not his type.'
B: 'Always a primate, never a bride.'

In this exchange, A and B flee the quicksand of nonconsummation by continually climbing to higher ground. A begins by suggesting that it is not anything particular about this relationship that appears to be failing, but the very genus of relationships among humans. Sensing that an interest in such anthropological claims cannot be shared in a satisfying manner, B mocks A's pretention with an ironic foray into comparative zoology. A responds by pretending to take B's suggestion seriously, pointing out a potential flaw in her plan, and B again seeks higher ground, this time in an absurdist variation on proverbial self-pity. What separates this movement from a simple process of finding shared interests is that A and B have ceased to hold out hope that they can find a higher union in their common appreciation of their condition. It is the movement away from fixed interests itself, the climbing out of the quicksand, that constitutes the intimacy of the ironic encounter. Thus even if the partners are clever enough to keep the irony going indefinitely, they will find that their fleeing is not shared, but merely sustained.

A fight, on the other hand, treats irony's reservation of an inaccessible interiority not as a ground for play, but as something to be resisted. In conflict the interiority of each partner is suspended, and the very resistance of each partner to the other constitutes the substance of the relationship. Let's imagine A and B's conversation continuing:

A: 'What the hell is that supposed to mean? You're the one who didn't want to get married.'
B: 'There you go again. Why do you always think marriage is the answer?'
A: 'So that's it: you don't want to marry me.'
B: 'I didn't say that. I'm only trying to get you to stop being so negative all the time.'

In this exchange, the climbing has ceased, and A and B have resorted to lobbing surface-level criticisms at one another. Yet it is not the desire for a common point of view, but the momentum of the argument itself that carries them along. They seek intimacy in the conflict itself.

Conflict thus occupies something like the place the inverted world occupies in Hegel's dialectic of consciousness.[5] After the failure of embedding's increasingly baroque and indirect paths to intimacy, conflict assumes that true intimacy is found in its opposite: the rejection of intimacy. While it might seem counterintuitive that intimacy could be built on the rejection of one partner by another, it is hard to find a theorist of friendship who has not commented on this process in some manner. When different matrices of embedding begin to overlap, as is quite common when a relationship is institutionalized, as in marriage, the stakes can become unbearably high. Montaigne, who felt the burden of an arranged marriage quite acutely and jealously guarded his friendship with Boétie from external encroachments, showed how periodic rejection is crucial to any fulfilling relationship.[6] One can find similar sentiments throughout Nietzsche's writings, but they share a common source with the claim that 'a grain of wrong actually belongs to good taste' (*Beyond Good and Evil*, §221).[7] Since submitting a relationship to the standards of some externalized conception of justice can place artificial limits on intimacy, conflict's very immediacy and renunciation of shared goals offers a relationship a perverse freedom. Its naïve hope is that intimacy comes, as the old tagline goes, when people stop being polite and start being real.

The dismissal

Though irony carried to its extreme tends to call into question the very desirability of intimacy, it sometimes pulls back to a rejection of *this* particular relationship. When one partner rejects the other not on grounds that she assumes ought to be shared by both partners, but on grounds that are open to questioning, what results is a new opening for engagement. Thus Kierkegaard's portrayal of Socrates in *The Concept of Irony* presents only a partial picture of the philosopher's techniques for establishing intimacy.[8] If Socrates were pursuing intimacy only through the generalized embedding of irony, his self-absorption would have eliminated the possibility of any real friendships. But Socrates does not just reject the external world in the company of friends; he rejects these friends as well. He continually mocks them, tells them their lives are worthless and even rejects their offers to help save his life. And yet it is this rejection, which is not a generalized rejection of everyone who fails to live up to his own standards but a series of specific dismissals of each of them in turn, that wins their affection. While in many cases it is possible to discern in Socrates' rejections of his compatriots a greater moral or pedagogical end,[9] it is also possible to analyse many of these moments, such as his rejection of Alcibiades in the *Symposium* (218e), as a dismissal: a rejection of a partner intended to bring about greater intimacy with him.

Kierkegaard's term for this process is 'rotating the crops', and he discusses it memorably in the essay from A in the first volume of *Either/Or*:

> People with experience maintain that proceeding from a basic principle is supposed to be very reasonable; I yield to them and proceed from the basic principle that all people are boring. Or is there anyone who would be boring enough to contradict me in this regard? (I: 285)

While this line of solicitation looks quite similar to irony in that it seeks to cultivate intimacy through a rejection of the entire community, it differs in that the proposed partner is explicitly included in this rejection and yet allowed an opportunity to prove his non-inclusion. Anyone who might be willing to challenge the assertion and thus engage in a debate has already been excluded as a worthy partner. And yet A goes on to insist that this dismissal does not give rise to an impasse, but is actually the beginning of all genuine motion. The assertion here is that only the repulsion of another can provide sufficient force for one to begin to develop the kind of negative relation to self that opens a place for genuine engagement. The essay as a whole plays on this transformation of irony into conflict, so A's assertion that all people are boring is also a challenge to the reader (whomever A might have intended in this role) to prove him wrong by engaging with the text. A tells the reader that she is boring and unworthy of his (or anybody's) time, which, through its very alienation, draws the reader in still further. Near the end of the essay, he extends this critique of boredom to a dismissal of friendship in general. While the ancients extolled the virtues of a friendship founded fundamentally on agreement, A rejects this stance and calls for a relationship with others founded on a bit of unpleasantness: 'The unpleasantness is indeed a piquant ingredient in the perverseness of life' (E/O I: 296). One thus ought to indulge occasionally in unpleasant interactions in order to 'rotate the crops' – to open oneself to a new set of possible relations to the world.

While such rotation may be personally renewing, from the standpoint of the dialectic of intimacy, the most salient characteristic of the dismissal is that it demands recompense and thus continues the interaction. Consider this scene from Tad Friend's profile of the actor Steve Carell:

> Life is a prolonged improv, in a sense, and Carell often pulls those around him into formalized theatricals. Recently, when his nine-year-old daughter, Annie, asked him, 'Daddy, how much do you love me?' Carell replied, 'I love you so much, you're the most important thing to me.' Then he sombrely shook his head, negating the compliment. She gasped and

laughed, then said with mock outrage, 'Daddy! That's terrible! How can you say such a thing?' Carell, instantly sunny, said, 'Oh, honey, you know, of course, that you're the most wonderful child.' After a beat, he shook his head again, starting the next round of the game. (52)

The dismissal works because it simultaneously gives Carell's daughter an opportunity to solicit further compliments and makes the original compliment gratuitous. By denying his love for his daughter, he shows that he is not simply responding because she has asked, but has some deeper, private reason for stating that she is important to him. In the process, he compliments his daughter's intelligence by assuming she can understand his irony. Their game, even if it gained some of its pleasure by being enacted before a journalist, showed itself to be based on a kind of private understanding, and yet it was not the private understanding of an irony that encloses the entire world in a shared bit of meaning, since any meaning that happened to be shared was secondary to the argument itself. What was shared was nothing: the negation of a compliment and the negation of this negation. This is even clearer in unspoken dismissals. The ingénue who playfully splashes her beau on their first visit to the lake is seeking to draw him out into some as yet undetermined form of intimacy by forcing a response.

The game of 'peekaboo' is perhaps the simplest form of an intimate dismissal. The child is drawn in as the parent wilfully withdraws her gaze. The parent emphasizes her withdrawal in the most obvious way possible, with hands or a blanket dividing the two, and the child is delighted that it is only temporary. While the parent's initial appearance of the day can also please the child, 'peekaboo' carries with it the added pleasure of the cancellation of an intentional withdrawal. Here it is not this feeling of pleasure and return that constitutes the intimacy, but the mutual recognition that there is a clear distinction between non-intimacy and intimacy that can be transcended at the simple discretion of one of the partners. The agent of the dismissal opens a place for intimacy by building a straw man that impedes the intimacy (a blanket, the agent's indifference, a belief that the relationship is star-crossed, etc.) and expecting the partner to deny it (the child pulls down the blanket, the beloved reaffirms the sacredness of the relationship, etc.). The dismissal thus depends on its own unseriousness. In Friend's words, it is a kind of 'prolonged improv', a place to say 'yes' that is opened up precisely by one partner saying 'no'. The 'no' and the 'yes' are not character traits or place markers in the relationship, since this would imply that each partner is simply acting out a role given independently of the relationship – the perversion of the neuter that Irigaray most feared. Instead, each 'no' and each 'yes' is an independent act, and the improvisation can continue only as long as there are new ways to say 'no' and 'yes'. Steve Carell is an exceptionally talented improvisational actor, but I doubt that his game with his daughter went many more rounds than Friend recounts.

The dispute

The dismissal tends to dissolve because it is merely playing with conflict. Being dismissed offers a partner the opportunity to respond, but because the dismissal always contains an anticipated response in its very structure, it does not take a stand on the relationship as a whole. When, however, the argument concerns more consequential matters, the invitational structure of the dismissal seems unseemly and the possibility emerges of ending the relationship entirely. When this threat is allowed to show itself along the edges of the discussion, it becomes clear to each partner that any assertion poses a potential danger to intimacy, and yet for this very reason everything that matters to each partner has a place in the dispute. Because the set of concerns at issue both shapes and is shaped by everything else that matters to each partner, a genuine dispute can go many more rounds if both partners are willing to explore and express the preoccupations that bubble up in this dispute. We find an excellent example of such a dispute between partners sincere, self-aware, and angry enough to follow out its logic in Todd Field's 2001 film *In the Bedroom*, in which a married couple struggle to reestablish intimacy after the murder of their twenty-two-year-old son. The title of the film itself points to the threat to intimacy posed by the involvement of a third party in any relationship[10] and thus speaks to the complexities of embedding, but the most memorable scene in the movie centres on a dispute. The main characters, Matt (Tom Wilkinson) and Ruth (Sissy Spacek), have to cope with Frank's death even as his murderer is set free on bail and thus occasionally visible in their small Maine town. In this scene, Matt, who has himself been preoccupied with revenge fantasies, confronts Ruth for having withdrawn from him and the world in general in her grief. Eventually their dispute centres on the son's relationship to his older girlfriend, whose ex-husband ultimately killed him.

> [Matt enters the kitchen]
> Matt: How did it go today?
> [no answer]
>   Something wrong?
> Ruth: Wrong? What could be wrong, Matt?
> [pause]
> What do you want?

Matt: I want to know what's going on.

Ruth: Oh, right.

Matt: You're obviously upset. Is there something we can talk about?

Ruth: Talk? Who, us? What if somebody walked in? They wouldn't recognize us. They'd think they were in the wrong house.

Matt: Do you want to talk or not?

Ruth: Oh, you mean about our dead son? We haven't before. Why should we bother now?

Matt: What can I do, Ruth?

Ruth: Forget it, Matt. Why don't you just go?

Matt: What do you want from me?

Ruth: I want you to stop acting like nothing's happened. That's what I want.

Matt: Why, because I'm not bouncing off the walls?

Ruth: No, Matt, that would require feelings. We don't want you to hurt yourself.

Matt: Do me a favor. If you want a grieving contest, go find someone else.

Ruth: Oh I know how you grieve. Go have another beer.

Matt: What the hell is that supposed to mean? What do you know? You know nothing. You don't know what I go through.

Ruth: No, I don't know what you go through, Matt, or if you go through anything! But that's your choice, dear, not mine.

Matt: You're goddamned right. My choice is not to scream at the world. Maybe one of us has to be reasonable around here, you ever think of that?

Ruth: Reasonable? Gee, Matt, I don't know about you, but I miss my son. I'm glad you have time for reason. That's what you imparted to Frank, that sense of reason. Oh, he thought you were very reasonable.

Matt: What are you talking about?

Ruth: Nothing.

Matt: Are you saying that I – that I'm the one responsible? Is that it? Well, let me tell you something. Let me tell you something: you got it backwards! I know what you think, that I was too lenient! That I let him get away with...

[Ruth throws a plate to the floor, smashing it]

Ruth: Everything! Everything!

Matt: Yes, yes, yes, and why? Why didn't he ever come to you?

Ruth: He wouldn't listen to me! He didn't trust me. You made sure of that.

Matt: Because you never listened to him.

Ruth: No, but you did. You were winking at him the whole time. You encouraged him. You wanted what he had. Her.

Matt: Oh my God, you've gotta be kidding!

Ruth: You know it! You wanted it and you couldn't get it. That's why you didn't stop him. So you could get your kicks through your son. You can't admit the truth to me or to yourself... that Frank died for your fantasy piece of ass!

Matt: You want to know why our son is dead? You really want to know? He was with her not because of me. He went there because of you.

[Ruth scoffs]

Yes, he did. Because you are so controlling, so overbearing, so angry that he was it! That he was our only one.

Ruth: That is not true!

Matt: Oh yes, it is. Yes, it is. Even when he was a kid, you were telling him how he was always wrong. I remember. One time you yanked him out of a Little League game and sent him home for throwing his glove in the dirt. He was what? Nine years old! Everything he did was wrong. Well, what was wrong with him, Ruth? You're – you're so unforgiving. You are. That's what he said.

[Ruth looks stricken]

And you're pulling the same shit with me. And that's a horrible way to be. It's horrible. You're bitter, Ruth. And you can point your finger at me all you like, but you better take a damn good look at yourself.

Ruth: I just wanted to talk about what happened, Matt.

Matt: You want me to be open with you, embrace you? You scare me. How can I talk to you? Sometimes I – Sometimes I can't even look at you.

The conversation at this point is interrupted by a young girl selling candy to fund a trip for her gymnastics team. Neither Matt nor Ruth finds the interruption particularly unwelcome, since both have been exhausted by the conversation. When Matt returns from the door, he apologizes for the vehemence of his claims, and Ruth cuts him off, accepting his criticism in a gesture that is at once theatrically self-mortifying and openly contractive, allowing Matt to end the dispute by taking the role of the expansive partner. Yet though the conflict ultimately dissolves into the rhythms of the heartbeat, while it persists it is driven by a unique form of striving for intimacy. It is clear from the beginning that both partners know what to look for in setting up the fight. When Matt enters the room he carefully tests Ruth's receptivity to an argument, asking guardedly if something is wrong. His tone is patronizing, but rather than closing off her lines of response by opening with a criticism he leaves her an opening to respond with a grievance. She initially rebuffs his offerings under the guise that she's occupied with putting away the groceries, so instead of pushing further, he waits for her to establish an opening of her own. When she asks him what's wrong, he asks, again somewhat patronizingly, 'Is there something we can talk about?'

Her answer is the first genuine opening of the conversation, an ironic doubt about the very possibility of openness between them. 'Talk? Who, us? What if somebody walked in? They wouldn't even recognize us.' Despite its bitterness, this is a merely formal complaint that does not get to the core of her grievance, so Matt asks for a clarification: 'What do you want from me?' Given Ruth's icy tone, Matt acknowledges by even asking this question that he is willing to open a genuine dispute, in which each partner shapes her arguments neither to achieve some concrete goal of mollifying or further angering the other partner nor to convince some imagined independent judge, but in the blind hope that some satisfactory resolution might emerge from the expression of partial and one-sided points of view. This mutual commitment allows Ruth to express a previously unacknowledged grievance: she believes Matt's reserved manner of expressing his grief constitutes both a dismissal of their son and an indictment of her own mental health.

At this point Matt feigns unwilling to have the conversation under these terms: 'If you want a grieving contest, go find someone else.' This time it's Ruth's turn to keep the discussion alive. She snares him with the unfair accusation: 'Oh I know how you grieve. Go have another beer.' At this point, the argument can continue on its own momentum, as both parties have the licence to air the grievances they have been nursing. To signal that nothing matters more at this moment than the confrontation itself, Ruth breaks a dish and then storms out of the room, forcing Matt to follow her to show his own concern for the debate over the mess in the kitchen and the rest of the world in general.

While it might seem odd to anyone seeking the necessary and sufficient conditions of intimacy that Matt and Ruth only manage to break through the fog of grief through outright condemnations of each other, for the dialectician this is no great mystery. Because their love had previously always been mediated by their care for their son, his death has left them with no shared world that does not in some way refer back to him. This scene is so passionate because it shows them learning for the first time how to share this absence. They are not simply 'getting things off their chests', as the self-help industry might encourage, but forming a new sort of between that is neither grief nor nostalgia. As Matt seems to intuit, basing their intimacy on any kind of feeling would devolve into a 'contest', as the sheer privacy of grief would continually remind each that the other could not possibly be feeling the same thing. Instead, what they share is a kind of negativity itself, in which the intimacy is propelled forward by a mutual disgust with their situation.

The argument gets even more heated as Matt answers Ruth's allegation that he recklessly encouraged their son to cultivate the fatal relationship with his own claim that she pushed him away with her constant criticism, but Matt makes a fatal mistake by appealing to their son as an independent judge. There is a noticeable change of tone in the argument when Matt ceases to represent his criticisms as merely his own and claims that Frank himself had called Ruth unforgiving. To this point, their intimacy has been structured by the argument itself – that is, by their mutual commitment to rejecting their condition – but since the logic of an argument calls for a resolution, Matt stabs at a potential clincher. He loses sight of the dispute's pure negativity and imports an incongruous set of rules in the effort to reach an affirmative conclusion. It is not entirely clear how fair his accusation is, but what is clear is that it dissolves the intimacy of the encounter. While Frank's memory is fair game for dispute, his words are not. The argument never called for resolution or proof, just commitment.[11] It is only the interruption of the gymnast *ex machina* that allows something like a rapport to be restored.

But it is difficult to imagine how the intimacy of the argument could have been maintained within the context of the dispute, no matter how committed each partner was to continuing it. While this example shows how remarkably fluid disputes can be, they must still be *about* something, even if this includes disputes over the right to make various claims within the context of the dispute itself. Unlike in irony or dismissals, there is never really a *meta*-dispute. Any dispute over how the parties conduct the dispute instantly sublimates into the rest of the dispute's content. Because the object of the dispute is not to achieve concord over some basic principle (or to achieve concord about how the dispute over this principle will be conducted, and so on), but to drown opposition and indifference in pure negativity, it makes no sense to make any one part of the dispute primary to or incumbent upon any other. The disputants seek intimacy in their commitment to positing and questioning the grounds of their distinctness, not in finding a particular result. If any point of genuine agreement happens to be found, it is put to the side as irrelevant to the activity of the dispute itself.

Violence

Because disputants actively seek out points of contention and reject grounds for agreement as betrayals of intimacy, disputes have no natural endpoint. They can end[12] in distraction (as in the example of Matt and Ruth), in the physical exhaustion of both parties, or, when one or both parties want to demonstrate that their commitment to the conflict exceeds the power of words, in violence. Violence has already made an appearance in the dialectic of touching, where the urge to wound one's partner grows out of the desire for a contact that exceeds all other forms of contact. There the wound is a manifestation of the search for immediacy, but here violence is demonstrative: in much the same way that Ruth breaks the dish as part of the escalation of her argument with Matt, it aims to show that nothing is more important to the violent partner than the confrontation at hand. Such a demonstration would not aim to kill, overpower, or even impress the victim, since these ancillary goals would be at odds with the movement toward intimacy. Without these other forms of desire for recognition to whip the violent partner into a frenzy of self-conceit, violence should show itself almost immediately to be a dialectical dead end.

If the violence is one-sided, the bilateral conflict is transformed into the meaningless act of a single partner. Each partner has a different relation to the violent act, and the violated partner shows that he has withdrawn from the dispute's open-ended commitment to mutual rejection. If, on the other hand, the violence is reciprocated, it still shows itself to be less intimate than the dispute, which at least took stock of what each partner cares about, even if only to reject it. The violence remains utterly dumb, and unlike in the *mêlée* (see Chapter 8), even the instant of transgression is not shared.

Withdrawal

Like violence, withdrawal also brings to conflict a perverse repetition of earlier moments in the dialectic. In the dialectic of the gift, the giver saw absence as a necessary step in purifying the gift of any vestige of self-interestedness. And in the dialectic of the between, withdrawal was a necessary moment of all togetherness, both to keep mutual presence from becoming too claustrophobic and as a consequence of intimacy's need to maintain some degree of separation. In both of these forms of withdrawal, the impulse was not to deny intimacy to one's partner, but to seize hold of the absence that intimacy entails. The gift and the between each call for a non-presence that is not simply chosen by one of the partners, but is part of the very structure of intimacy.

In conflict, however, withdrawal is a weapon that can be powerful in wounding but not in fostering intimacy.[13] Refusing to engage one's partner explicitly in a dispute calls attention to the limitations of verbal argumentation as a means for achieving the goals of conflict. While the partners show their commitment to rejecting every external factor that could interfere with the relationship, the withdrawal of one partner shows the emptiness of the form of the dispute: what is all this talking supposed to accomplish anyway? It is a provocation in the manner of the dismissal, but it leaves no means for the response to the provocation to present itself. Any assertion, question, or command that responds to such a withdrawal has been declared meaningless before it is even uttered.

The withdrawal does, to be sure, call on the speaking partner to take on an expansive role and attempt to argue from both perspectives at once. This can make a few moments of silence a powerful tool in any dispute, but complete withdrawal from the conversation leaves no path back to reengagement. Thus it fails to foster either the dismissal's solicitation to further engagement or the dispute's fluidity of personal commitments. It is a pure negation that has lost sight of the intimacy that the negativity of conflict was supposed to induce.

Yet there is also a formal contradiction in confrontational withdrawal that lays the groundwork for a more structured form of conflict. To the extent that withdrawal is a form of rebuke, it can be called out as such. The withdrawal would, after all, fail if it were not made completely plain to the other partner.[14] The partner who does this calling out is, to be sure, shown to be the kind of chump who continues arguing even when it is precisely arguing that is being mocked. But by accepting this rebuke and showing that the withdrawing partner is also continuing argumentation by other means, the speaking partner shows that the dispute is only possible in terms of a publicly discernable logic. 'Yes, our dispute has gotten us nowhere,' she says, 'but the fact that you're giving me the silent treatment shows that this dispute still matters to you. You thus must be trying to tell me something, so we should figure out what that something is.' In its rejection of engagement as such, withdrawing is an essentially ironic gesture, so it can be colonized through conflict in the same way as ironic embedding. In the process the dispute becomes a debate. No longer simply an exercise in mutual rejection, it now involves an antagonistic yet collaborative effort to arrive at the roots of the conflict.

Debate

If reaching a point of agreement were the primary goal of an argument, then the process of argumentation would resemble nothing so much as a fetish. One can imagine two scientists developing a genuine rapport as they argue for hours over data until one discovers the crucial evidence that makes his side of the argument indisputably correct. At this point, there is nothing more to be done and said, and the scientists can give each other one last high five before heading home to their respective families. It is likely here that their activity is not purely utilitarian and approaches a kind of intimacy, but there is nothing to distinguish it from any other project undertaken in common.

The scientists draw near to one another through their relation to a common interest, but this interest remains external to both of them. Some arguments, however, aim at an intimacy that would be achieved not in any conclusive answer, but in the very practice of argumentation. Indeed, I suspect that anyone who has made it far enough through this book to be reading these lines finds the sincere and critical engagement that attends philosophical debate one of the most rewarding forms of human encounter.[15] Or consider the *Monty Python* sketch in which Michael Palin enters a clinic for the sole purpose of paying for an argument. He clearly is not interested in establishing the truth of any matter as such, and his frustration with the office worker who allows the argument to descend into mere bickering shows that he is seeking quite a bit more from a genuine debate. Such debate differs from the utilitarian discussion of our two scientists[16] in the assumption that arriving at the correct answer is not the primary aim of the activity. Debate is not fetishistic in that its partisans do not necessarily hope for reconciliation and even assume that their individual differences will never be resolved into a single common position. But unlike a dispute, a debate is not structured by the opposition itself, but is always *about* something.

The object of the debate is thus never fully present for the partners, but neither is it a mere vanishing moment in the discussion's interplay, as in a dispute. To be sure, almost every conversation that partners care to engage in responds to a variety of different motivations. Speakers want to be recognized as intelligent or passionate and for their positions to be accepted. They want to serve as examples of the kinds of discursive habits that help build communities and to work on improving their own discursive habits to measure up to the examples that have inspired them. They want to change the world with their words and gather information to know how to change themselves with their actions. And sometimes they just want to pass the time or ensure that the conversation is predictable enough to be completely forgotten. I believe many of these desires can be accounted for by a more thorough tracing of the dialectic of recognition, but my interest here in the dialectic of intimacy is considerably narrower.[17] In this context, a debate seeks intimacy in a managed conflict.

In such a context, any assertion can function as a solicitation to further engagement. Just as Fichte's appeal or summons (*Aufforderung*) calls for the freedom of its respondent by allowing her to respond either affirmatively or negatively, an assertion opens a vast field of assenting, contradicting, qualifying and modifying responses.[18] And because any response would have to rely on a similarly vast network of commitments, it too will open up a range of possible responses.

Of course, these possibilities are not endless. Every response must at least maintain the antagonistic structure of the discussion, for simply following thoughts where they took the partners would at best be a kind of fetishism and at worst a pair of unrelated streams of consciousness. But the antagonism is never absolute. Unlike disputants, debaters recognize that their conflict always assumes a much vaster web of agreement. There need not be any single proposition that the debaters take to be unquestionable, but the debate must be conducted in the currency of reasons.[19] The reasons do not have to be fetishized as postulates, stipulations, or ideals, but they must in principle be sharable. Once someone makes an assertion, her partner can demand reasons for it, give reasons against it, or assert that it is bound up with reasons that ought to be rejected. The debate can continue to be about these reasons, and because the debate does not have as its object the testing of any central master claim, there is not necessarily an infinite regress as the partners debate the reasons given for the reasons for an assertion, and so on. To assume an infinite regress in this situation is to assume a fixed point from which the debaters are regressing, but the intimacy of the debate depends on there being no such point. The goal here is not to find an ideal speech situation[20] from which all threat of force has been removed, but for the partners to engage one another continually through reasons. The fact that such reasons themselves call for reasons allows the partners to explore a web of significance without the apocalyptic stakes of the dispute.

While reasons do not have to be fixed, they do at least have to be sharable, and for them to be sharable, there must be a distinction between those reasons that are acceptable and those that are unacceptable.[21] Because stipulations about how the debate is to be conducted are inseparable from the other kinds of reasons given in a debate, the risk is that these stipulations calcify into a *pro forma* structure that the debate must follow. There is of course a kind of intimacy in the pair of friends who carry an ongoing and good-natured political dispute over a number of years or the married couple who cannot get by without their formalized disagreements, but the conflict in these cases has been stripped of all its risk. Here Barthes helps set the scene:

> When two subjects argue according to a set exchange of remarks and with a view to having the 'last word,' these two subjects are *already* married: for them the scene is an exercise of right, the practice of a language of which they are co-owners; *each one in his turn*, says the scene, which means: *never you without me*, and reciprocally. This is the meaning of what is euphemistically called *dialogue:* not to listen to each other, but to submit in common to an egalitarian principle of the distribution of language goods. (*A Lover's Discourse*, 204)

Of course, adherence to formal procedures is not in principle a bar to intimacy. In Chapter 1, for instance, we saw that even completely predictable instances of ritualized gift-giving established the continuity of engagement necessary for Aristotelian συνηθεία. Similarly, even predictable debates force partisans to listen to one another, respond to particular turns of phrase, and so on.

Yet such ritual is uniquely at odds with the demands of conflict. Since conflict grows out of embedding's realization that partners cannot meet each other in the setting up of a common space, it cannot assume that simply being together and answering one another's arguments is enough for intimacy. There must be a continual movement of self-assertion and cancellation of this self-assertion for conflict to distinguish itself as a form of intimacy. When debate is formalized, it becomes clear that either the self-assertion or its cancellation (or both) is merely feigned and thus that the debate is either superfluous or ironic. Reasons are the lifeblood of vibrant debate, but they are also maddeningly contingent. To prevent debate from being bound to formal requirements, the reasons must always be questionable, but the giving of them must always be a form of self-assertion that opens itself to contradiction. The questionability of reasons must thus be both hidden and apparent in any assertion.

Even more damningly, every appeal to reasons in a debate implicitly imagines an independent third party who serves as judge of the argument. While in a dispute such a judge is irrelevant (witness how Matt's appeal to Frank's words causes Ruth to withdraw), debates assume an ideal judge to whom the *right* reasons would be perfectly compelling if only they could be found. The structure of the debate is thus the reverse of embedding. Rather than taking a third party as the content of an intimate dyad, the debate takes a (real or imagined) third party as the measure of the relationship. What matters most is not what is inside the relationship, but what is outside. With this reversed triad, the debaters find themselves just as alienated as the ironists were. They recognize that their aims are to resolve their differences, but since these differences have governed how they define themselves to each other, they do not yet grasp how they can deny their differences without denying themselves.

8

The *Mêlée*

In dismissal and debate, the search for intimacy does not take the form of agreement or disagreement, but appears rather in the ongoing process of positing and abolishing grounds for disagreement. But in the scorched-earth conflict of the sort we saw in *In the Bedroom*, intimacy is sought in the combustion of the conflict itself, and any contribution that is not fuel for the conflagration is irrelevant to the project of intimacy. Disputes thus either exhaust the partners and return them to the progressive-perfect of the heartbeat or transform into the more stable but calcifying format of a debate. If, however, the partners wish to preserve the uncompromised negativity of the conflict but are willing to suspend the personal commitments that make disputes so fiery and debates so open-ended, they can enter what, for lack of a suitable English equivalent, I am calling the *mêlée*.

The English 'melee' gives only a shadow of the sense of the French *mêlée*. As in its English equivalent, a *mêlée* is sometimes a descent into conflict without order, but it need not be an outright battle. It involves a mixture, a *mélange*, and thus appears whenever there is meddling. When Nancy gives his 'Eulogy for the *Mêlée*' in Sarajevo (*Being Singular Plural*, 145–58), he is of course describing a chaotic conflict, but he is also describing the totalitarian need for connection that underlay it. He initially distinguishes between the *mêlée* of a fight and the *mêlée* of love[1] but quickly concludes that each is inextricably mingled with the other.[2] This is also why he works to distance the concept of *mêlée* from a simple mixture (*mélange*). Whereas talk of a *mélange* implies a relatively easy process of coming together and mixing, '*mêlée*' highlights the chaos of a coming together that is not sure in advance if intimacy is even possible.[3] A *mêlée* is never something unitary, since 'in a *mêlée* there are meetings and encounters; there are those who come together and those who spread out, those who concentrate and those who disseminate, those who identify and those who modify – just like the two sexes in each one of us' (BSP 151). But far from fragmenting the partners into a sense of lost intimacy, the *mêlée* serves rather to counteract the fragmenting tendencies of fetishism and conflict.[4] When partners meet in a *mêlée*, the collapse and waste all around them allows for a suspension of the distinction between individuality and collectivity. Indeed, in a *mêlée* even the between collapses, rendering presence and non-presence mere abstractions. Conflict's work of disentangling the embedded relationships that seem to make irony our fate has already been accomplished. The *mêlée* appears as the very possibility of an intimate encounter.

The *mêlée* thus appears in the interruptive time of the event. Rather than positing a time or space in which the intimacy will be or has been consummated, the *mêlée* is only ever an interruption of everything that impedes intimacy.[5] It is the moment of revolution, when the combatants are bound not by their common aims or the society that will one day unite them, but the sheer giddiness of all the little things ceasing to matter. The *mêlée* is thus not tied to any particular subjectivity, but posits a presubjective space from which subjects have somehow settled out. By reentering this space, partners hope to find an intimacy that their self-centred projects have denied them.

Consumption, destruction and waste

In intense conflict, the membrane of one's partner's impenetrability is stripped away, but what remains is still not an open site for engagement. Instead, the conflict's intimacy only lasts as long as the promise that a future membrane could be torn away. When, however, the site of this membrane is posited as one's own self-seeking, stripping away this self-seeking might offer the same possibilities for intimacy as conflict without the need for further conflict. In *The Accursed Share*, Bataille describes the intense intimacy that arises between the Aztec warrior and the prisoner he intends to sacrifice. According to Bataille, this intimacy derives not from the mutual recognition that one is the victor and the other the conquered, but from their mutual renunciation of concerns for the future. The warrior renounces all the value that could be extracted from a potential slave, and the prisoner renounces all hope for a life beyond ritual consumption in the present (51). All myth and religion, Bataille contends, longs to suspend the movement by which people became obsessed with mere things: 'In his strange myths, in his cruel rites, man is *in search of a lost intimacy* from the first' (57). In modern capitalist countries we make gestures toward this need for sacrifice in parties and occasions for conspicuous consumption, but our hearts are rarely in it. When I consume all that I have without concern for tomorrow, I show that things are nothing to me and I am concerned only with laying myself bare (58–9). This intense consumption, however, is pure violence in that it leaves no place to join in this new intimacy, which is why there must be an organized festival of sacrifice. The gesture of openness must be put in its place; destruction must be given its due (59).

Our most common bourgeois rituals of consumption offer little recognition of this necessity of destruction. Doing shots of expensive alcohol can consume no more than a day's wages for the bourgeois information worker, and the ensuing hangover will compromise at most a morning's worth of productive labour. When 'party' has become a verb, ritualized consumption is part of the normal course of life for which we can make relatively simple allowances. While a general fellow-feeling is not all that difficult to secure with a little well-chosen food and music, the *mêlée* calls for more than just feeling – which, after all, could only ever be private. It is not just our love of the food and music that binds us, for these are mere fetishes, nor is it the generosity of the host to which we are each responding, for this is a variation on the (non-)intimacy of the gift. Indeed, the more we emphasize the music's brilliance or the host's beneficence, the more we reduce the συνηθεία that the party makes possible to a series of transactions: a great deal of planning and money went in to making it possible for us to release ourselves temporarily from our private strivings, so the least we can do in return is help with the dishes. The *mêlée* asks for something more: an intimacy prior to all transactions.

Of course, parties need not involve such bourgeois hand-wringing, and contemporary class divisions likely make the contradictions of modern parties seem more pervasive than they are.[6] There is no intrinsic contradiction in partners gathering together for the sole purpose of squandering resources. Augustine's theft of the pears was pleasurable precisely because he acknowledged but did not have to involve himself with the work it took to cultivate the orchard. And as he says, alone he would not have done it (*Confessions*, II: vii [33]). Teenagers squatting and partying in a foreclosed house are able to consume without having to commit themselves to production, yet even here they find themselves caught up in the general movement of production and do not simply annul their private projects. Not only do they have to seek out new houses to trash, but they have to frame the chaos in terms of their particular roles in the destruction. The objects of consumption and waste are still fetishized, and thus their destruction takes on a mechanical and even organized flavour. Tom is in the pantry peeing on the dry goods, Sally is spraypainting the walls in the living room, and I'm on the porch shooting skeet with the china. We are as alienated from one another as factory workers.[7] The intimacy of the *mêlée* thus cannot appear in the consumption and destruction of external objects. So long as waste, consumption and destruction are our purposes, we do not find intimacy in their process any more than we find it in love of or obsession with objects. While they aim at a general condition for togetherness, consumption and destruction are always too specific in their choice of objects to find it.[8]

This is true even when we make the objects of destruction our own bodies. The obverse of the gym rats sharing the fetishization of their bodies is the expression of total unconcern for one's own and others' bodies found in mosh pits and purposeless combat. Such exertions are exhilarating in their release from fetishes and touching's desire for immediacy, but they are only intimate in the vanishing of concern for one's body. Showing you are willing to suspend your self-concern to the point even of sacrificing your bodily integrity is only significant if body-fetishism also persists.

Laughter

Laughter, in contrast, can emerge as a more generalized negativity. Laughter appeared once before in the dialectic, in the woundless affection of tickling, and I think it is no accident that the curious physiological response of laughter is elicited by tickling and humour alike. I suspect that there are evolutionary ties between our responses to tickling and humour,[9] but for now my aim is only to outline their dialectical homologies. Kant famously defined laughter as 'an affect that arises if a tense expectation is transformed into nothing',[10] but this overlooks the extent to which this 'nothing' is not an emptiness or isolation, but a negation of our standards of judgement that itself can be shared. Humour surfaces when our expectations are challenged in a way that calls into question our usual standards for ordering the world, yet does so in a way that seems sharable. Children's puns and riddles play on the arbitrariness of the linguistic order they have inherited, and the more world-weary humour of a Mark Twain questions whether it is reasonable to attribute a moral order to the world at all. But both only work because the unexpected dissolution of sense belongs to something that is shared, whether the polysemy of our language or the hypocrisy of our institutions. In contrast, a crisis in faith is not generally experienced as humorous, but when framed against (say) the tendency of undergrads to fall into such crises right around exam time, it very well could be. Given the difficulties of controlling for cultural differences, I am suspicious of the widely cited figure that people are thirty times more likely to laugh in the presence of others than they are alone, but it does at least evince the fact that humour is irreducibly social.[11]

Yet while Kant's account of laughter misses this social aspect, its contrast between the 'strained expectation' and the 'nothing' does highlight humour's tendency to spread beyond any isolated 'butt' of the joke. In the setup to a joke, the 'strained expectation' – or the 'committed active belief', as Hurley, Dennett and Adams more aptly describe it[12] – calls to mind a determinate conceptual field. By releasing us from this field, the joke does not just replace it with a more adequate one, but shows the expectation to be 'nothing'. That is, the feeling of mirth is a feeling of unconstraint. If this particular strained expectation has shown itself to be ridiculous, what is to save existence in general from ridicule? Yet mirth has a positive valence, because in cases of humour, this 'nothing' is confronted by everyone. The shareability of the experience of ridicule does not make the dissolution of meaning any less obvious, but it makes it endurable by showing that it is shared.

Thus humour plays upon the dialectical structure of not only tickling, but irony – which also can elicit laughter. Even when we only joke to ourselves, humour depends on a playful dismissal of our community just as irony creates and dissolves a community in a single gesture. As the tickled partner shows her receptiveness to touching, humorists show their receptiveness to radical reorientations of meaning in their lives. As in irony, when we laugh together at something humorous we celebrate our mutual suspension of the community, but this celebration pulls our focus from the relation itself to the between. We laugh more easily together because in laughter we share the ecstasy of collapse. Bergson's claim in *Le Rire* that the object of humour is typically a mechanized version of an ostensibly free action is well known, but it has been less remarked that Bergson sees something mechanical in laughter itself. According to Bergson, laughing occurs at the moment when the body comes to resemble a machine no longer in control of its own destiny.[13] Laughter is infectious because it is not simply the projection of an individual feeling onto an event but a suspension of all the projects and intentions that individuate us.

Both irony and humour gain their intimacy from a shared occasion, but whereas irony depends on a message from one partner, humour reacts to an absurdity independent of either partner. Even when one partner tells a joke, what is pleasing or striking about the joke is not its teller or the fact that others are excluded from making sense of it, but something generally accessible. Inside jokes can muddle these categories, since they combine delight in some absurdity with the intimacy of a conspiracy, but their humour still depends on something independent of the couple. It is thus possible to tell a joke one has heard elsewhere without dissolving its impact in the least. Formal jokes are assumed to be part of the general ether, and before telling one, we only have to ask 'Have you heard the one about …' to remind the audience that humour is less a subjective production than a collective realization. With irony, on the other hand, attributing the ironic observation to someone else only makes sense if the observation itself belongs to something that can be shared in a unique way. The ways I can make you laugh by pretending to be someone I am not are almost endless, but as soon as I imply that my pretence could be universally acknowledged, the irony is lost.

In this way, humour shows itself to be not just a collective fetish, but a *mêlée*. Like orgies and mosh pits, rooms full of laughing partners seek intimacy in their disindividuation. Just as the mosh pit promises an intimacy in the temporary destruction of its members' independent aims, mirth only overtakes an entire room when its occupants are primed to dissolve their objective striving entirely. Kierkegaard describes such dissolution into humour as a rediscovery of the childlike, though not of childishness (CUP 551). Appreciating humour involves a suspension of the certainty of adulthood that nevertheless does not respond to everything with the sheer wonder of the child. If Gervais and Wilson are right that ritualized laughter developed in hominids long before language began to evolve (411), then Kierkegaard's analysis of humour takes on added significance, and humour points us to a form of sociality before or beyond linguistic determination itself. In irony, on the other hand, both partners recognize the ultimate irrelevance of their private desires, but they nevertheless need their partners to affirm the relevance of this irrelevance.

If there is anything special about the intimacy of roaring laughter, it is that it depends on no sharing at all. There are often things we share in laughing at a joke – a culture, common assumptions about the world, a set of experiences, and so on – but the intimacy of the joke is that it leaves all of these things behind. All of the experiences and ideals we share in common are just fetishes and therefore separate us as much as they link us, but humour promises an intimacy in our very openness to the world and thus calls for a suspension of our ideals in order to make our connection possible. To be sure, humour can serve to help structure group identity. A group of friends may routinely gather every Friday, and around 11:30 Jim may be asked to 'tell the one about the coconut and the starfish'. In this case, it is not the experience of humour itself that the group longs for, but the familiarity (Aristotle's συνήθεια) of always having laughed at the joke together. In this case the fact that it is a joke that they all share is largely indifferent. They could just as easily be singing a song or recalling an old sporting triumph. However, when it is the humour itself that structures the intimacy, the only thing to be shared is the movement away from self-determination. This movement, however, can only last a moment. While a little humour tends to prime us for more, so that we can continue laughing for a while – for me about ninety minutes is the absolute maximum before I begin to cramp up painfully – the intimacy of laughter only creeps in at those moments of retreat from self, and the vast majority of the time is spent either in solipsistic enjoyment or in appreciation of a common spectacle, either one of which is ultimately isolating. The intimacy of humour itself comes and goes in flashes that leave the moment of humour incomprehensible. There is neither a simultaneous vision of what it means to be together nor an ongoing rejection of the conditions that impede intimacy, but just a timeless intimation that perhaps our distinctness does not matter so much after all.

Frenzy

Frenzy, in contrast, aims to undermine not just the factors that make us distinct, but the very time in which we might mark the oscillation between togetherness and distinctness. It is no accident that modern raves tend to combine endless pulsing rhythms and drugs that alter consciousness of time. The rave, perhaps like its Dionysian forebears,[14] aims to blur not only spatial, but temporal boundaries. The Burning Man festival, for instance, centres on a vast conflagration on its final night, but just as crucial to its success is the endless and undifferentiated expanse of desert it occupies. Communities of tents and vehicles tend to cluster at irregular intervals, but the overriding effect is one of de-spatialization. Likewise, the pulsing beats and indistinct melodies of house music, trance music, and their offspring[15] create a kind of anti-time in which there is neither an expectation of progression nor even a sense of passage. When the music is sufficiently loud or the ground sufficiently conductive, bass beats can overwhelm both mental timekeeping and the ability to perceive one's own corporeal rhythms, such that one's heart beats outside of one's body. Psychotropic drugs can magnify this feeling of externality, making it seem only natural that everyone would share the same heartbeat. It thus should not be a surprise that frequent rave attendees report them to be profoundly intimate affairs, despite the anonymity and impossibility of extended conversation. Indeed, it is the very breakdown of everyday pursuits of intimacy that allows the frenzy to present itself as an evasion of traditional blockades to intimacy.

If this heartbeat were experienced as completely universal, however, there would be no experience of intimacy with one another, but simply nondifferentiation.[16] Thus it is crucial that the frenzy be experienced as a *breaking down* of internal time and space in order that an anti-time and de-spatialization might be left over. Without this transition from private timespace to public timespace, the *mêlée* would never appear as a unique site of intimacy. Thus frenzy is not the experience of always already having broken down interpersonal distinctions, but a transition out of time that must nevertheless be accounted for within time. Through the course of the frenzy there may well be an extended feeling of ecstasy, but this ecstasy is only intimate when it is shared. Participants may anticipate the event with others and after the fact recall the special conditions (the weather, the band, the drugs, etc.) that made it possible, but such fetishizing activities are parasitic on the intimacy of the *mêlée*. Unless they contain comic elements (which would excuse their lack of success), stories of frenzies are generally boring because they must pass over precisely what in the moment seems to make these events special: the surprising breakdown of individuality that could not be predicted from the sum total of conditions.[17]

The structural problem here is not just that the breakdown that makes the frenzy intimate is ineffable. After all, there is no reason why intimacy would have to be communicable to the outside world. Partners who share secrets are willing to accept that intimacy must remain confined between two people, so perhaps the *mêlée* is similarly an event *you had to be there* to share. But the intimacy the frenzy longs for is not just private and unexpressible, but impossible. Because it requires a transition out of time, it cannot even enact the surprise that would call it forth as a genuine event. While communal acts of destruction bring partners together in moments of transgression[18] that show themselves to be isolating, the frenzy never brings partners together because the frenzy disrupts the very temporality that would make being closest to one another possible. The alienation of the ruffians trashing the home, for instance, was relative to their objects: they could not help but relate to the house and the activity of destroying it in different ways. The alienation of the frenzy, on the other hand, consists in the fact that it promises a breakdown that is always to-come but pretends to fulfil this promise only by disrupting partici-pants' senses of time and with it the desire to look to the future for a genuine disruption. The frenzy fails to allow participants to live in the moment because it takes away the temporal span in which the moment could have a meaning.

Nancy sees a similar impossibility of coming together in a *mêlée*, but he frames it as an ontological impossibility:

> The *mélange* does not exist any more than purity exists. There is no *pure mélange*, nor is there any purity that is *intact*. Not only is there no such thing, this is the very law of *there is not*: if there were something that was pure and intact, there would be nothing. Nothing exists that is 'pure', that does not come into *contact* with the other, not because it has to border on something, as if this were a simple accidental condition, but because touch alone exposes the limits at which identities or ipseities can *distinguish themselves* [*se démêler*] from one another, with one another, between one another, from among one another. (BSP 156).

Nancy helpfully observes here that despite its ability to dissolve the illusion of absolute separation, a *mêlée* can never establish an ultimate intimacy because it is premised on the universality of nonidentity. But it would be a mistake to conclude from this breakdown that dissolution and nonidentity compose the universe. Within the context of the present investigation, it does not follow that because the frenzy fails to find conditions of intimacy in its suspension of the time and space of laughter there must be an inherent fissure in the space and time of our togetherness. Nancy's conclusion, 'if there were something that was pure and intact, there would be nothing', makes the opposite mistake of the virgin bride: it assumes that nonconsummation is what gives the world its meaning.

To some extent, this is just a difference between Nancy's ontological-deconstructive project and my dialectical one. For Nancy, the nonconsummation of the *mêlée* is a necessary feature of human existence. 'In and of itself transcendent, the subject is born into its *intimacy* ('*interior intimo neo*'), and its intimacy wanders away from it *in statu nascendi*' (BSP 78). Intimacy is thus for Nancy a state to which human beings can never return. But as I have tried to show, it makes no sense to conceive intimacy as a consummated state of affairs, even in some mythical and nonexistent past. Such an ontological account would tie us to the aporetic attempt to conceive the *mêlée* as a nonconsummating drive for consummation. My dialectical account finds no need to hypothesize an inborn state of intimacy and instead traces its multiple breakdowns. But I think we cover over something important in the frenzy in particular and the *mêlée* in general when we ignore its dialectical structure. A *mêlée* needs to be enacted. If it found our nonconsummation always already to lie between us like an open wound, the *mêlée* would lose the actuality that comes with the destruction of boundaries. The *mêlée* longs for a destruction of individuality and cannot find it in the realization that individuality was always already fissured. Since the immemorial past is tainted by all of the habit and compromise that impedes intimacy, the *mêlée* must thus attempt to find the conditions for the elimination of subjectivity somewhere else. Rather than attempting to tie itself to a lack of differentiation that leaves no room for activity, it posits the future as the time in which subjective differences might cease to matter.

Millenarianism

Looking to the future does not, however, always mean embracing it as a field of shared possibilities. If partners embrace the fissure between the present and the future, then they have already entered the next dialectical stage: the future. But it is still possible to hold on for a while longer to the *mêlée*'s urge for dissolution. If disaster is imminent, then we are free to plan for the future in any way we wish, since none of it will matter anyway. Since our plans have already been thwarted, we can revel in the meaninglessness of the *mêlée* while still recognizing that this revelling is itself a production of meaning. We are not simply recognizing an already existing dissolution of our differences by enacting it by embracing its imminence. At the same time, we do not have to fear that unexpected events might disrupt our togetherness, since the future consists of nothing but the end of our present differences. Imminent death gives immunity to all illnesses.

Yet the freedom that this immunity brings still does not allow partners to approach one another openly. When we party like it's 1999, we take the apocalypse not as a purely negative project of destruction and consumption, but as a shared future. The projects and perspectives that used to divide us have been dissolved into the coming ecstasy. But with so little time there is little to be shared, so planning to spend judgement day with only a single partner would be a rather dull affair. The millenarian needs to gather with as many people as possible to obscure the emptiness of the future she shares with everyone else. There is an implicit hope that the days remaining might be multiplied to something approaching infinity by sharing them with an indefinite number of other empty futures.

Intimacy, however, is not a geometric sequence. It can be added to with familiarity, but active being together also requires being toward a future, which here is absent. Millenarianism thus devolves into the same stuporous activity of every other form of *mêlée*: its participants continue on with the destructive, derisive, or ecstatic activities that once promised a coming freedom in a gently nostalgic malaise. The *mêlée* can thus persist for a while as a kind of arrested dissolution, a suspension in the chemical sense. Our transgression binds us not just because it is transgression (which is necessarily fleeting), not just because it is *ours* (which would give it the structure of a fetish), but because it elevates the between from a place of wonder to a place of development. In the 1981 film *Reds*, Warren Beatty and Diane Keaton's snowball fight amidst the October Revolution is in part a celebration of life in general, but it only achieves its ecstasy from the sense of mutual determinacy that washes over the couple. While as a child Augustine grew giddy from the mere act of transgression with his fellow pear thieves, revolutionary fervour is heightened by the sense that the transgression will bring determinate but as yet unknown rewards.[19] Our millenarians and corybantes find that the *mêlée*'s event of shared transgression never appeared in any time that could be shared. It can only be sought in the future.

9

The Future

In millenarianism, the attempt that began with irony to find intimacy in the abandonment of all fetishes reaches its limit. By rejecting not only their individual goals, but the possibility of anyone's goals mattering at all, the millenarians promise themselves an ecstasy so total that just to acknowledge it is already to share it with everyone else who does as well. What they find, however, is not apocalyptic ecstasy, but the dull and merely numerical intimacy of a crowd. Without projects that the partners can pursue together and according to their private impulses, there is nothing rapturous at all about the end of times, but just a boring wait for nothing at all.

Nevertheless, millenarianism's decision to look to the future for an activity that transcends mere fetishization proves to be a promising one, for the future is never simply a projection of the present, but continually surprises us as it confounds our expectations. When partners try to share a fetish, they treat the object as a static one that binds the partners together through their respective relations to one another. Millenarians have at least grasped that intimacy cannot be found in the brute presence of any object and that the unpredictability of the future allows intimacy to be stretched across time. As such, sharing is no longer simply an either/or proposition. When a shared object is assumed to be structured by an uncertain future, the likelihood of a common plan being frustrated is built into this sharing. The question of whether the relationship finds its fulfilment in any particular object becomes increasingly irrelevant and the standards for sharing life more flexible. Once the millenarian assumption of an empty future is eliminated, the partners can begin attempting to fill it, and their struggle to do so in a way that can be shared according to the superlative standards of intimacy constitutes the dialectic of the future.

The test

While the future initially appears as a release from the fetishized object, the simplest way to conceive a future together is to fetishize it. I want to know that my partner will be there in every case, and so I take one case in the present or immediate future to stand in for an entire future of expected responses. To find this case, I may act unpleasantly or place an unusually difficult demand on my partner under the assumption that if she is willing to meet this demand, she will be willing to endure more or less similar unpleas- antries or meet other more or less similar demands as well. There are obvious practical problems with this approach, since it is unlikely that anyone can anticipate the range of possible threats to a relationship and, even if she can, it is even more unlikely that she will be able to formulate tests appropriate to this entire range. Moreover, there is the affective problem observed by Kierkegaard that any love that must be put to the test loses itself in uncer- tainty over one's partner's motives and one's own ability to detect them.[1] The test is far more likely to breed doubt than certainty. But the structural problem of the test goes deeper than either of these challenges. As we have already seen, uncertainty about one's partner is probably unavoidable in any relationship, and the beyond can never be completely collapsed into the between. But to subject intimacy to a test is to treat the future as something that can be secured in the present. It reduces something futural to a present perfect: *I know we are intimate because she has passed a test*. Thus the more perfectly a test can predict a partner's likelihood of meeting one's expectations, the more thoroughly it closes off the future. In the limit case in which I am able to articulate fully what I expect out of the relationship, devise a series of tests so psychologically sound that my partner's ability to pass them guarantees that she will meet my expectations, and observe my partner pass them with no ambiguity, I have succeeded not in securing our future together but in limiting it solely to what is predictable.

Such a limit case is, of course, implausible. Far more often tests are proffered half-heartedly and indiscriminately, so that neither the criteria nor the implications of a failed test are worked out in advance. Such tests want both to insure against the future and bring it about more quickly, and while their arbitrariness at least prevents the complete closure of the limit-case test, they offer nothing that is shared by the partners and only a vague anxiety in the tester that none of his tests have been adequate. Such anxiety is found, for instance, in Woody Allen's observation in *Annie Hall* that, like a shark, a relationship must always move forward in order to stay alive. The irony, which I suspect Allen intended, is that Allen's character Alvey's very understanding of this 'forward' presumes a progress that can be tested at discrete moments of the relationship, a presumption that implies a breach through which wonder will slowly leak out. Indeed, it is not just the anxious need to know the future in advance that closes it off, but the supposition that it can be measured according to some standard of progress. Alvey assumes that the stasis in the relationship arises from some particular dimension of his relationship to Annie rather than an untenable understanding of what progress and stasis involve. Alvey is the shark's killer, not just its pathologist. To correct this error, he would need to conceive a future that is not measurable either according to a series of discrete benchmarks or according to a generalized need for progress, but by attempting to incorporate the uncertainty of the future into the relationship. Such a measure could only be sought in a commitment.

The commitment

In Chapter 5 we examined the promise as a kind of fetish. When I make a promise to you, I put before both of us (for the promise does not exist as such to the promiser before it is uttered) a statement that will serve as the measure of my future actions. I thus intend us to share a common relationship to this statement – we understand it in the same way – which in turn governs my future behaviour. Our attitudes toward this behaviour, as we have seen, will not be identical. Typically, I will assume an attitude of resoluteness toward it, and you will anticipate or expect it, though the range of attitudes can vary broadly. The promise was intended to neutralize this necessary difference by locating our intimacy in our common understanding of its expression, but my future behaviour itself was left beyond the scope of this revised conception of intimacy. By making a promise to you, I give you a standing point of access where you can engage me if I fail to live up to it, but the relevance of this access point extends only as far as the meaning of the promise. While this divergence of attitudes poses no necessary threat to the intimacy of the promise as long as the partners understand each other's respective role in promise-keeping, the fact that the promise appears amidst a vast network of events and values means that neither partner will understand it in precisely the same way. It thus stands out as a linguistic artefact that allows varying interpretations.

A commitment is different from a promise in that it does not tie itself down to any particular statement of intention and assumes in its very constitution some level of divergence between the partners' interpretations of it. Where the promise demands that the promiser do what she said she was going to do, the commitment can be fulfilled in a number of different ways. Its intimacy thus consists not in its having been made and understood but in the continued progress toward its fulfilment. Moreover, this standard of continued progress is considerably more flexible than the standard of promise fulfilment. My commitment to my students is not abrogated if I miss a class to attend a conference, for instance, even though appearing regularly in class would have to be included in any reasonable articulation of this commitment. My students and I understand that I am fulfilling my commitment to them through a large array of activities, and this mutual understanding is the basis of our intimacy.[2]

Nevertheless, the meaning of a commitment cannot be infinitely flexible, since this would reduce it to the pure unexpectedness of the between. Even if they are entirely implicit, there must be some measures according to which my partner and I understand the commitment, and over time my partner and I will still have to use them to evaluate my behaviour. If the partners maintain a relatively high level of agreement on these measures of the commitment and on whether they are being adhered to, the commitment can yield a zone of free play, wherein small disagreements about the nature or success of the commitment can help fill out the content. Such disagreements offer a particularly promising path to intimacy, since they combine the safety and stability of a debate's search for common reasons with the immediacy of a dispute's confidence that it is the relationship itself that is at issue. Moreover, the fact that the commitment may be uneven or that each partner may have different attitudes toward it does not necessarily pose a threat, since, unlike a promise, commitment does not assume that intimacy is found in consensus.

Despite this broad leeway, to have any force at all the commitment must be taken by both partners to determine their future together. And given the ambiguity inherent in a commitment without explicit promises and the tendency of mutual understandings to drift, the commitment also needs to be periodically articulated and reaffirmed, either in the medium of language or with some other sort of sign. This sign would not constitute the full meaning of the commitment, since many other possible signs would suffice in its place – a gift and a wink might work equally well. Yet the sign must still be something present and thus is vulnerable to the dialectic of the fetish. The problem is not that the partners' expectations, desires and lives diverge, since this divergence is built into the very structure of the future. The problem, rather, is that while a commitment is not as static as a promise and is intended to adjust to changing circumstances, it still has to treat expressions of commitment as means of securing the future. When differences can be interpreted as a failure of the commitment rather than a difference in priorities, the partners fail to share the future. The commitment is as close as we have come so far in the dialectic to a pure συνηθεία, a being together that is not structured by any external assumptions about what would constitute intimacy, but it still assumes that intimacy involves living up to *some* standard. Without either a way for the partners to express this standard that does not simply take shelter in a fetish or some greater articulation of the relation between commitment-making and commitment-following, the commitment risks meaning nothing at all.

There are two possible responses to this crisis in meaning. The partners could, on the one hand, suppose that there is simply no distinction between the sign of a commitment and its enactment. The intimacy of the couple would thus be found in the 'I love you' or handshake or 'Go Buckeyes' or whatever it is that marks the commitment, and this would differ from the fetish in that it has no meaning at all outside of its expression. There would be no test for commitment, for every expression of commitment would be a condensation of the partners' entire future. To express commitment would be to *be* committed. Yet this effort to capture the future by fiat hollows out that future by denying the vicissitudes that make συνηθεία possible. By denying the possibility of a divergence in meaning, it has regressed to a pre-ironic stance that is unable to appreciate difference.

The other possible response to the crisis in the commitment's meaning is to treat the future as something that is continuously created by both of the partners acting together. The commitment would not just be one partner's actions in accord with a vaguely defined sign accessible to both (or all, in relationships larger than couples) partners, but a series of coordinated activities confronting an unpredictable but still imagined future. In order to maintain the intimacy when there is no longer a sign of the commitment tying the partners together, this process of confronting the future would have to be managed by both partners together, though their contributions would not have to be equal. As long as the partners work to agree on their respective roles, their possible approaches to the future would be infinite. In such a commitment, the sign or gesture of commitment would itself drop out as irrelevant, and the constitutive activity of the relationship would be what we generally call planning.

Planning

In seeking a way for partners to embrace an unpredictable future together without relying on the already given understanding of a promise, planning must address each partner's finite particularity. The future does not eschew particularity itself – these particularities are what give it life. Your love of baking means we *could* open that cupcake shop we talked about, but your erudition means we *could* also sit and talk about Milton forever. But this unexplored particularity only becomes intimate to the extent that it is shared by the partners. I may find you fascinating if you exhibit a manifold of potential courses of life, and I may even be excited if some of these courses are compatible with my own interests, but we still need to engage in planning together for this potential to be something shared. This, in turn, requires an investment from each of us to show that neither of us is trying to preserve our indefinite potentiality at the expense of a plan that we work out together. Our intimacy would be both comparative and superlative because each of us forecloses other possible futures to embrace a shared future. I have to know that it is really my partner who is sharing this future with me, which means I need to identify her by her finite particularity. I need her at once to be that finite particularity (so I know it is *she* with whom I share it) and to eliminate that finite particularity (so I know that the particularity of our future remains indeterminate).

This does not, to be sure, require either perfect knowledge of the future or perfect execution of the plan. Both of these perfections would turn planning into a kind of fetishization, the first because it treats the plan as something on which perfect concord is possible and the second because it treats the carrying through of a plan as the mutual adherence to a preordained reality. Even if Mom and the twins endorse Dad's vacation itinerary down to the last bathroom break, they have not embraced the futurity of their planning unless they assent to the possibility of slippage. Planning thus seizes on what Žižek has called 'the realness of the virtual' (in opposition to 'virtual reality', which posits a virtual experience almost as good as the real). It embraces the fact that what is virtual – what activates a potential – is just as real as reality itself (Gabriel and Žižek, 109). The plan is not deprived of intimacy just because it has not yet been put into effect and will never come to presence in precisely the way that it is expected. Rather, its very virtuality is the condition for intimacy. The partners embrace the future plan as futural. Because planning does not require commitment to a future state of affairs, it is no indictment of the process of planning that the partners' schemes gang aft agley. Rather, planning is exciting precisely because of its virtuality.

This virtuality, in turn, is only shared when the partners embrace not only the plan itself – to which they can never commit themselves fully without cancelling its virtuality – but the conditions under which their partners embrace the plan. I choose this plan (or its vague, modifiable outlines) because I think it is *good* for you, not in the sense of Heidegger's 'leaping in' (*einspringen*) for you, but in the sense of 'leaping ahead' (*vorausspringen*) of you.[3] In other words, I think about all the things that you would want with an implicit understanding of why you would want them and we each try to formulate plans that would be good for both of us without presuming *a priori* that we know what each other wants. Our actions are also not strictly creatures of mutual beneficence, since the intimacy of planning also consists in the very process of *determining* what is good for each of us. In planning I am looking for the intimacy of negotiating our future, not necessarily the best result for either of us. Planning thus answers the gift's future-perfect perspective with a simple future. As we have seen, the gift treats the process of deliberating about one's partner's interests either as one that has already been undergone by the time the beneficent action has been undertaken or as one conducted privately as part of the extended process of beneficence. Planning, however, places beneficent consideration (developed in concert with one's partner) at the centre of intimacy and treats its carrying out as secondary.

Since it is the very process of determining what is best for each partner that matters most, planning can paradoxically blind itself to the consequences of its decisions. If what matters is that we care about one another and show that we care about one another, we will only distract ourselves from the intimacy of planning by seeking to determine what is objectively best for everyone involved. When we say that 'love is blindness', this is at least part of what we mean. In the giddiness of a caring that is its own end because it is shared, partners tend to dismiss questions of the rightness of their ends. When the stakes are low, this can give rise to the absurdity of a reverse-dispute, in which each partner is so concerned to defer to the other's interests that she is unable to conceive of any interests that might be relevant to either party. When the partners contemplate going out to a restaurant, for instance, their immediate impulses are to defer to each other's desires, however microscopic and provisional they might be. But when the partners try to reconcile these competing acts of deference, they have no principles on the basis of which to deliberate, and a stalemate of bland assurances of deference arises.

On the other hand, when the stakes are high, it may be difficult to deliberate effectively without reintroducing the conventions of debate. When intuitive beneficence and reflexive deference fail to yield immediately obvious plans, the partners have to incorporate the weighing of possible options into their mutual activity of planning. A debate, as we have seen, requires an ongoing search for reasons, which would have to be valid independently of the activity of planning. Thus the partners cannot be united in their immediate orientation to the future until the grounds of their common orientation can be excavated, but this, as we have seen, is a never-ending process.[4] Rather than drawn together in a sober and measured meditation on their common future, they are pulled apart by the need to bring this sobriety and measure to the process of planning.

Identification

But perhaps the problem is not that debate over plans tends to pull the partners apart, but that they need to deliberate about what matters to them and how they intend to live their lives at all. If intimacy were simply defined as the orientation toward a shared future that generally does not require deliberation, then the need for debate over plans could be taken as evidence that the partners do not yet know each other well enough to be intimate. The thesis of this book, after all, is not that intimacy is rare or even entirely absent given our mortal, fallen, and/or late capitalist existences, but that intimacy is contradictory in its very structure. Thus we need also to consider the possibility that true intimacy consists in both partners already knowing what is best for each of them and working to bring those goods into effect, even if circumstances tend to make that knowledge rare. It is not uncommon for a partner to tell the other: 'I shouldn't have to tell you what I want; you should just know.' I take this statement to mean at least in part that true intimacy involves an identification with one's partner so deep that both partners consider their interests inextricable and for the most part can identify what these interests are.[5] Such identification is different from the partners thinking of themselves as identical or as composing an unbreakable unit, since this would be a denial of intimacy as such: partners must be distinct to be intimate. Identification with one's partner instead assumes that their future together is a common one even as they remain distinct. To be sure, there will be pleasures and pains that are accessible to only one of the partners at a given time – or at least do not yield identical sensations in each partner[6] – but these fleeting, individual experiences would be extrinsic to the future the couple is building together. Their intimacy would consist not just in their planning the kind of life they want to live together – though some deliberation could occasionally be required for more difficult decisions – but in responding to the vagaries of life with an already given understanding of what matters to them.

Such partners, we might think, are finally examples of the superlative closeness for which intimacy strives. Unhampered by intervening fetishes, they would be *most in* or *most upon* one another in that what they care about is limited to what they can care about together. Everything that affects one of the partners in any way that matters would affect them both, and, conversely, everything that only affects one partner (such as a fleeting thought never shared) would not really matter. Intimacy would involve embracing all the achievements, disappointments and surprises that the partners confront together and brushing off everything that tends to draw their attention away to the mere particularities of their bodies, histories, and so on. It should thus be clear that the future they share would not just be passively encountered.

The partners are not just similarly affected by the passage of time, but seek to activate a future that can be shared in common.

Thus identification in this robust sense would be resistant to the dialectic of the fetish. The partners would of course come to the relationship with different attitudes toward it that arise from different biographies, just as the music lovers discussed in Chapter 5 approach the artist they admire from different perspectives. But unlike the music lovers, the partners who identify with each other would not be divided by their differing histories and perspectives.[7] These differences are not just static facts about the partners but are important figures in the future of the relationship that can be mined as part of the common project of identification.[8] If, say, one partner's traumatic experience is so obtrusive that the partners find they cannot genuinely consider their future a common one, then this would be a failure of intimacy, but so long as they have reasonable confidence that they are on the way to reconciling, we cannot assume their identification is doomed just because they come from different places. It is not even a fatal objection that both partners will inevitably die (one likely before the other), thus permanently interrupting the constitutive activity of reconciling their differences. Identification is not like a debate, where the goal is to reach a common set of basic reasons to adjudicate differences. It treats the entire future as its object, and the past from which both partners approach this future is part of the future itself. The fact that this activity will continue indefinitely, but not infinitely, is exactly what makes it possible for the partners to engage in an ongoing process of identification.

Again, the fact that identification establishes a high bar for what counts as intimacy is no argument against it. There is nothing incoherent in the suggestion that intimacy is a pretty rare phenomenon that may or may not be worth all the trouble. Nevertheless, the particular requirements of identification as a form of intimacy prove to be unsustainable in a way that cuts to the very heart of the dialectic of the future. First, it is noteworthy that unlike a commitment, identification would have to be fairly symmetrical in order to be intimate. A parent who identifies almost entirely with the success of her child, for instance, would work alongside the child for the child's well-being and feel distressed when the child suffers, but insofar as this identification is asymmetrical, she would find no reason why her identification with her child is greater than other possible instances of identification.[9] The superlative dimension of intimate identification would require some way to distinguish this from other possible identifications. In Hegelian terms, she would be like the slave, whose capacity to provide recognition is not itself recognized.[10] Someone else could be devoting just as much effort toward the child's success, and so long as the child thinks primarily of her own future, there would be nothing special about the parent's contribution. While the parent and child can each be warmed by the parent's commitment to the child, a unidirectional pursuit of identity would deny the very fusion of identities that makes identification compelling as a form of intimacy.

The partners' contributions to the intimate identification do not, however, need to be equal, and it is not even clear what it would mean within the context of such identification for the partners to be equally invested. The question is not one of commitment, since identification does not require adherence to some expression of what the relationship means. When the partners' shared object is the relationship itself, even their unequal contributions to various shared goals can become part of the relationship, much as their diverse pasts become fodder for discussion. In identifying with the relationship, the partners have already posited that what cannot be shared is irrelevant to who they are.

Despite this indifference to questions of equity in contributions to the relationship, the problems with asymmetrical attempts at identification point to a larger problem with identification in general: it cultivates an arbitrary blindness to what is outside the relationship. We last saw an attempt at enveloping the whole world into the relationship in embedding, which treated the limitations of the external world as the content of the relationship. Identification has abandoned this search for content, since it recognizes that content *qua* content cannot be shared. But in its constitutive assumption that everything the partners will never share can never matter, identification posits whatever is not part of the partners' ongoing process of identification as an empty externality. What matters to us is not limited to what either of us wants or even what we have promised one another, but lies instead in the future that we continue to build together. But this supposition throws off a remainder of every possible life that we are not living together, everything that we might care about but do not, and everything that we might think of as informing our identities but choose not to. This remainder is not just what happens to be left behind in the vast and ongoing project of intimacy, but is part of its very constitution. Finding intimacy in our identification is only intelligible if the process of identification is always excluding other possibilities to make *this* one the intimate one. Even if we posit that it is not our choices that matter so long as they are *our* choices, treating them as choices assumes that there are alternate and excluded possibilities.

The project of identification ultimately collapses because it cannot incorporate these possibilities into the activity of the partners. If they pre-exist the relationship and the process of identification involves choosing among them, then they stand as an indictment of this particular relationship: how do the partners know that *this* is the closest relationship and not some other configuration of plans and significations? If, on the other hand, the alternative possibilities are created as the partners go about the daily process of choosing how to live, then to whom do they belong? If the partners assume that in their collective activity they are constantly creating new possibilities that through their decisions remain purely virtual (for instance, if buying a house also means choosing not to buy all the others that could have been bought with the same investment of time and money), then are all of these unexplored possibilities also part of their shared future? Perhaps, but what of the possibility that one partner might simply decide to walk away from the relationship? If this possibility belongs to both partners together, then it is not a real possibility, since the partner who might defect would have already committed herself to the assumption that any decision to walk away would be part of the movement of identification. The relationship would not have been ended, but conducted for an extended period in the modality of absence. Walking away from the relationship would still be part of the relationship, and nothing could ever sever the tie between the partners. This determination of the future would be meaningless, because every relationship would be equally intimate.[11] If, on the other hand, the (unrealized) possibility that a partner could leave the relationship belongs only to him (and the corresponding possibility to his partner), then identification would involve only sharing the positive possibilities, not the negative ones,[12] and thus would explicitly divide between the realms of the shared and the unshared, returning to the dialectic of the between.

Anticipatory mourning

With this splitting of the realm of the partners' shared possibilities, the work of identification is once again privatized. I try to find a way to incorporate all the negative possibilities by which my partner distances herself back into my own consciousness. And in order to avoid falling back into private longing, I try to make her absence something I can share with her. Because I cannot embrace every aspect of every possible life I may share with my partner, much less embrace the absenting that entails that in many of these lives we will have little to do with one another, I have to find some way to appropriate her absence as my possibility as well. The most direct way to do so is to imagine her death (or some other occasion for her indefinite absence) in order to distil these manifold possibilities into a concentrated future. She could die tomorrow in a car crash, or slowly waste away from an incurable disease, and in each case I would be left to mourn: in the former in an acute moment of shock and in the latter over an extended period of coping and caring for her. These fantasies are not just ways to heighten feelings of intimacy by contrasting them with their opposite – the salty food that makes a cold drink more refreshing. They are attempts to pull together the entirety of a relationship's intimacy by the law of the excluded middle. If at any given time our relationship either will be or will not be, then if I can think the relationship's being alongside its nonbeing, I therefore am able to appropriate it in its entirety. While our future together will be limited in some ways that we can control and some that we cannot, I can at least know with perfect certainty the most important fact about it: one day it will cease to be. By playing out the various permutations of this knowledge, I can make its unpredictability my own, and by longing for my partner while she is right beside me,[13] I hope to enact the most intense form of intimacy.

Anticipatory mourning can be seen as an amplification of the impulse Freud observed when his grandson would roll his spool of string back and forth, saying 'fort ... da' (gone ... here) to mimic his mother's comings and goings.[14] In the same way that the boy gains a feeling of control over his relationship with his mother by grasping the difference between presence and absence in simple spatial terms, we can seek to understand the entirety of intimacy by alternately imagining its presence and absence. 'Fort ... da ... tot ... da.' This game would not need to be explained by any special drive or 'pleasure principle', since it is a straightforward development of intimacy's turn to the future. In imagining my partner's death, I realize that while I have no control over the events that will one day take my partner away from me, at least I can understand what it means for us to be together in grasping the inevitability of losing her. But this is less a condensation of intimacy than a fantasy or schema of it. While the anticipatory mourner is in Irigaray's terms acknowledging the inevitability of both a between and a beyond in the relationship, she treats each as something entirely in her kin, which actual death belies. Death comes to a relationship not as its dénouement, but as the shock that shows just how incomplete the law of the excluded middle is. The being and nonbeing of the relationship were never the only options, and neither seems to have the slightest thing to do with its actual course. Intimacy breaks down because its various attempts at a closeness beyond closeness prove to be incoherent, not because being intimate and not being intimate are equivalent logical possibilities.

Anticipatory mourning thus reveals the limitations of treating intimacy as a form of play. There is, to be sure, much that is promising in this approach. By treating intimacy as both playfully open-ended and yet confronted by inexorable boundaries, anticipatory mourning opens up a space for intimacy to come into its own without the danger of overextending itself. Intimacy will always get bogged down if it is treated as necessary according to its own inner principles or as confined to a pre-given pattern of development. Yet it is equally misleading to treat it as a space of play that one can enter, leave, and prolong at one's pleasure. Death is a genuine affront to intimacy, and its appearance shows that there are limits to the kinds of closeness that can be achieved through the imagination. No matter how fearlessly a partner throws herself into a relationship, the possibility of it ending by the forces of nature, history, or the other partner's whims is never absent, and to pretend that the possibility of this end is just part of the game is to ignore the collective activity that goes into making a future together. Knowledge of this possibility may help prepare a partner psychically, but such knowledge is no more intimacy than knowledge of a vessel's leaks makes it seaworthy.

10

Mourning

The death of one's partner is an incomplete refutation of intimacy.[1] Upon the death of a childhood friend, Augustine wondered how love is possible at all between friends who will die: 'I was surprised that any other mortals were alive, since he whom I had loved as if he would never die was dead.'[2] The fact that one partner can die while the other lives on – indeed, that this *must* happen to one partner or the other, even if one survives the other only momentarily[3] – appears to show that intimacy was always bound to be temporary and thus ultimately drawn up into the greater narrative of the surviving partner's life. Even if I am not the one who constructs this narrative and I steadfastly refuse to engage the rest of the world on any other terms than the plans that my partner and I developed while he was still alive, these plans no longer give us the same connection, and I have to recognize myself as his survivor. So long as I persist in identifying intimacy with our organizing a life together, I am forced to admit that all of the adjustments we made in order to establish a future together merely concealed the fact that this future was never wholly ours.

Mourning, however, begets a new form of intimacy – one that abandons the future's assumption that intimacy requires an open-ended future together and thus distinguishes itself from all the preceding moments of the dialectic in that it does not take itself as necessary for intimacy. This is not as counter-intuitive as it might seem. While the death of the loved one might seem the antithesis of closeness to her, there are undeniable emotional charges (both erotic and benevolent) attending death. The charms of a dying lover are well known to authors of mass market romances, and one of the surest ways to remind ourselves to appreciate friends and family members is to imagine them dead. Death interrupts every plan, but it also structures and motivates many of our living desires. Bataille, for instance, notes that sexual reproduction depends on death not only as its reason for being, but to provide the species with organic material with which to continue reproducing itself.[4] At least in the sexual sense, the desire to come together is not a denial of death, but an embracing of it. Love may be a desire to achieve immortality by giving birth in beauty, as Diotima's speech in the *Symposium* has it (206b), but love also desires death itself as its necessary complement. In suicide pacts of all kinds, lovers may long for death as the only possible way their distinctness can be overcome.[5]

We need to be careful, however, not to confuse the general circulation of organic matter with intimacy. The universal overcoming of distinctness we find in death is not intimacy, but a condition that makes it impossible.[6] Regardless of what produces our erotic urges or the vast context of organic forces in which they appear, intimacy's need for a closeness beyond closeness is neither bound nor resistant to the prospect of immortality. If partners ever do seek death to restore them to intimacy, they are enacting a form of planning based upon a metaphysical assumption about the nature of people that is extrinsic to the dialectic of intimacy. Mourning responds to the dialectic of the future not by seeking out death's limitations, but by acknowledging them. The mourner seeks closeness with her lost partner by alternately expanding indefinitely to occupy the space of the dead and contracting into a superlative interiority in which they might at last be alone together, but she does not long for them never to have been distinct in the first place. This latter wish, as the *mêlée* showed, rips away not only the conditions of their separation but the conditions under which intimacy might mean anything at all.

But if mourning declines to accept death as an indifferent unity in which all individual identity is purged, it also rejects the therapeutic assumption that mourning is simply a process that everyone must pass through to restore their mental health. While the 'work of mourning' can teach valuable lessons about one's place in the world and the contingency of life, such lessons are beside the point as far as intimacy is concerned.[7] To avoid reducing the dialectic of mourning to a clinically observable process, we should distinguish among 1) the 'truth' of mourning, or the wisdom that the process of mourning ultimately reveals to the bereaved, 2) the structure of mourning as a moment of the dialectic of intimacy, and 3) the feeling of intimacy that attends mourning. It can be surprising for those who have not recently mourned that the death of a loved one sometimes brings stronger feelings of closeness to her than any previous moment of the dialectic. These feelings are, to be sure, interspersed with an opposite feeling of alienation, but they are powerful enough that they deserve some consideration. It is often assumed that the feelings in 3) have an essential role to play in arriving at 1) either as indicators of what is to be cognized or as obstacles to genuine recognition. We learn from our sorrow, for instance, how much our partner meant to us and thus how valuable life in general is. Or perhaps our intense ambivalence impedes us from seeing the need to reengage with the people who are still present and matter a great deal to us.

Yet often our feelings of closeness and separation are instead indications of 2) the dialectical structure of mourning. While we ought not to confuse the feeling of intimacy in mourning for its dialectical structure, an undue attention to the work of mourning can obscure the experience of mourning itself. Mourning is 'work' only if we aim to achieve something independently of it, but we often mourn just to be close to the one we have lost rather than to grow in insight or achieve psychic equilibrium. This closeness, to be sure, would have to take on a vastly different form than the models of intimacy we have considered so far. There is no hope, for instance, of sharing a touch with a corpse or of cultivating the expansive-contractive interplay of the heartbeat. But we have already seen that none of these models succeeds as a self-contained route to intimacy, and they differ to such a great extent that it would indeed be odd to say that because they are lacking (even though they are already internally lacking), intimacy is impossible between a mourner and the one he mourns. Mourning is no less a dialectical development of intimacy than any of the others, and its failure cannot be reduced to a lack of mutual presence or interaction. The failure of mourning to articulate and achieve its proper form of intimacy introduces something new to the dialectic.

But this dialectical perspective carries its own danger of occluding the phenomenon of mourning. If it tries too hard to explicate a general *course* of mourning, with all its pitfalls and achievements, then it is nothing but another reflection on the work of mourning. By focusing on the general process of mourning, it would, as Nancy explains, ignore the very form of intimacy at which mourning aims:

> True mourning has nothing to do with the 'work of mourning': the 'work of mourning', an elaboration concerned with keeping at a distance the incorporation of the dead, is very much the work of philosophy; *it is the very work of representation*. In the end, the dead will be represented, thus held at bay.[8]

Mourning succeeds in illuminating the dialectic of intimacy only when it succeeds in highlighting the mourner's desire for intimacy, but this highlighting always risks being condensed into a mere representation of the path of grief.[9] An account of mourning would be *my* account and would remain self-centred even when it ventured into hyperbolic elegy. This is especially problematic because, unlike most previous moments of the dialectic, mourning tends to involve a great deal of philosophizing. In throwing oneself into mourning one cannot help reflecting on what it means to mourn.[10] It is thus crucial to avoid confusing the dialectic of mourning with the searching and self-centred reflections of the mourner by maintaining a clear distinction between the experience of mourning and its dialectic – what Hegel might call 'spirit for itself' and 'spirit in itself', respectively.

Gathering and retraction

The death of a partner does not end the striving for intimacy all at once. It can even be a spark that sets in motion an avid period of gathering. We pull together artefacts and memories of our time together, sometimes imagining an indeterminate future use, sometimes not even bothering with the pretence.[11] To explain why it is so important to accumulate so many letters, photographs and stories about her, we may propose that we intend to produce a memorial of some kind or want in some more abstract way to 'hold on to her memory', but there is no illusion that any intimacy will be found in the memorial or even the memory. It is in the act of gathering itself that intimacy is sought. Jean-Luc Marion describes the process of mourning as a vast forensic investigation in which various particles of evidence are sorted for reliability and assembled and reassembled into competing interpretations of the deceased (*In Excess*, 123). This is the moment in which Marion's notion of a saturated phenomenon is most appropriate to a relationship. According to Marion, a saturated phenomenon is one in which the experiencing subject's intentionality is overwhelmed by the content of the object. When the partner is alive, allowances for saturated phenomena choke off the play of expansion and contraction necessary for genuine interplay. With the partner's death, however, there is no space for contraction, no one to follow you back into yourself. There is only pure expansiveness without return into a world that is alternately sublime and disorientingly beautiful.[12] Mourning thus appears with an intensity with which no prior moment of the dialectic of intimacy can compete. Whereas the between sought an indefinite site in which the partner's infinite retreat could be modulated, death presents only the partner's retreat and suggests that if we are ever to meet again, it will have to be solely through the surviving partner's effort.

But this very boundlessness inspires an equally intense contraction in the mourner. In her magnificent 'epitaph' to her late brother Michael, Anne Carson suggests that contraction is the only possible response to a death:

I wanted to fill my elegy with light of all kinds. But death makes us stingy. There is nothing more to be expended on that, we think, he's dead. Love cannot alter it. Words cannot add to it. No matter how I try to evoke the starry lad he was, it remains a plain, odd history. (*Nox*, 1.0)

When it becomes clear that no matter how far we expand to reach our partner we will never reach him, we retract into the tiniest of selves. We close off all windows to our grief and jealously guard this feeling as one that ought to be inaccessible to anyone else.[13] Yet Carson's very care in composing the 'book'[14] commemorating her brother belies her claim of stinginess. Such a marvellously nuanced and innovative work is the very opposite of stingy. If the work at times comes off as 'stingy' to the reader, it is because Carson has ventured off into her brother's absence and left only traces to follow her path. Like many of the best works of mourning, Carson's book comes across as an ambivalent and indirect solicitation of intimacy. One who mourns is expected to be stingy and thus calls for an immense expansiveness to meet her own – one that recognizes it has no right to reciprocation from the mourner.

Because the mourner cannot help but feel stingy for her inability to reach far enough into the absence of the loved one to reestablish the intimacy, she takes her limitless expansion for contraction. Witness Roland Barthes's reaction to his mother's death:

> A stupefying, though not distressing notion – that she has not been 'every-thing' for me. If she had, I wouldn't have written my *work*. Since I've been taking care of her, the last six months in fact, she *was* 'everything' for me, and I've completely forgotten that I'd written. I was no longer anything but desperately hers. Before, she had made herself transparent so that I could write.[15]

The opacity of Barthes's mother's death has suddenly awakened him to his contractive tendencies. While he professes to feel that his focus has narrowed, it has actually expanded so far beyond himself that work has become impossible. In a relationship with a living partner, this diastolic pressure would gradually be modulated and moderated as the two partners sought out a sustainable heartbeat, but in mourning the absence of the partner yields only a contradictory unity of attraction and release. Again Barthes:

> On the one hand, she wants everything, total mourning, its absolute (but then it's not her, it's I who am investing her with the demand for such a thing). And on the other (being then truly herself), she offers me lightness, life, as if she were still saying, 'But go on, go out, have a good time ...'[16]

Because his mother is no longer present to speak for herself, he puts himself in her role of calling him to task. He must gather all he can to understand what she would have wanted from him but also must sheepishly remind himself that it is only he who is investigating her desires. The only possibility of a synchronous heartbeat is with those who are still alive, but the pull of this attraction and release so overshadows the moderate demands of intimacy that the mourning continually dissolves and reintegrates itself as an endless longing.

Note here the bivalence of the relation. The space between the bereaved and her partner can appear as an immense chasm, but the activity of mourning consists of a continual oscillation between expansion and contraction. To be sure, this expansiveness frequently drives mourners to ontologize their need for intimacy to an extent equaled only by erotic love. Levinas, for instance, compares the transcendence of the Other to the uncomfortable collective consciousness of loss: 'The void that hollows out is immediately filled with the mute and anonymous rustling of the *there is* [*il y a*] as the place left vacant by one who died is filled with the murmur of the attendants.'[17] Because the expansive moment never reaches so far as to bring the dead back into the fold, it can seem that existence itself has been fissured. But as Carson's reflection shows, it is just as easy to assume that the fissure lies not in existence, but in my shallow, self-interested self. Indeed, all the connections that anyone makes are vanities: insipid projections of our own need for recognition masquerading as nonsensical 'connections' to others.

Mourners are often aware of how unreasonable it is to oscillate between such extremes,[18] but this realization offers no path to intimacy. It is far beyond the scope of my project to determine whether it is healthy or unhealthy to achieve an equanimity about the lost partner's importance to you, but such equanimity is certainly not intimate – at least not with the one who has been lost. Any 'perspective' that comes through the 'work of mourning' will be private; it will not be coming to terms in the sense of a contract negotiation, with each partner budging slightly from their optimal price. Rather, the terms to which the partners come are put forth and accepted entirely by the mourner.

Thus the gathering of details about the lost partner's life and death seeks intimacy not in the work of developing a livable perspective, but in the unregulated heartbeat that goes out into unbounded beneficence and returns to unreasonable selfishness. Yet the fact that the dead partner is not present to moderate these movements does not in itself mark the process of gathering and retraction as a failure of intimacy. The external perspective that sees this movement as a self-centred submission to private feelings assumes that the intimacy of the relationship had all along had the structure of the heartbeat: a pattern of continual readjustment to one another punctuated by sudden bursts of wonder. In the intensity of gathering and retraction, the mourner finds that the progressive-perfect rhythm of the heartbeat was at best an oversimplification of the temporality of the relationship, and mourning instead carries a temporality that resists compressing continuity and rupture into mere aspects of the present. Unlike the stalker, who imposes a mere simulacrum of a relationship onto his distant partner, the mourner seeks intimacy with a partner who really does respond and withdraw, though not in the temporality to which she is accustomed.

This new temporality rejects the assumption that intimacy with one's partner can be expressed in the aorist/preterite or past perfect. The mourner does not simply retreat into what *has been* – though it often appears this way to the outside observer: *why can't he just get on with his life?* Mourning appears at times in the anti-time of the frenzy, which throbs incessantly to a rhythm that does not keep time, and at times in the dull continuity of the long-accustomed touch, which oppresses not with its pain, but its inexorability.[19] The oscillation between these times and the regular temporality of workaday life is not evidence of a natural sequence to the mourning process, but a manifestation of the mourner's inability to find a time in which the intimacy which is her only possibility (though it also seems impossible) might manifest itself even fleetingly. If mourning thus comes to an end, it is not because it has passed through all its necessary stations or stages, or even because it grows frustrated that its gathering never really *gets* it anywhere. Rather, it comes to the conclusion that in all its biographical excursions and subsequent retreats into stinginess it has not even known *where* to look for the missing partner.

Haunting

The inherent disorientation of mourning is one of the most overlooked insights in Freud's 'Mourning and Melancholia', which spends a surprising amount of energy musing about the *place* of the melancholic's grief. While *Totem and Taboo* treats the phenomenon of haunting more directly in its analysis of 'primitive' manifestations of grief,[20] throughout the book Freud remains confident that the myths and customs that tend to spring up around grief can be fully accounted for as investments of psychic energy. 'Mourning and Melancholia', in contrast, takes on the disoriented position of the mourner and is thus a thoroughly haunted text that never quite manages to gain its bearings. Far from offering a cold diagnostic standard by which a healthy course of mourning can be distinguished from a descent into melancholia, Freud attempts to work through the distinction almost as a mourner herself might do, gathering insights from here and there but always aware of how disoriented he is.[21] He initially proposes that the most striking difference between ordinary, healthy mourning and melancholia is the extremity and even 'violence' with which the melancholic contracts into herself (247). For the melancholic everything that is wrong with the world can be connected to some defect in the self. The mourner, in contrast, ought to be able to see through the kind of self-abnegating obsessions that we saw in Carson's emphasis on her 'stinginess' in grief and appreciate the distinctness of the mourner from the dead.

Freud famously revises this account in *The Ego and the Id*, where he posits the melancholic disruptions of mourning as part of the very structure of intimacy, but even in 'Mourning and Melancholia' he works to undermine his own distinction almost as quickly as he draws it. Freud's initial schematic explanation for the emergence of melancholia is that whereas the mourner finds the world empty without the lost partner, the melancholic locates this emptiness in himself. The melancholic carries on an unresolved debate with his absent companion and thus cannot release his connection to someone who is so deep inside himself. The work of mourning would thus consist in filling the empty place the departed has left behind, and the melancholic would fail to complete this work by displacing the loss. Melancholia arises when the normal process of mourning has broken down and,

> owing to a real slight or disappointment coming from this loved person, the object-relationship was shattered. The result was not the normal one of a withdrawal of the libido from this object and a displacement of it on to a new one, but something different, for whose coming-about various conditions seem to be necessary. The object-cathexis proved to have little power of resistance and was brought to an end. But the free libido was not displaced on to another object; it was withdrawn into the ego. There, however, it was not employed in any unspecified way, but served to establish an identification of the ego with the abandoned object. (248)

The standard translation 'cathexis' here is misleading. Freud's term, *Besetzung*, while not quite an everyday German word, is not that uncommon either, and Freud uses it to refer rather straightforwardly to an investment of libidinal energy. In the German term it is hard not to hear the root *setz*, which underscores that this is a *placement* of energy. Freud has thus explained the emergence of melancholia as a failure of the normal process of displacement, whereby the bereaved learns to place her libidinal energy onto a new object because the object that has been lost is too tied up with her own conception of self. Freud points to factors that can aggravate the melancholic tendency, such as feelings of disappointment or strong ambivalence to the one who has been lost, but he soon realizes that strong investment in the lost partner is unavoidable. After wondering whether the fact that the melancholic places his loss inside rather than outside himself implies that melancholia could be brought about without any external stimulus (through a fluctuation in brain chemistry, for instance), Freud observes that 'normal mourning, too, overcomes the loss of the object, and it, too, while it lasts, absorbs all the energies of the ego' (254). Why, then, does the (healthy) mourner not launch into a manic period of release from all melancholia? Freud declines to answer and instead surmises that the mourner is very much like the melancholic in that he locates his loss partly inside himself and partly elsewhere.[22] What has been lost is both an object in whom he has placed a great deal of psychic energy and that part of his identity that is bound up with this object. Freud's only remaining explanation of the distinction between mourning and melancholia is that mourning eventually goes away – an unsatisfying symptomological answer rather than an aetiological one. And yet Freud does not give any temporal criteria to explain even this weak, surface-level distinction, for, like mourning, melancholia tends to disappear after a time, sometimes leaving barely a trace (251).

In the end, Freud concludes that the processes of mourning and melancholia are likely quite similar, in that each must gradually extricate its psychic energies from an object whose 'significance is reinforced by a thousand links' (255). Melancholia, however, has an extra feature: an element of ambivalence to the object (256). But insofar as mourning and melancholia alike assign their object a thousand-fold-linked significance, it is difficult to see how ambivalence could ever be absent from mourning. Ultimately, Freud betrays so much sympathy for the melancholic that it is not at all clear whether the mourner or the melancholic understands her situation better – whether loss opens up a hole in the world, in the ego, both, or neither.[23]

This is the question that the dialectical move out of gathering opens for the mourner. For the haunted, mourning is not a matter of coming to terms with the departed (as in the gift), since it is unclear what it would even *mean* to have a healthy relationship to her grief. Mourning instead involves a careful watchfulness just in case the dead might show her true location. Like the melancholic, the mourner can't help but be bothered by the question of Freud's *Besetzung*: *Where exactly is the object I am mourning – in me, or outside?* But because this question reveals that there was never a simple distinction between myself and my partner, because we were linked in a thousand ways, the question is replaced with a vaguer one: *Now where did I put that?* The activity of gathering responds in an inchoate way to this question, but it loses itself in wondering precisely what the *that* is – what is it that the partners shared or that made the dead partner unique, or what is it even that the bereaved is *looking* for? Haunting suspends this search out of a more basic disorientation that prevents the mourner from telling her inside from her outside. Because the mourner is (in Freud's terms) responding to a loss of a direction for her libidinal energy – however we wish to interpret what was even for Freud a placeholder for a theoretical construct that continually needed to be reworked – she is not just missing something important to her but is missing her very principle of orientation.

Part of this disorientation is an uncertainty over whether the bereaved even wants intimacy with her dead partner. She may attempt to index her desires to temporal distinctions, assuring herself that 'it is better to have loved and lost ...' or that she has to 'look forward', but the implication of these bromides that intimacy once was present but now has passed away posits a temporality alien to mourning. The haunted partner can look neither back nor forward for a resolution to the relationship because the one she has lost remains conspicuously present in his absence. While it would be satisfying to be able to condense this presence and absence into a single moment in which to say goodbye, such a moment proves just as illusory as the inaugural moment in a relationship. For Jean-Luc Marion, because a person's life can only be gauged in its last instant, 'to love would mean to help the other person to the point of the final instant of his or her death. And to see the other finally, in truth, would mean, in the end, closing his or her eyes' (*In Excess*, 123). Only in this last instance would one perhaps 'strip it of all that would cover it up and deliver it in its naked truth' (*In Excess*, 123).[24] But this conclusion is, as Marion himself notes, a false closure, one that does not survive the conversations that must continue with the dead. Instead, the mourner is haunted, compelled to recall his partner and their relationship in a sequence that offers no easy narratives of togetherness and loss.

Because this haunting continues even as the mourner has given up searching in frustration, it seems to be imposed from the outside. While the longing for intimacy has up to this point been associated mainly with each partner's agency, from the gifts one gives to break the ice to the destruction and planning the partners attempt together, in haunting intimacy appears imposed from without. The partner who is haunted appears not to be *doing* anything at all, but is periodically visited by memories and expectations that she cannot control. The time she spent with her partner appears not so much as a series of places she can visit at will as a single place whose boundaries she can never escape. Yet such haunting does not appear as a call from outside the mourner that would name and implicate her. It is too indeterminate to tell her who she is or what does or ought to matter to her. While Iris Murdoch is perhaps right in her claim that 'The bereaved cannot communicate with the unbereaved', this is not because the bereaved have finally been able to recognize themselves for who they are, but because they have experienced a haunting that resists articulation. Put another way, haunting does not reveal what intimacy wants so much as the difficulty of knowing what intimacy wants.

Singularity

Haunting thus acts like a dampener on the dialectic of intimacy. Whereas fraudulence shocked the ironist back into intensified engagement with her partner, haunting diffuses the urge to engagement to the point where both the nature and point of engagement are so thoroughly questionable that intimacy seems both unavoidable and impossible. The intrepid optimism of the gift, which saw intimacy as a project, has been replaced with the vague sense of intimacy as a general miasma. At the same time, haunting continually pulls the mourner back to the partner in his particularity. If I am not solely responsible for my very own drive for intimacy and if the meaning of my partner's life cannot be assembled into a coherent explanation of why he mattered so much to me, then there must be something ineffable about him that drives our continuing intimacy even now that he is absent. Thus in response to haunting's anomie, there is a renewed focus on the singularity of the partner as what breaks the possibility of the between. No matter how expansive the mourner becomes in her task of determining who her partner was and why he matters, she never arrives at an adequate understanding of what went wrong or what went right or even want simply *went* in the relationship. The dead partner, it becomes clear, is inaccessible. When this inaccessibility becomes the very meaning of intimacy, the mourner treats the dead as a singularity: as an utterly unique person who may have resembled others and played important roles in their lives, but whose being exceeded all these resemblances and effects. Like an astrophysical singularity, his being can be deduced from what is observable in the relationship but cannot itself be observed. Rather than gathering disconnected tokens of his memory, the mourner now commits to observing all the ways he exceeds these tokens. The task of the bereaved is thus not to understand him but to commemorate him for his singularity. She may thus grow frustrated when others fail to observe this singularity, but she must also acknowledge that the others' memories themselves are mere tokens and thus that seeking to correct them is as misguided as the gathering of more physical tokens. Still, she has long since abandoned the hope of being closer to the dead by embedding the superficiality of everyone else's relation to him within their own. These others thus cannot bring the mourner closer to her partner no matter how they express their own grief. They are only irritants who remind the mourner of the impossibility of an adequate commemoration.

This commemoration is not the rupture's generalized recognition of commonality in radical difference, but a specific appeal to the dead partner as the one who makes their intimacy possible. In the rupture, in contrast, I suspend my search for what is wondrous about anyone in particular because I realize that strangeness belongs to the very fact of our being together. Rather than always already together, we are always already accessible to one another even though being completely together is impossible. In commemorating the singularity of my partner, on the other hand, while I also recognize the impossibility of my plans ever coming into complete accord with my partner's, I am unconcerned either with our always already being together or with our always already being strange to one another. While I recognize that many others have been in my place before and that I have no good reason to prize our relationship more than theirs, I nevertheless posit that an intimacy such as ours never could have been possible with anyone else than my partner. In this way, Heidegger's observation that I can never die in someone else's place expresses only half of the insight of singularity.[25] The fact that each of us dies utterly alone does indeed show the superfluity of every effort to express the meaning of someone's life for the community. To recognize someone as one's intimate entails recognizing that the future belongs to each of you separately. But to treat this separation as absolute is essentially an ironic gesture: it seeks credit for authenticity in its refusal of any explicit conditions of togetherness. The dialectic of intimacy, however, calls for a suspension of this irony and thus continues to strive to express the meaning of intimacy. Though I cannot express the meaning of my partner's death, I nevertheless need to express its inexpressibility, even though this latter expression assumes that intimacy, if not mourning, must be generally expressible. Call it the law of our included middle: though the dead was not *unlike* others in that any trait I could ascribe to him is more or less similar to traits that many others have shared, neither was he *like* anyone else. To mourn him I must hold onto this paradox – not because I feel obligated to do so as proper acknowledgement of his gift, but because I take our intimacy to lie *inside* this paradox.

Any commemoration, however, will fail to live up to my partner's singularity. It should be clear that to eulogize my partner in public is to reverse the embedding relationship, so that I cannot help betraying my partner in any effort to share my grief with others or to work together to understand the partner we have lost.[26] As Brault and Naas put it, 'Each time we mourn, then, we add another name to the series of singular mournings and so commit what may be called a sort of "posthumous infidelity"'.[27] Yet even if I only commemorate our relationship to myself, I still seem to be betraying my partner's singularity. In Derrida's words, the worry is that in the absence of a partner to contradict them, efforts to express the meaning of the departed's life will take 'the form of a personal testimony, which always tends toward reappropriation and always risks giving in to an indecent way of saying "we", or worse, "me"'.[28] If I have managed to come to terms with my partner's role in my development, then I have not simply bracketed it as something in my past; I have abandoned it as a mode of intimacy. Even if I acknowledge that there is something utterly ineffable about how he made me who I am, I have ceased to engage his singularity as one that calls me beyond myself.

Yet when attention is deflected away from the dead and to the act of mourning itself, what appears is not its necessity but its contingency. Well-meaning acquaintances of the mourner may pass it off as wisdom that everyone must die, but it does not therefore follow that everyone must mourn. Even when mourning has brought on a new and intensified moment of intimacy, it would be ridiculous to say that the partners would not have truly been intimate if the survivor had not had this opportunity to mourn. Derrida is among those who have noted that it is constitutive of every friendship that one partner will one day have to mourn the other's passing,[29] but the reverse is closer to the truth. While sudden deaths and lapses in communication can sometimes arrange it so that neither partner sees the other die, *at least one* partner will always escape without having to mourn the other's death – which equally means that at least one partner will only be able to mourn the other's death in anticipation. Mourning thus reveals the contingency of every prior moment of the dialectic of intimacy as well. Just as someone does not *have* to mourn her partner in order to participate in the dialectic of intimacy, neither does she *have* to touch or fight him. The hypothetical structure of each moment traces what intimacy must look like *if* it seeks to find closeness in a gift or *if* it wants immediacy through touching. While irony would lose much of its flavour if it were not contrasted with the more direct approaches to intimacy that precede it and the *mêlée* would lose its desirability without its opposition to ironic indifference, this does not imply that one who has never given a gift, for instance, has never even begun with intimacy. With planning's transition into mourning and the latter's eventual non-resolution, intimacy shows itself as something that is never consummated – not because it sets coherent goals that happen to be unreachable in the span of human lives but because it cannot even express its goals coherently.

This realization shows why irony and anticipatory mourning are too hasty in their assumption that intimacy is simply impossible. While haunting and singularity never manage to articulate an account of what complete and unproblematic intimacy would consist in, their unwinding does show that it was presumptuous to assume that such an account could be found in sharing objects, relationships, or future plans. Because there are no longer grounds to imagine a theoretical apex of intimacy either within or beyond this world, neither are there grounds to suppose that in any particular case intimacy has either run or failed to run its course. Once it has been dialectically stretched, the contradiction at the heart of the concept of intimacy is beside the point. Or rather, it comes off as a senseless truism. The claim that intimacy is never consummated and therefore that no one is ever intimate with anyone else papers over the fact that so much of the search for intimacy assumes and suspends this very fact. We laugh together and fight one another and mourn one another in a way that does not quite measure up to intimacy's call for a closeness beyond closeness but for that very reason is also not non-intimate. The very failure of intimacy in mourning shows that we have been looking for it in the wrong way. As Blanchot puts it, 'Death, the death of the other, like friendship or love, clears the space of intimacy or interiority which is never (for Georges Bataille) the space of a subject, but a gliding beyond limits'.[30] Indeed, mourning also contains an impetus away from isolation, so that, almost like a slingshot, the mourner is pulled away from and then back into the arms of the community. Judith Butler has explored the political potential of this tendency and argues that grief allows us to perceive that all people are bound together in their common physical vulnerability.[31] For Butler, a refusal to mourn can be a reflection of a 'fantasy of mastery' of the sort that led the United States into two wars following the 2001 terrorist attacks, but when we attend to the actual experience of grief we can be sufficiently shaken to register our common vulnerability with those around us.

We should be careful, however, to avoid turning this realization into its own justification. Because the dialectic of intimacy does not allow its reduction to a simple course, we cannot simply say that the trauma of mourning is either an ontological condition of our being together or a challenge to the integrity of consciousness that needs to be worked through. Loss can *feel* all-consuming, but the very fact that we can have and articulate this feeling shows that loss leaves much behind that has not been consumed. We need to consider mourning to fully articulate the dialectic of intimacy, but the fact that mourning cannot be universal shows it is not a necessary step on the way to some totalized intimacy. To be sure, no relationship is completely intimate without it, but its very possibility also makes every relationship incomplete. If anything, the haunting that accompanies mourning reveals the vibrancy of every prior attempt at intimacy. There is a temptation to ask mourning, because it is temporally the final stage in a relationship, to be its fulfilment. Even when we are not under the illusion that we can perfect the relationship at this final stage, we at least want to know that we gave our best shot to come to terms with what it had been. Because life passes so quickly, we want this chance to grasp the full nature of the relationship, even in all its imperfections. Being haunted, however, has shown that there was never a moment at which the relationship might be consummated. By their very structures, the gift, touching, and so on preclude perfect intimacy, but if incompleteness belongs to every form of intimacy, there is no reason to dismiss these early forms as privative versions of a higher ideal. Every moment of the dialectic is thus allowed to shine in its own light rather than the reflected light of a neat narrative summation.

Since mourning in its finality does not have any ultimate priority over previous forms of intimacy, a stretched dialectic even allows them to appear alongside one another. Though mourning tends to consume the exclusive attention of the mourner even more than embedding did, to the extent that the work of gathering and attending to singularity virtually closes off the outside world, mourning can also allow itself to fall back into the *mêlée* in the form of indifferent promiscuousness or gallows humour. We joke about ourselves and the dead not just as a technique of embedding but as a response to the contingency and incompleteness of mourning. The small gesture of betrayal does double duty in suspending one's engagement with the one who is lost. On the one hand, it serves to embed the relationship to the lost within relationships to the living. When I make fun of my late father's fastidiousness, I reaffirm my connection to my compatriots, who recognize the camaraderie entailed in my flouting of elegiacal conventions. On the other hand, this minor betrayal helps extend my relationship with my father as one that is still living enough to be capable of being betrayed. It is incompatible with the assumptions of embedding that one can share intimacy with someone who is no longer able to share in your mocking of others, just as it is incompatible with the assumptions of mourning that memories of the dead can be shared with the living, and yet these moments can appear side-by-side.

Thus while Freud half-heartedly suggests in 'Mourning and Melancholia' that mourning succeeds in overcoming grief primarily through its 'respect for reality' (243), the dialectical wisdom of mourning is precisely its lack of respect for reality – at least as determined by its prior failures. Mourning reopens and flattens the dialectic of intimacy by refusing to accept the various hypotheses of intimacy it has thus far explored as its absolute limit. In Fredric Jameson's words, it realizes that

> the dialectic is not a thing of the past, not some chapter in the history of philosophy, but rather a speculative account of some thinking of the future which has not yet been realized: an unfinished project, as Habermas might have put it; a way of grasping situations and events that does not yet exist as a collective habit because the concrete form of social life to which it corresponds has not yet come into being.[32]

While dialectics cannot specify with any certainty what future conditions might finally allow intimacy to appear, it at least is not confined by the hypothetical limitations it has posited for itself.

Because of this flattening, intimacy also does not easily submit itself to a succeeding and higher stage that would replace it. While I have treated intimacy all along as a form of recognition and thus linked it to more complexly political ways that we develop our identities through engagement with others, the fact that intimacy is never consummated does not imply that one *must* seek recognition in other forms. The transition from intimacy to value (which I take to be the next stage of a dialectic of recognition) will still be a hypothetical one: *if* one seeks a fixed public measure of one's value to compensate for the incompleteness of one's self-identification through intimacy, *then* one ought to pursue the dialectic of value.[33] But there is no need to get ahead of ourselves. The time for a deepened engagement with the dialectic of intimacy has not yet passed.

Afterword

When Goethe wrote that anyone who cannot draw wisdom from three thousand years of Western culture is living hand to mouth, he spoke to an age of cultural bounty, yet one in which involuntary spiritual starvation was still a real possibility for many. Today, with the internet beginning to approach true ubiquity, even the pickiest of consumers is forced to limit his gluttony with arbitrary refusals of certain foods. In some respects, this is not a rich man's problem; it is no problem at all. The inability to sample everything worth sampling is no limitation of power, but an expression of the indefiniteness of our potential. But in a more important sense, this vast bounty challenges the contemporary author to demonstrate that he is not putting forth cultural junk food that might stand in the way of someone's genuine sustenance. After all, myths of indefinite potential tend to wither under dialectical scrutiny, and I can no more rest content that I have entered into *some* kind of dialogue on intimacy than the gift-giver can rest content that he has fulfilled his part of the bargain and allowed the recipient to respond any way she wishes. Instead, I need to be specific about what the dialectical account of intimacy I have developed over these pages has to offer.

I promised in the introduction that this book would offer a distinct perspective on intimacy, and, as with any promise, its full meaning is only becoming apparent now that I am forced to own up to it and negotiate its implications. I promised that this book would not be a typology, critical anthropology, or deconstruction of intimacy and would develop instead a dialectical study modelled most closely on the approaches of Hegel and Beauvoir, but also quite substantially on those of Plato, Schelling, Marx, and others. Yet though the book was propelled by the identification of contradictions in various hypotheses of what intimacy might consist in, most of the philosophical sources I consulted served much more as friends than enemies, and when I gave explicit arguments against them, they were generally more programmatic and clarifying than propulsive of the dialectic. This is not a threat to the dialectic itself, since the rejection of a hypothesis is perfectly compatible with affirmation of an indeterminate horizon of interpretation, as when I have affirmed Derrida, Beauvoir, Freud, etc.'s analyses of the limitations of various forms of intimacy, but from the beginning of this book I have promised the reader that there is something determinate about the dialectical approach to intimacy. All determination is negation, and so, for all my positive debts, I have committed myself to saying something negative about alternative approaches to intimacy.

Deconstruction in particular deserves more than my appreciative attention since it, too, finds the same sorts of breakdowns, and it is just as willing as the present account to renounce the exclusivity of its own observations.[1] The latter trait implies that dialectics and deconstruction could actually share the insights of this book without having to divvy up credit for any of them. Because dialectics and deconstruction both reject the goal of identifying an objectively present set of facts about the world and the possibility of developing a method to identify those facts, both are likely to retreat quickly from claims to discover truths that could not have been grasped in any other way. For the same reasons, it would be difficult to find any propositions that one would univocally endorse and the other univocally reject. Thus I'm happy to defer to anyone who reads Derrida and Nancy as having already worked out every essential development of the dialectic I trace. Great minds, right?

Still, as reassuring as such concord would be, I do not think it is or even could be complete. While my emphasis has been on the breakdown of these ten hypothesized forms of intimacy, my search for meaning in the dialectic of these breakdowns would likely be anathema to a committed deconstructionist. Though there is much more to be said about the ontological meaning of this claim, I am still committed (in all the senses of Chapter 9's discussion of the commitment) to the claim that *there is* a dialectic of intimacy, without any of those words being put under erasure. We might say for this reason that deconstruction goes a step further than dialectics insofar as it shows not just a series of contradictions, but the contradiction of building philosophy on a series of contradictions. But if this is a step further, it is not a step that we *have* to make or even that we can be sure we *can* make. I take the dialectic of mourning to have shown that it is presumptuous to jump from the observation that the meaning of the term 'intimacy' breaks down in a variety of interpretations to the assumption that meaning therefore *must* break down. The latter claim is one that deconstructionists have also had to fight,[2] but the hiatus it imposes on grand narratives of philosophy's promise leaves room for a humbler dialectics of the sort I am endorsing.

Mourning's flattening of the dialectic of intimacy cannot be said to establish its limits – much less advance from the negativity of dialectics to a genuinely positive philosophy that would reveal intimacy as it actually appears. Either goal would require a conclusion about the structure of the dialectic itself – what Hegel would call a 'science'[3] – which would show the necessity of the subject alienating itself from its self-sufficiency. This is the sandbar on which German idealism foundered, and I am not equipped here to dredge it. What I am more interested in pursuing is how, given this alienation, the capacity to recognize and be recognized begins to emerge along with our provisional conceptions of ourselves.

Though intimacy has shown that it cannot live up to its own demands, recognition of this failure does not simply liberate one from these demands. Because the dialectic does not present itself as a whole, it does not offer the freedom of a psychoanalytic *amor fati* that would excuse our failures as products of human nature. It is tempting to conclude from this long sequence of attempts at intimacy that could never quite get a grip on what they were asking for that the quest for intimacy was doomed from the beginning or that evolution has dealt us an unwinnable hand. But the haunting of the mourner has shown that at least as long as we strive for intimacy this anthropological perspective is not available to us. Because intimacy was never the self-assigned project of an ambitious (if naïve) subject, it cannot simply be abandoned as a grand dialectical mistake. The critic who assumes that the untenability of intimacy can be read off the concept in its totality has been insufficiently attentive, for the failures of intimacy each appear as particulars.

I stated in the introduction that I wanted this book to do more than just cultivate a mindfulness to the contradictions of intimacy that might attune us to its ever paradoxical emergence in our life. Such mindfulness is the worthy contribution of so many recent phenomenological and deconstructive approaches to intimacy, but I hoped it might also be possible to contribute to the sum total of our *wisdom* about intimacy, in spite of all the usual caveats that terms like 'total', 'wisdom', and 'our' deserve. A dialectical approach, I asserted, promises to preserve the wisdom contained in a hypothesis even as it shows its systematic failure. To a degree, I think the dialectic of mourning helps articulate why this is possible. Because the intimacy of mourning does not appear as a necessary capstone to a relationship, but as an utterly contingent haunting that no one seems to have chosen, it shows both the possibility and necessity of thinking concepts like intimacy that cannot be coherently articulated. In place of either a systematic account of intimacy's necessary and sufficient conditions or an intimation of its utter senselessness, it offers wisdom about a problematic concept.

It might sound from this that my dialectical reading of intimacy is all just a fancy way of saying: 'Intimacy may work in practice, but it'll never work in theory.' But I think this interpretation is misleading, both because I have tried to avoid assuming such a distinction between theory and practice and because I have tried to show how difficult it is to determine whether any relationship 'works' in practice. If the measure of a successful relationship is its intimacy, then there is no way of stating consistently what this would even mean. Dialectics is not the disenchantment of intimacy, but a more determinate account of what it is asking for.

The question with which we began, however, still nags: since intimacy asks for something inconceivable, how is it even *possible*? This framing of the question is fundamentally Kantian, since it seeks a critical position as an antecedent for any responsible study of intimacy. But the Kantian urge to establish once and for all the conditions for the possibility of intimacy, to survey its limits without exceeding its boundaries, and to make perfectly transparent what we may hope for subordinates the dialectic of intimacy to an a priori conception of what philosophy ought to be doing with its concepts – as if some all-seeing shift manager had assigned us the task of pre-testing our concepts before they left the factory floor. Such an assignment might indeed be comforting, and it could help combat the vertiginous sense that dialectical thinking might not be good for anything, but it would be a task that could neither be assigned nor received by anyone.

Rather than having been assigned, the question of the possibility of intimacy is instead one that haunts us.[4] The dialectical approach to intimacy was never just an application of one of several philosophical methods to a particular problematic, and we cannot claim to be intrepid investigators for having braved it. My desire for a suitably critical position from which to assess the meaning of the dialectic of intimacy as a whole has instead been shown to be unsustainable. It would provide a nice sense of what the self-help books call 'closure' to this dialectic if I could simply wrap up this book and move on to the next one, secure in the knowledge that my commitment to this project is now a thing of the past. What I would like, I can now see, is for my mourning of the book to secure our relationship. I may not have been its greatest friend, but at least what we had was something genuinely *had*. No one can take that past away, I would like to say. But if this is true, then it is only in the sophistical sense that this past was never fully present. If anything, I can only mourn the various moments of the dialectic as ghosts to which my expression remains inadequate. I would like an expression of modesty to be able to excuse the incompleteness of this work – to be able to say that because dialectics are never complete, because meaning is always deferred, because all writing comes from a contingent perspective, that therefore even if this book could have been otherwise, this fact that it could have been otherwise could not have been otherwise. But this would rob my mourning of its singularity and dissolve it into an indifferent 'life goes on'. Our dialectical perspective thus requires of us a great deal of humility, both as writers and as readers. If any wisdom has been expressed in the past ten chapters, it is not yet clear to whom it belongs. To the extent we are able to see ourselves in these dialectical moments, it is only with a glimmer of recognition.

Notes

Introduction

1 As Kristeva puts it, 'Are not two loves essentially individual, hence incommensurable, and thus don't they condemn the partners to meet only at a point infinitely remote?' (*Tales of Love*, 35).

2 *Works of Love*, 23.

3 Montaigne, 'On Friendship'.

4 See, for instance, Markell's *Bound by Recognition*, Williams's *Hegel's Ethics of Recognition*, and my 'Multivalent Recognition'.

5 Honneth, *The Struggle for Recognition*.

6 In the analytic tradition in particular, there have been some careful recent efforts to disentangle these various senses, including Helm's *Love, Friendship, and the Self* and Abramson and Leite's 'Love as a Reactive Emotion'.

7 In addition to the philosophers who have built these distinctions into their own ethical systems, see especially Vlastos's *Platonic Studies* and Gordon's *Plato's Erotic World* for particularly incisive discussions of how these distinctions function in Plato's texts.

8 Though my first encounter with his work was relatively late, my position on the dialectical structure of recognition is closer to Markell's than to any of the other thinkers named above. In particular, I want to hold fast to his insight that for Hegel recognition is limited not merely in the practical difficulties of everyone pursuing it, but in its very contradictory structure (*Bound by Recognition*, 94). I do think his emphasis on tragedy is too constrictive on the possibilities of recognition, since what Ricoeur called the 'course of recognition' cannot be summed up in its downfall, and I think that many of the insights that he associates with 'acknowledgement' are bound up in the dialectics of recognition, but I am willing to follow him quite far in his reading of Hegel.

9 In *Atmospheric Disturbances*, Rivka Galchen explores the profound threat to intimacy that can be posed by diseases like Capgras, but she also notes the relative triviality of the mere *feeling* of intimacy: 'But with that photo it was more than just an appearance, it was also a feeling, a *family feeling*. A feeling that at least seemed to be responding to something beyond mere appearance, though at times such 'feelings' – such limbic system instinctual responses – are the most superficial and anachronistic of all, like the feeling a baby duck must have when it responds more strongly to a stick painted red than to the beak of its own mother' (27).

10 V. S. Ramachandran, *A Brief Tour of Human Consciousness.*

11 It would be an interesting empirical question to investigate whether those more prone to feelings of familiarity (whether on account of drugs or innate brain chemistry) develop more intimacy in their relationships – though I am unsure how this could be tested given the multiple and conflicting layers of intimacy I will discuss in this book – but for the time being it is enough to note that however tight their empirical correlation is, intimacy and familiarity are phenomenologically distinct.

12 Bennett Helm obscures this point by identifying intimacy with the 'felt evaluations' by which one becomes aware of it (181). While I am sympathetic to Helm's treatment of intimacy as essential to self-identity (though not to his appeal to evaluative concepts, which I think constitute a distinct dialectic of recognition), his linkage of intimacy to its feeling obscures its dialectical structure.

13 Heidegger, *Sein und Zeit,* 25.

14 *Kritik der reinen Vernunft,* A61/B86.

15 While this project is indebted to Hegel more than any other thinker, I do not think that the dialectic of intimacy as worked out here has a particular place in Hegel's system. Hegel himself treats intimacy most explicitly in the context of the family (see Ciavatta, 'The Unreflective Bonds of Intimacy'), but the movements traced out in the book before you correspond variably to moments in what Hegel calls anthropology, self-consciousness, reason, *Sittlichkeit*, morality, civil society, and others.

16 Marx was, of course, a thinker whose account of fundamental philosophical methodology changed over time, so any reference to his view of dialectics has to be accompanied by a fair number of caveats. I would, however, like to distance Marx from the distinction between historical materialism and dialectical materialism popularized by the Soviet reading of Engels. Such a reading, which would hold that under dialectical materialism there exists a single dialectic in nature according to which the evolution of human economic relationship necessarily unfolds, lacks a firm basis in Marx's writings and is in any event far afield from the senses of 'dialectics' that I am attempting to locate in Plato, Hegel and Marx.

17 See Jameson, *Valences of the Dialectic,* 320. As Amy Wendling has recently pointed out, *Capital* itself is structured as an analysis of economic relations *if one assumes* the political economy of industrial capitalism (Wendling 10).

18 In the *Phaedo* as well, Socrates uses ὑποτίθημι in this more provisional sense of 'putting something down' rather than establishing it for all time (100a). For more on Plato's use of ὑποτίθημι and ὑπόθεσις, see Sallis, *Logic of Imagination,* 10.

19 Hegel, *PhG* 433, ¶807. All references to Hegel's *Phenomenology* give the page number of the critical German edition and the paragraph numbers found in the Miller and Pinkard translations. See also my discussion in *Suspension of Reason,* 94–106.

20 Gadamer argues that Hegel's dialectic shares Plato's reception of the Eleatic emphasis on contraries, but in its 'monological' form fails to appreciate the role of dialogue and interplay in dialectical learning (Gadamer, 'Dialectic and Sophism', 93–4). Hegel contends, however, that his conception of dialectic improves on Plato's by incorporating its emphasis on dialogue without unduly privileging fixity. For Hegel, Plato's dialectic is of only limited utility because it ignores the plastic and dynamic aspects of dialectical progression:

The concept's moving principle, which not only dissolves but produces the particularizations of the universal, I call 'dialectic', though I do not mean that dialectic which takes an object, proposition, etc., given to feeling or, in general, to immediate consciousness, and dissolves it, confuses it, pursues it this way and that, and has as its sole task the deduction of the contrary of what it starts with – a negative type of dialectic that frequently appears also in Plato. Dialectic of this kind may regard as its final result either the contrary of a representation, or, if it is as incisive as the skepticism of the ancients, its contradictory nature, or again, in a feeble manner, an 'approximation' to the truth, a modern half-measure. The higher dialectic of the concept consists not simply in producing the determination as a contrary and a restriction, but in producing and apprehending from it its positive content and result, because through this alone is it a development and an immanent progress (Hegel, *Philosophy of Right*, 36).

While Hegel ignores much of Plato's fluidity in focusing on Socrates' demand for a non-hypothetical first principle, he is right to resist claims (like the one Gadamer later advances) that his is a monological dialectic. Because Hegel wants to preserve even the partial insights of his interlocutors, it is fairer to say that he offers a polylogical if not always dialogical dialectic. The passage above also helps correct the common misconception that dialectical always begins from the postulation of two opposing positions. While some notable oppositions (master and slave, faith and pure insight, etc.) headline Hegel's dialectical approach, there are plenty of dialectics (desire, phrenology, etc.) that collapse under the weight of their own contradictions.

21 Popper, 83.

22 D. P. McAdams, 'Human Motives'.

23 Karen Prager, *The Psychology of Intimacy*, 1.

24 The emerging field in psychology of 'relationship science' has much to offer a dialectical approach, but it is not entirely clear what dialectics has to offer in return other than the clarification and reorganization of some guiding concepts. It does not attempt to ground such a science and prefers the anecdotal to the rigorously experimental, so it could be that it simply works at cross purposes with psychology. See Debra Mashek and Arthur Aron, eds, *Handbook of Closeness and Intimacy*.

25 Cf. Levinas, *Otherwise than Being*, 6.

26 As such, dialectics gives no special place to any particular *mood* with which we might welcome the other or cultivate intimacy. There are of course manifold ways that the moods of fear, apathy, and so on can close off genuine encounters with our partners, but intimacy need not start with any particular mood and will generally outlast any particular attunement. Indeed, a fixation on one attunement among others can easily become an impediment to intimacy, as even wonder tends to linger longer than it needs to on intimacy's doorstep.

27 The phrase is Levinas's (*Otherwise than Being*, 6), but the ambivalent relation to play could just as easily have come from Schelling. See my 'Reason at Play'.

28 Cf. Merleau-Ponty, *The Visible and the Invisible*, 77.

29 For Jean-Luc Nancy, it is only natural that intimacy's focus on what is inmost should most commonly be applied to something prevailing among multiple people, since isolated individualism is self-contradictory: 'If intimacy must be defined as the extremity of coincidence with oneself, then what exceeds intimacy in interiority is the distancing of coincidence itself … it is no accident that we use the word "intimacy" to designate a relation between several people more often than a relation to oneself. Our being-with, as a being-many is not at all accidental … *The plurality of beings is at the foundation of Being* (*Being Singular Plural*, 11–12). Here Nancy is making an important observation about the inadequacy of any account that seeks to define intimacy as the closeness of two self-sufficient beings, but I do not wish to take the ontological step of concluding that plurality (or anything else) is at the foundation of Being.

30 Fredric Jameson makes a similar comparison of dialectics to deconstruction, but he contends that what I am calling deconstruction's higher metabolism actually reflects a different methodology. While both dialectics and deconstruction show the structural incoherence of any idea they confront, dialectics pauses upon this realization until a new idea or ideology emerges to critique and 'deconstruction races forward, undoing the very incoherence it has just been denouncing and showing that seeming analytic result to be itself a new incoherence and a new "contradiction" to be unraveled in its turn' (*Valences of the Dialectic*, 27).

31 This continual striving for more is not present in every form of the search for recognition. With legal personhood, for example, I can be content with a certain level of recognition and be indifferent to any more. This is why I think that a theory of justice can be organized metaphysically along Kant's model and does not have to dip its toes in dialectics so long as it recognizes that it concerns only recognition of one's legal personhood and not other forms of recognition. Intimacy, however, has no exemplar and thus keeps looking for something closer.

32 In this way my approach roughly follows Hegel's in the *Phenomenology*, in which the subject develops as the dialectic proceeds. See Butler, 'Longing for Recognition', 288.

33 Marion, *Being Given*, x.

34 As I hope will be apparent in any event simply from the ways I bring other figures into my argument, the order in which I address these figures is not meant to imply anything about their internal completeness or the level of esteem in which I hold them. I am not giving a surreptitious history of the concept of intimacy, but am just referring to philosophers in the contexts in which their insights are most relevant.

35 Hegel, *Philosophy of Right*, 10.

36 In his late philosophy, Schelling goes further to distance his approach from dialectics, deriding the latter as merely *negative* philosophy. Such philosophy does not rely on any external source of revelation and thus can make no claim to describing the world as it exists. At best it can find order among all the worlds that might be. Feuerbach went even further to dismiss such thinking as empty play. For Feuerbach, 'Dialectics is not a monologue that speculation carries on with itself, but a dialogue between speculation and empirical reality' ('Towards a Critique of Hegel's Philosophy', 110). But this notion of dialogue miscasts the relationship of philosophy and speculative philosophy. To the extent that empirical reality is 'speaking', it is already engaged in philosophy. In attuning itself to the manifold *possibilities* expressed in a particular hypothesis, dialectics opens up a space for engagement with the world but does not in so doing claim to speak for it. To this extent, it is fairer to follow Aristotle in noting that dialectics differs from sophistry in its 'choice of life' (τοῦ βίου τῇ προαιρέσει) (1004b 24–5). Rather than simply seeking to make a point, dialectics chooses and commits to the openness of life itself.

37 Schelling, *Weltalter*, 5. A slightly expanded version of the same passage also appears in the 1815 *Ages of the World*, SW 8: 201.

38 It seems clear that Hegel is a primary target of Schelling's contempt here, and it is possible that Schelling's own early work, especially his *Identitätsphilosophie*, is also under the knife. As should be clear from the discussion above, I find Hegel's approach to the dialectic more dynamic than Schelling does, but I do not wish to refight this battle here. For more, see my *Suspension of Reason*.

39 Benjamin, *Like Subjects, Love Objects*, 21.

40 Approaches like Lacan's, which problematize the relationship between the real and the symbolic, complicate the picture, since they disturb the (admittedly oversimplified) contrast I have been drawing between dialectical and empirical approaches to intimacy. Given his lifelong commitment to uncovering the ontogeny of psychosis, I am inclined to include even Lacan in the class of psychoanalysts whose work contrasts with my own dialectical approach, but I would not rule out *a priori* the possibility of a purely dialectical psychoanalysis. I will, additionally, have more to say on the mirror stage in future work on value.

41 While my critique is not nearly as strident or univocal, I do entertain some of the same suspicions as Deleuze and Guattari in *Anti-Oedipus* (47). To the extent that psychoanalysis attempts to grasp intimacy as a need whose non-fulfilment results in pathology, it will tend to ignore the complex dialectical path by which intimacy continually struggles to appear.

42 A psychoanalyst might diagnose this dialectical commitment as a way of delaying or diverting the desire for consummation, much as the courtly knight occupies himself with ever new quests in order to delay his union with his beloved (see Žižek, *Tarrying with the Negative*, 35). But this is exactly the kind of move that I find suspect in the investigation of intimacy. Since the goal of intimacy cannot be coherently named in advance, assuming that it must nevertheless guide our actions as a purely negative position closes off the playfulness with which dialectics can tarry with the possibilities of intimacy.

43 See also the work of Helen Fisher.

44 *Attachment*, 210–20.

45 Bowlby does not take behaviours that can be accounted for by other drives, like feeding and reproduction, as instances of attachment behaviour (*Loss*, 39).

46 Eppel, for instance, is among the psychologists who at times seem to conflate intimacy and attachment. Eppel interprets Harlow's studies with cloth and wire monkey mother surrogates as supporting the hypothesis that the monkeys primarily seek attachment (*Sweet Sorrow*, 4). But why not conclude that what they seek instead is touching? Without a much richer theoretical edifice to determine that attachment is more important to the drive for closeness than the various dimensions of intimacy I will discuss, this emphasis on attachment is unwarranted.

47 One psychologist who does attempt to delineate the conceptual structure of intimacy is Karen Prager, who defines an intimate interaction (as opposed to an intimate relationship) as a dyadic verbal or nonverbal exchange in which one or both partners share something personal or private (Prager, *The Psychology of Intimacy*, 28). But despite her care in avoiding essentialism in her definition, she still falls back on an undefined conception of the 'private', which presupposes an ability to distinguish what makes each partner distinct. Prager later compounds the philosophical difficulties by specifying that an intimate interaction must be 'positively cathected' (67), which would require a way of distinguishing positive from negative affects. The broader problem with such accounts, I will argue, is that intimacy cannot be defined by a set of conditions even in the sense of a family resemblance concept (cf. Prager 16) because the very conditions intimacy sets for itself are contradictory.

48 In *The Struggle for Recognition* Honneth undertakes an ingenious effort to find common ground between typological and dialectical approaches to recognition through what he calls 'a phenomenologically oriented typology' (93). In Hegelian terms, he is attempting to confirm through the understanding the conclusions that Hegel and Mead have reached in general terms through reason. Such comparisons are certainly interesting, but they will only be dialectically relevant once the terms of recognition have been systematically secured.

49 I take this to be the approach of Montaigne in his famous essay on friendship.

50 *Beiträge zur Philosophie*, §250.

51 *The Way of Love*, 44.

Chapter One

1 For reasons that will become clear as this chapter proceeds, it would do my project no good to begin with an account of the transcendental conditions for the possibility of a gift or of the meaning of the term 'gift' in ordinary language. I begin instead with an initially unanalysed gift given for the purpose of instituting an intimacy. While such a beginning is anathema to some philosophical traditions, I do not think it is entirely discontinuous with twentieth- and twenty-first-century discourses on the gift. As Derrida notes, even Mauss bases his ostensibly structural analysis of gifts across world cultures more on ways that the word 'gift' can be used than on what the gift itself is (*Given Time*, 55). Similarly, my aim is not to uncover some essence of the gift, but to trace its failures in establishing an ultimate intimacy.

2 Sight can, of course, confer its own limited form of intimacy. If we do not privilege the initiating moment, then the sight of one's partner can give the seer a sense that the seen has been apprehended in her totality. As Husserl long ago showed, however, total vision is impossible, and no matter how much is stripped away from the seen to elicit a perfectly nude vision, objects are only ever seen in partial adumbrations.

3 Such is the power of the 'meet cute'. Here Barthes is particularly instructive: 'the first thing we love is *a scene*. For love at first sight requires the very sign of its suddenness (what makes me irresponsible, subject to fatality, swept away, ravished)' (*A Lover's Discourse*, 192). This sign of love's suddenness, however, is an inoculation against the development of one's partner. It treats the partner as an Other who wounds the lover, only to retreat to an original space of non-connection.

4 Beginning here has the additional advantage that the gift's onesidedness marks a stark contrast to the mutual interactions of a more developed relationship. In comparison to touching or mourning, the gift is underdeveloped.

5 The recent furor on college and high school campuses over 'sexting' (the practice of sending sexually charged images of oneself over mobile phones) largely overlooks the fact that such 'sexts' have the prototypical structure of a gift. The sender divests herself of something judged to be valuable with at least some doubt over whether it will be accepted or rejected, kept private or disseminated. The possibility of dissemination doubtlessly raises the stakes, but this is also true of any gift (such as an honest and personal love letter) that wins its intimate currency by bestowing unusual trust on the recipient.

6 Fichte, *Naturrecht*, 193. For more on Fichte's distinction between the formally common will and the materially common will, see my discussion in 'States of Peace'.

7 Fichte, *Naturrecht*, 207. See Williams, *Recognition*, 63.

8 For a helpful explanation of why the gift for Mauss both creates and forestalls intimacy, see Godelier, 'Some Things You Give'. According to Godelier, what Mauss did not fully understand was that to repay in kind is structurally different from an economic exchange.

9 Derrida, *Given Time*, 14.

10 From this perspective, every gift would be founded on a kind of hypocrisy as its very condition of possibility. Or in the words of Marcel Mauss, 'Society always pays itself in the counterfeit coin of its own dream'. Thus such encomia to unconditional gifts as Lewis Hyde's praise for a son who

donated a kidney to his mother would be open to mockery (Hyde, 71). According to the logic of the gift, if the son expected anything in return, then the gift would have been cancelled, because it would merely be part of an exchange. But since his mother had borne him and he knew he could count on her love in the future, he felt organ donation was more than called for. As Derrida points out, this means that the kidney donation was not really a gift under the son's own conditions (*Given Time*, 17–8n.). In the son's line of thinking, it was a kind of repayment for the mother's past and future sacrifices. It could only be treated as a gift under the condition that the son not articulate what exactly was being repaid through the donation. Here unconditionality is only a useful fiction, and the gift succeeds (if this is even the right word) only if the son pretends that the relationship that has made the gift meaningful plays no part in it.

11 Often translated as 'summons', Fichte's term *Aufforderung* indicates something between a request and a demand. The *Aufforderung* is most effective when it manages simultaneously to convey that the request matters a great deal to the appellant and that the appellee is completely free to grant or deny the request.

12 Tip O'Neill famously observed that people like to be asked for things, and I take Fichte's account of the *Aufforderung* to provide one of the most compelling reasons why. We enjoy being asked because the appellant is recognizing our freedom.

13 We find a small version of this interaction on Facebook. Even when nothing else is shared, there is a kind of minimal intimacy developed when one partner asks another if she would like to be a 'friend'. Yet what is in danger of being lost in a system like Facebook friending is the risk of the request. To the extent that conventions emerge regarding whom one does and does not 'friend', accepting a friend could become automatic in some cases, thus stripping meaning from the recognition of both the appellant and the appellee.

14 In the *Foundations of Natural Right*, Fichte is quite clear that he is describing a *political*, not a moral relationship, by which he means that he is concerned only with how persons motivated only by selfishness can develop institutions of mutual respect, not with how individuals might become less selfish (Fichte, *Naturrecht*, 150).

15 In the following paragraphs I will be giving a simplified and perhaps even idealized version of Bourdieu's account of gift relations. While Bourdieu emphasizes the unanticipated nature of gift-return, he often (and frustratingly) lapses into structural analyses that make it seem that recipients somehow manage to find the only possible return for any gift. For a more fully developed version of this critique, see Anthony King, 'Thinking Bourdieu Against Bourdieu'.

16 It should be noted that this appeal to unreflective actions does not depend on the positing of a metaphysical or psychological unconscious. Indeed, for Bourdieu, to appeal to the unconscious to explain the ways that the gift exceeds the self-identification of a culture is a copout. Although it is certainly true that many cultures do not make explicit the conditions for giving a gift, any reference to a vast storehouse of implicit thought is a misconception. The influences of the past upon me are great compared to the influences of the present, but this is only because it takes a while to become habituated to the strictures of a culture (*Logic of Practice*, 56). Far more useful as an explanation of the operations of a social condition is what Bourdieu calls *habitus*: 'The *habitus* – embodied history, internalized as a second nature and so forgotten as history – is the active presence of the whole past of which it is the product. As such, it is what gives practices their relative autonomy with respect to external determinations of the immediate present. This autonomy is that of the past, enacting and acting, which, functioning as accumulated capital, produces history on the basis of history and so ensures the permanence in change that makes the individual agent a world within the world. The *habitus* is a spontaneity without consciousness, or will, opposed as much to the mechanical necessity of things without history in mechanistic theories as it is to the reflexive freedom of subjects 'without inertia' in rationalist theories' (*Logic of Practice*, 56).

17 The necessity of this time lag is a subject to which Mauss also devotes attention. For societies such as those indigenous to the Northwestern United States, for instance, since barter is mostly unknown, no transfer of goods can occur without a sufficient amount of time between the initial gift and its return (*The Gift*, 35–6). Contrary to the armchair anthropologist's assumption that 'primitive' societies would only ever exchange something of value for something else of value, he contends, for these societies the uncertainty that the temporal lag introduces is essential to the exchange itself.

18 The anthropologist Parker Shipton gives an example of this need for a concealment of the principles of exchange in his account of his time with the Luo people of Southwest Kenya. For the Luo, it is inappropriate to exchange a daughter's hand in marriage for grain, but in times of famine such exchanges can be organized under the condition that there be a delay between the handing over of the daughter and the delivery of the grain. In such an arrangement, both parties acknowledge that this is not an exchange at all, but a mutual showing of good faith and openness to an ongoing relationship (Shipton, *The Nature of Entrustment*, 213).

19 *Nicomachean Ethics*, Book 8, Chapter 3 (1156b 26).

20 This magnification seems to be the goal of contemporary 'secret Santa' festivities as well. Because a participant is ignorant not only of who will be receiving her gift, but of what she will be receiving in return and who will be giving it, the space of play is significantly magnified. Yet since such festivities are often organized among work colleagues or other groups on only slightly intimate terms, they are prone to dissolution under the strain of the forced intimacy. The uncertainty will only be pleasurable to the extent that no gifts will be grossly inappropriate, which occasionally calls for explicit rules, which reduce the uncertainty and extension of time.

21 However, while they both refer to a necessary hypocrisy in the circulation of gifts, there is a crucial difference between Derrida and Bourdieu's accounts. For Derrida, it is calculation of the rewards and consequences of a gift that annuls the functioning of the gift (GT 91). A gift ceases to be a gift

whenever I use it to attempt to delineate what is yours and mine and what will come back to me through the gift. For Bourdieu, on the other hand, the more relevant concern is not whether a genuine gift is in fact possible, but what contrivances of *habitus* and conversions of economic into social capital are required to make gifts function (in Schrift, 240).

22 'On the Gift: A discussion between Jacques Derrida and Jean-Luc Marion', in Caputo and Scanlon, 67.

23 See, for instance, Hyde, *The Gift*, 58. John Milbank takes this position to an extreme, suggesting that continuous gifts are *necessary* for love: 'We have inherited a contrast between *agape*, a "giving" love, and *eros*, a "desiring" love, but human erotic attachments are only sustained by the incessant exchange of gifts, which are always tokens of further, future gifts, such that desire is never fulfilled as possession, for a constitutive lack in desire will always prove its own thwarting. If desire does know moments of fulfillment, then this is in the coincidence of giving and giving back' (Milbank, 'Can a Gift be Given?' 124). Such an emphasis on the necessity of the gift for intimacy faces the same limitations as Fichte's emphasis on the necessity of the appeal.

24 One could argue that the latter case does not reflect the nature of the gift in general but points to a unique historical situation in which market-based exchange has become so dominant that any charitable giving brands the recipient a stranger (cf. Hyde, 139). But such a position would already assume what this chapter aims to show: that intimacy does not consist in the exchange of gifts itself, but requires additional dialectical manoeuvrings.

25 I do not wish to go so far as Joseph O'Leary and argue that Marion's ignoring of Hegelian questions of historicality point twenty-first-century phenomenology in the wrong way (*The Gift*, 148–9). In *Being Given*, at least, I do think there is a careful consideration of the role of gifts in actual human relationships. But I do contend that Marion embeds these discussions in a phenomenological framework that is foreign to my project.

26 Marion, *God without Being*, 104, cited in Horner, 112.

27 In an essay that is otherwise critical of Marion, John Milbank extends on this position, arguing that 'to receive the *other* in receiving his gift demands that the distance of the other remains in place – to try to possess the other and his gifts, to receive them as exactly due rewards, or as things we do not need *to go on* receiving, would be simply to obliterate them' (Milbank, 'Can a Gift be Given?' 132–3). Ultimately, Milbank concludes that Marion errs by emphasizing the withdrawal of the donor over the space that remains between donor and recipient and alone makes this withdrawal possible.

28 Of course, gifts are often given for the sole purpose of deferring intimacy (witness the apathetic husband buying jewellery every Valentine's day or the second-place job candidate overladen with praise), but it would be overly cynical and empirically unjustified to assume that *all* gifts are given merely to defer intimacy.

29 To be sure, Marion does not speak unequivocally against an intimacy developed through unconditioned giving. In *The Erotic Phenomenon*, he even defines the lover as the one who is willing to suspend all economy and give unconditionally (78). But what Marion calls love is not the only form of intimacy, and I take his account of the gift to represent a distinct, though still flawed, form of intimacy from his erotic phenomenon.

30 Marion, 'The Reason of the Gift,' 105–6.

31 Here I do not pretend to speak to the phenomenological aspects of Marion's theory that givenness always exceeds a gift. I am not discussing the possibility of a gift's appearance, but the breakdown of giving's striving for intimacy.

32 Nancy, *The Experience of Freedom*, 146–7; see also Derrida, *On Touching*, 21.

33 This desperation poses a similar problem to the Fichtean ego's desperate efforts to secure recognition. Because Marion believes that the meaning of the *cogito ergo sum* can only be secured by the hope of intimacy, intimacy is not only something strived for, but something demanded. Just as Fichte thought that the requirement of recognition for all human freedom justified totalitarian measures to punish failures of recognition, Marion asks us to cling to love at all costs in order to secure a phenomenologically coherent conception of the self.

34 I suspect that this advantage of the text is in part responsible for the renewed appreciation for cellular text messages among the younger generations. While those of us accustomed to the flexibility of phone calls find texting absurdly inefficient, those who have grown into adulthood with the medium may find intimacy in the self-conscious retreat of the texter.

35 For this reason the theatrical renunciations of the gift of writing by Barthes's unnamed lover ring hollow. Unlike the gift of (say) a slipper, he complains, the written, dedicated text makes no effort to fit its recipient: 'there is no benevolence within writing, rather a terror: it smothers the other, who, far from perceiving the gift in it, reads there instead an assertion of mastery, of power, of pleasure, of solitude. Whence the cruel paradox of the dedication: I seek at all costs to give you what smothers you' (*A Lover's Discourse*, 78–9). Like every gift, a piece of writing will prove less than completely adequate to the complexity and personality of the partner, but it smothers only to the extent that the reader denies or forgets that it is a text, projecting incomplete futures and demanding incomplete allegiance.

36 For instance, at 241c: 'So keep these things in mind, my darling boy [ὦ παῖ].'

37 While I have reviewed all translations to follow, I have relied to a great extent on Stephen Scully's translation of the *Phaedrus*.

38 Later Lysias is even more emphatic about the importance of carefully assessing the value of one's chastity, warning against the pain that follows when the beloved has 'given away freely what is most important to you [προεμένου δέ σου ἃ περὶ πλείστου]' (232c).

39 See Scully in Plato, *Phaedrus*, 15 n39.

40 Socrates would likely have ambivalent feelings about Phaedrus's description of him as 'most out of place' (ἀτοπώτατός) (230c). On the one hand, his atopicality is a precondition for the excessiveness of his gift, but on the other he seeks to establish a place where he and Phaedrus can share a meaningful conversation.

Chapter Two

1 *The Body in Pain*, 166.

2 Nancy, *Birth to Presence*, 204.

3 Thus I find quixotic Marion's attempt to find in the phenomena attending eroticism and sex some ultimate evidence that the lover and beloved are sharing in the exact same touch. His postulation of a 'phenomenological requirement of an erotic univocality of the taking of flesh, which, without exception, is the condition for its accomplishment' (ER 125) imposes too great a burden on the sexual relation. As we will see below, there are both good and bad reasons for positing sexual touching as more intimate than other forms of touching, but even in the (in my experience rare, but then again I am not French) phenomenon of simultaneous orgasm (cf. ER 145), it is not sensation or even ecstasy that is shared, but a wounding touch apparent from two distinct sides. It is doubtless the case that lovers often long for the 'final immanence' of mutual climax (ER 128), but we should be suspicious of any analysis that posits an actual consummation in this event.

4 Merleau-Ponty, *The Visible and the Invisible*, 140–4. From Merleau-Ponty's perspective, there is, of course, more to the story than the mere non-coincidence of my touching and being touched. These phenomena point to a general 'reversibility' of being, between touching and being touched, seeing and visibility, etc. Claude Lefort has argued that Merleau-Ponty overestimates the general applicability of this peculiar example ('Flesh and Otherness'), but for my purposes it is enough to say that touching and reversibility are two different ways of conceiving intimacy. Whereas the former seeks intimacy in immediate contact, the latter seeks it in the oscillation between expansion and contraction that I consider in Chapter 3.

5 It should go without saying that my use of 'intimacy' here differs from Merleau-Ponty's. When he states that it is 'as though there were between [the visible] and us an intimacy as close as between the sea and the strand' (*The Visible and the Invisible*, 130–1), he posits an intimacy that precedes sensible experience yet retreats from it. I will consider an intimacy with this general shape in the next chapter, but it will not be the sort that could exist or develop between inanimate objects.

6 Derrida extends on this analysis in *On Touching*: 'Even between me and me, if I may put it this way, between my body and my body, there is no such "original" contemporaneity, this "confusion" between the other's body and mine, that Merleau-Ponty believes he can recognize there, while pretending he is following Husserl' (Derrida, *On Touching*, 193).

7 Nancy, *Being Singular Plural*, 11–12.

8 This is not to say that a phenomenological account of being with others would not be valuable for other philosophical ends, but merely that we cannot achieve intimacy by delving deeper into the ontology of being together.

9 Here the example of the prosthesis is also instructive. When I touch someone with a prosthesis – say, when I grab my wife's backside with a novelty plastic pincher – it is neither immediacy nor the sensation itself that I seek, but a kind of closeness. And the fact that I am immediately inclined to do so when I always have the option of touching her 'directly' with my hand suggests that immediacy is not always the goal of touching.

10 This added layer of complexity is the primary reason I have not attempted parallel accounts of the dialectics of seeing or hearing. Many people do indeed seek intimacy in seeing a partner's nude body, for instance, but the reasons why this fails are easy enough to extrapolate from the dialectics of touching and the fetish (Chapter 5). Not all of the failures of touching, on the other hand, could be extrapolated from a dialectic of seeing.

11 For a further reflection on the opposition of tact and immediacy, see Scarry, 9.

12 The desire for intimacy is not necessarily the only drive at work in such phenomena. In the fetishization of virginity, for instance, men may also be guided by a need for recognition of their power, a pre-Oedipal desire for connection with the mother-figure, and other drives.

13 Elaborate myths have also been built up regarding anything touched by menstrual fluid. Often anything to come in contact with a menstruating woman is viewed as contaminated or even dangerous. There is such a substantial disproportion between the unclean woman and the ones who would touch her that even 'indirect' touches carry the risk of contagion.

14 This difference between the Eucharist and more lasting forms of intimacy is something Nancy himself has noticed, particularly in the context of sexual love: 'Thus the bodies of lovers: they do not give themselves over to transubstantiation, they touch one another, they renew one another's spacing forever, they displace themselves, they address themselves (to) one another' (*Corpus*, 9). To be sure, Nancy's project is one with which I sympathize. He wants to show that the Christian promise of an ultimate unity with God is in principle unfulfillable. Just as he showed in his early work that the romantic hope for a return to a community unified by common origins and interests has always been a myth and its corresponding take on contemporary society as an alienating jumble of nonidentities is a gross exaggeration that nevertheless keeps reappearing, in what he calls his 'deconstruction of Christianity' he seeks to show that Christianity makes promises that its flesh can't cash. The very nature of intimacy is such that it is structured by a contradiction. I want my touch to prove that my partner and I or God and I are really *one* even as I realize that such oneness would annul the possibility of any touching.

But Nancy takes this carefully developed observation in directions that I find unsustainable. In showing that insufficiency belongs to the very nature of intimacy, he implies that our goal ought to be to develop a static, ontological account rather than a dialectical one. Rather than trace the ways that various forms of intimacy can break down and transform into other forms, he seeks to show that intimacy in general is always already broken. In demonstrating this brokenness, Nancy does not mean that there is no such thing as intimacy or that it never appears in the world. Partners everywhere somehow manage to find some intimacy despite the fact that the very conditions we set for a perfectly intimate touch would seem to imply that it could never actually happen. For Nancy this means not that we should reject the empirical evidence for intimacy's existence, but that intimacy can only ever appear when we abandon the assumption that we can know what will constitute a true instance of intimacy or even that we will know it when we see it. It is a recognition that the future will and must surprise us and an openness to being confounded.

But I think that philosophy can provide something more than mere bafflement with intimacy. And here again I think that Beauvoir offers us an innovative and productive approach. In her more explicitly existentialist works, Beauvoir, like Nancy, is eager to show that there is no ultimate unity that human beings can hope to achieve and thus no perfect community that could justify violence in the present. While she never endorses Sartre's more extreme position that we are fundamentally alone in the world, she does aim to prove that our relations with others are by their nature fundamentally ambiguous and resistant to any consummation. She thus sets out to give an account of human nature even as she denies that we could ever appeal to such a nature in understanding ourselves. But in *The Second Sex*, Beauvoir develops a dialectical approach much more along the lines of a Hegel than a Sartre. *The Second Sex* is not a practical guide to navigating the dilemmas created by our sexist culture, but it does seek to show how human subjects attempt to wriggle free of its strictures, at times succeeding and at times exacerbating the problem. Rather than attempting to delineate the conditions for the possibility of intimacy, it aims to show how intimacy tends to break down and redevelop in unexpected ways. The subject matter for *The Second Sex* is of course far vaster than my concerns with intimacy, but on each occasion where the book does address intimacy, it takes it to be problematic rather than impossible. Its aim is not just to prove that intimacy of any sort must be fleeting, but to find different reasons for why different kinds of intimacy are fleeting and to find those times when intimacy really does appear.

15 In *In Excess*, Jean-Luc Marion makes a similar point: 'But what one sometimes still names the "carnal union" is characterized precisely by the fact that it provides us with the most unquestionable proof that the flesh of the other remains absolutely inaccessible to me, like mine to him or her. Pleasure is not divided, especially if two pleasures stimulate each other and are accomplished simultaneously' (98). With this last thought, however, he reengages the myth, seeking a more primordial sort of flesh in which both partners find a kind of unity. While I am sympathetic to Marion's resistance to reducing the bodies of the self and other to dull mechanical *Körper* and agree with him that the intimacy of a touch does not just consist in the respective sensations of two bodies, this emphasis on the ecstatic pleasure of a single moment engages in the same sort of mythmaking Beauvoir criticizes. It seeks a touch beyond touch that would establish an intimacy greater than any old ordinary touch.

16 As Bataille puts it, 'what attracts isn't immediate being, but a wound' (*On Nietzsche*, 22). Or as Jason Winfree summarizes Bataille's position, 'Community is constituted in the overlapping of wounds, the sharing not only of what cannot be shared, but the sharing of a suffering that is neither mine nor yours, a suffering that does not belong to us, but which gives us to one another, and in doing so both maintains and withdraws the beings so configured' (Winfree, 41).

17 'Unless I see in his hands the mark of the nails, and place my finger into the mark of the nails, and place my hand into his side, I will never believe' (John 20.25).

18 For Hegel this image of God wounded on the cross was one of the primary ones that lifted Christianity above other religions and made it the very consummation of religion. Other religions have found material objects or even people that allow us to come into contact with God, but only Christianity explores the full depth of suffering that humanity shares with God. See also Lauer, 'Sovereign Gratitude'.

19 Since Levinas imparted so much philosophical weight to the term 'caress', it seems important to distinguish my use of the term from his, which on my reading is not particularly intimate. For Levinas, the meaning of intimacy is so deferred to a future time that the caress, the very mark of mutual presence, is lost in a beyond: 'The caress is the expectation of this pure future (to come), without content' (*Time and the Other*, 89).

20 Cf. MacKendrick, 'Sharing God's Wounds'.

21 I borrow this turn of phrase from Andre Dubus III, in an interview with Eleanor Wachtel of the Canadian Broadcasting Corporation, 22 July 2012.

22 'In this case, and in that of laughter from being tickled, the mind must be in a pleasurable condition; a young child, if tickled by a strange man, would scream in fear. The touch must be light, and an idea or event, to be ludicrous, must not be of grave import' (Darwin, *The Expression of the Emotions in Man and Animals*, 199). Darwin finds it of particular interest that though the ability of a seven-day-old child to be tickled suggests that laughing is a mere reflex, tickling does not elicit laughter under every condition.

23 Cf. Meyer et al., 'How the Brain Laughs'.

24 Panksepp 2007; Panksepp and Burgdorf 2003.

25 See also Bataille's comment that 'what attracts isn't immediate being, but a wound' (*On Nietzsche*, 22).

26 Lucretius, *On the Nature of Things*, Book 1, Line 34.

27 In *Totality and Infinity*, Levinas combines this fixation on the feminine as vulnerable with a fetishization of virginity: 'The feminine essentially violable and inviolable, the "Eternal Feminine", is the virgin or an incessant recommencement of virginity, the untouchable in the very contact or voluptuosity, future in the present' (258). See also *Time and the Other*, 85–8.

28 I need hardly mention Elaine Scarry's momentous work on this point, but I want to call special attention to her contrast between the experiences of the prisoner and the torturer (28–9).

29 As Nancy has observed, 'Injury, the wound, closes the body, gives it the function of a sign. But the wounded body is still meant to be touched, it is still offered to the sense of touch, which restores its absoluteness. Thus, the body has been turned into nothing but a wound. We have not simply tried to dominate it through struggle, or hurt it, or even kill it; we have tried to take away its absoluteness from it' (Nancy, *Birth to Presence*, 205).

30 A similar phenomenon appears in popular depictions of psychological wounds. The intimacy we seek through them is somewhat different from touching, since it generally does not pretend to seek the immediacy of contact, but it finds itself attracted to woundedness all the same. In viewing daytime TV talk shows we may initially feel a thrill from being allowed into someone's trauma, but even in the presence of the most skilful interviewers the wounded person will generally retreat into a core of unknowable otherness.

31 For this reason I am sceptical of Irigaray's approach to the intimacy of touching, particularly her work in the past decade. While (as we will see in Chapter 4) her account of the 'between' has much to recommend it, her emphasis on the encounter of two already established subjectivities leads her to place the highest value on 'allying two intimacies,' not on engaging in the complex dialectical striving for a single intimacy between two partners (*The Way of Love*, 151).

Chapter Three

1 For an empirical study of partners who find themselves repeatedly 'seeing each other for the first time', see Halling, *Intimacy, Transcendence, and Psychology*, 15–40.

2 Seen in the light of this later stage of the dialectic, one way to read the failure of the gift was that it assumed intimacy is something that could be achieved in the future perfect: I will have given. The heartbeat, in contrast, posits its intimacy in the present progressive perfect, whose awkwardness in English foreshadows its unsustainability: we are intimate in my *continually having adjusted*.

3 Margaret Clark and Joan Monin advance a definition of love as 'Communal Responsiveness'. While their definition of communal responsiveness combines dialectical patterns I associate with the heartbeat with those of the gift and other dimensions of intimacy, and while I have already expressed my reservations against using the overbroad term 'love' to designate any particular dialectic of intimacy, their emphasis on beneficent concern for the other gets them much closer to the structure of the heartbeat than most other psychological accounts of love. Rather than prioritizing the attitudes the partners hold to the relationship, Clark and Monin emphasize responsiveness to the other's concerns.

4 Merleau-Ponty, *The Visible and the Invisible*, 11.

5 For this reason, the heartbeat continually interrupts jealousy even as it renews the urge to proprietary self-seeking. Barthes has described this phenomenon with the term 'tenderness'. In tenderness my partner and I find ourselves dissolved into each other. There is no distinction between gift, giver, and recipient, but precisely for this reason there is no way to exclude others from this transaction: 'tenderness, by rights, is not exclusive, hence I must admit that what I receive, others receive as well' (Barthes, *A Lover's Discourse*, 225).

6 For further reflection on Woody Allen's shark metaphor, see p. 126.

7 Except for the 1811 and 1813 editions of *The Ages of the World*, which appear in a Nachlassband edited by Manfred Schröter, all references to Schelling's texts will give the volume and page number for series I of K. F. A Schelling's edition of *Schellings sämmtliche Werke* (SW), which can be found in the Schröter edition and most recent English translations.

8 Schelling's most complete exploration of the interplay of expansion and contraction in the organic realm appears in the *First Outline of a System of the Philosophy of Nature*, in which he develops the late eighteenth-century physiological theory of 'excitability' (*Erregbarkeit* in Schelling's German) into an account of the receptive and irritable forces of organic nature (*First Outline*, 53–70; *Werke* 3: 69–93 and the entire Third Division). For a discussion of expansion and contraction in inorganic forces see *First Outline* 87n; *Werke* 3: 117 n.

9 For a defence of this term as a translation of Schelling's *Sehnsucht*, see Krell, *The Tragic Absolute*, 84–9.

10 On the other hand, Schelling is an incomplete and even dangerous ally for a project like the present one, since it is not his ultimate aim to develop what I am calling a dialectic of intimacy in any of the passages I am discussing. While he does a great deal to explore the contrary forces that that both support and inhibit an individual's efforts at individuation, his philosophical goal is usually not a description of this process itself, but an 'indifference point' that will make the possibility of individuation intelligible once and for all.

11 Neither of these claims is meant to endorse the common reading of Schelling as the most Protean of modern philosophers. He was certainly ambitious and even experimental, but elements of his interpretation of intimacy as heartbeat can be found throughout his long career.

12 I do not take it as especially problematic that much of Schelling's focus in these reflections on the possibility of intimacy before identity is on individual human souls rather than pairs of partners, for Schelling's very point is how inseparable the individual soul is from what is outside of it (see McGrath, 11). Beyond general references to 'love', Schelling does not talk much in *The Ages of the World* about concrete relations between partners, but I do not think this was because he did not mean to address intimate relations. Rather, his focus was on the more general project of explaining the conditions for the possibility of intimacy.

13 In each of the three versions of the *Weltalter*, Schelling explicitly contrasts his approach with that of dialectics. In the 1813 version, for instance, he writes that dialectics would not be necessary once true science is achieved and leaves us to assume that he is offering a 'scientific' approach to the past (WA 114; cf. WA 8–9). Yet since he is at this point only laying down the

conditions of possibility of revelation, he has not yet extracted himself from 'negative', dialectical philosophy, a point that he makes explicit later in the text.

14 In this way, Schelling's development mirrors that of developmental psychology over the second half of the twentieth century, which increasingly recognized the role of the infant as an individuating agent, not just a part of an undifferentiated unity with the mother (Benjamin, *Bonds of Love*, 18).

15 See *Stuttgart Seminars*, 7: 425.

16 While Schelling's account of the A^3 changed repeatedly, he gives a particularly lucid description of it in the *Stuttgarter Privatvorlesungen*, 7: 451.

17 For a more detailed discussion of this dialectic as it applies to natural life, see Lauer, *Suspension of Reason*, 33–55.

18 See Žižek, *The Abyss of Freedom*, 30.

19 A key difference between the heartbeat and the future is that the heartbeat takes intimacy already to be present between the partners and merely reawakened in experiences of wonder, whereas the future assumes that intimacy is found in the collective embrace of the future. Thus while the heartbeat treats the past as an unfathomable (un)ground for the relationship, the future treats the past as just another collection of individual differences for the partners to explore and develop together.

20 We see Schelling struggling with this difficulty especially acutely in the 1811 *Weltalter*. Though he realizes that his resistance to the idea of a single necessary development of nature stresses the very possibility of systematic philosophy, he struggles in vain for language to express the place of the subject in 'the development of protean nature' (WA 47).

21 Descartes, *The Passions of the Soul*, Art. 53. I will discuss Descartes's account of wonder more fully in the next chapter.

22 Consider Nietzsche: 'Life is *essentially* appropriation, injury, overpowering of what is alien and weaker; suppression, hardness, imposition of one's own forms, incorporation and at least, at its mildest, exploitation' (*Beyond Good and Evil*, §259, KSA 5: 207).

23 Derrida describes beautifully how absence or loneliness gives rise to the need for expansiveness, for pure giving: 'This effraction of the other, of what cannot return to self, is the condition of desire; it is the heart, this "organ whose symbolic renown has long been established". The thinker of the syncope is also the thinker of the diastole, of the gap or dilation without return, of this *other heart*, at the heart of which the diastolic difference or diastema does not let itself be gathered up or contracted in the relation to self, in the *syn-* of any systole, This thinking of dilation without return to self, without exchange, of a heart without circulation is the thinking of an absolute generosity, of a generosity more generous than generosity itself, which as its name indicates, would still be genial and too natural' (Derrida, *On Touching*, 282). But of course, such a movement is only part of the movement of the heart, and expansions and contractions always go together. Thus while the need to give a 'pure' gift can seem total and all-consuming, it is only a moment alongside more self-centred striving.

Chapter Four

1 Nancy, *Being Singular Plural*, 65.

2 J. Benjamin, 'Response', 300.

3 Marion, *In Excess*, 38

4 For Kierkegaard, this manifoldness is made explicit in the contrast he draws in *Works of Love* between 'non-preferential love' (*Kjerlighed*) and 'preferential love' (*Forkjerlighed*), and the distinction of each from sexual or erotic love (*Elskov*).

5 1 Corinthians 12.13; Romans 8.9.

6 Romans 8.1–5.

7 Hereafter WL and ESD, respectively.

8 In *Sharing the World*, Irigaray presents the child as a new link capable of '[e]stablishing or restoring human being between us' by reminding us of 'the elementary duties that can bind us to and with one another as humans' (40).

9 Descartes, *The Passions of the Soul*, Art. 53.

10 As I have already mentioned, *sexual* difference does not play any special role in the dialectical account I am developing. For my schematic purposes, any number of other sources of wonder could work equally as well. This allows me to avoid some of the disturbing heteronormative assumptions of Irigaray's account, but it also limits the wisdom it can offer on what Irigaray called 'one of the major philosophical issues, if not *the* issue, of our age' (ESD 5).

11 Hegel, *Philosophy of Right*, trans. T. M. Knox (Oxford: Oxford University Press, 1967), §168.

12 The insufficiency of the parent-child-parent relationship is a theme that Irigaray contemplates in many of her other works as well, but she does not always frame it so clearly in terms of the structure of the between. In *This Sex Which is Not One*, part of the problem is that the desires of the father and mother only meet indirectly in the child. No longer able to experience the wonder at their difference through simple touch, they must rediscover their alterity in their caresses of the newborn child (TSWINO 27). But it would be a mistake to assume that intimacy depends on the immediacy of desire, for the more immediate one's desire is, the less room there is for a partner to respond. On the other hand, as we will see in the next two chapters, complex and even fetishized ways of approaching one another can do wonders to bring two partners together.

13 Kierkegaard's account of the wedding rite is indebted to Hegel's account in the *Philosophy of Right*. Hegel suspects that positions like Friedrich Schlegel's that treat wedding ceremonies as obstacles to true intimacy are really just arguments for sensual immediacy masquerading as defences of love (*Philosophy of Right*, §164z). For Hegel, the view that love can be found in the immediate contact of lovers ignores the ethical aspect of love, which demands that partners learn to live with the contradiction that love requires both self-effacement and the plea that one be recognized as an individual (§158).

14 This insight relies upon Kierkegaard's special understanding of the aporia of the gift. While I incur in love an infinite debt to the other, it would be insulting to wish to repay this debt completely (WL 173–4). I should instead wish to repay the debt and still remain in debt. For Kierkegaard the insult of returning a gift too readily consists in assuming that the relationship is a finite one, since 'An accounting can only take place where there is a finite relationship' (WL 174). To love the other is to deny that such finitude is possible and thus to take every gift of love as being unrepayable even as it demands repayment.

15 Despite the fact that *Works of Love* was published in two separate parts, I am reading a unity of intention into Kierkegaard's plan for the book.

16 For a particularly cutting example of this movement, see Kierkegaard, *Either/ Or*, I: 345.

17 To be clear, the standpoint of the rupture is not identical with Nancy's development of this term; rather, Nancy is the most careful explainer of the structure of the rupture. The term is introduced in *The Inoperative Community* (6) and developed further in *Being Singular Plural* (10).

18 Levinas, *Totality and Infinity*, 50.

19 To be sure, Levinas's conception of the (non-)relation to the Other developed a great deal over the course of his career, and there may indeed be much a dialectical study of intimacy can gain from his conception of the singularity of the Other in particular. But because the present study begins with the hypothesis of intimacy as a goal, Levinas will always be an unreliable ally.

20 Butler advances a similar claim in *Precarious Life* (19–49). Thus I think that Butler is further from Levinas than she lets on (and closer to Nancy's notion of the rupture) when she proposes that it is my very difference from myself that allows me to recognize the difference of the other: 'I find that my very formation implicates the other in me, that my own foreignness to myself is, paradoxically, the source of my ethical connection with others. I am not fully known to myself, because part of what I am is the enigmatic traces of others ... I am wounded, and I find that the wound itself testifies to the fact that I am impressionable, given over to the other in ways that I cannot fully predict or control' (*Precarious Life*, 46). Neither the impulse to intimacy nor its possibility could be said to come from me, for I do not know who I am prior to this rupture. But nor can it simply be said that this urge and possibility come from beyond me, for intimacy is part of the dialectic of recognition by which I become myself.

21 Nancy emphasizes that his project is to think human beings not in terms of their 'perspectives' or 'views' of the world, but in terms of their openness to the world (BSP xii).

22 As Maurice Blanchot has shown, Nancy's conception of the original rupture of the self (at least in its early incarnation as the 'insufficiency' of being) also cannot be taken at face value, since the mere feeling that something about my own being or being in general is incomplete is not enough to establish lack as the basis of common being (*Unavowable Community*, 3–8). This is a dialectical development that could be pursued further here to illustrate the rhyme structure of the dialectic, but since it resembles the movement of irony in Chapter 6 I have elected not to discuss it here at length.

23 Here Nancy's reasoning reiterates one of the lessons of the dialectic of the gift, only from the other side: 'In fact, the pure outside, like the pure inside, renders all sorts of togetherness impossible. They both suppose a unique and isolated pure substance, but pure in such a way that one cannot even say "isolated", exactly because one would be deprived of all relation with it' (BSP 60).

24 *Being Singular Plural*, 78. While on the previous page Nancy gives Hegel credit for laying out the basic structure of the dialectic (BSP 77), here he suggests that Hegel's entire project falls into the trap of positing an independent self encountering and overcoming obstacles. The former claim is probably fairer to Hegel's account of absolute knowing as 'self-sacrifice' and general resistance to immediate self-awareness (*Phänomenologie* 433, §807), and Nancy develops a more nuanced account of this movement over the course of *Hegel: The Restlessness of the Negative*.

25 'The fact that the intimate, the absolutely proper, consists in the absolutely other is what alters the origin in itself, in a relation to itself that is "originally plunged into mourning". The other is an originary relation to death and in relation to originary death' (BSP 78).

26 In *Fear and Trembling*, Kierkegaard describes the interesting as the *confinium*, or border category, between esthetics and ethics (83). It is a kind of self-cultivation that does not quite take stock of one's relationship to world. In Kierkegaard's depiction, the merely interesting are obsessed with newspapers and think endlessly about everyone's place in the world without deciding to make for themselves a place in that world. See also *Either/Or*, I: 339, where A counsels against becoming too interesting, since this involves a solipsistic reflection into oneself.

27 Spinoza's ideal of social existence as a life in which a person strives to cultivate new affects in order to be on common terms with as many like-minded people as possible would be a useful model here, though of course the Spinozan ideal of power is far from intimacy as I have been describing it.

Chapter Five

1 *De Rerum Natura*, Book 4, lines 1205–7.

2 See Žižek, *Indivisible Remainder*, 4.

3 The latter aspect of Freud's approach to fetishes makes his entire account foreign to my own dialectical approach, since it must assume ontologically real drives grounded in a larger biological theory of human nature. Nevertheless, I share Freud's distantly approving attitude toward many fetishes, as expressed in this passage from the first of the *Three Essays on the Theory of Sexuality*: 'The point of contact with the normal is provided by the psychologically essential overvaluation of the sexual object, which inevitably extends to everything that is associated with it. A certain degree of fetishism is thus habitually present in normal love, especially in those stages of it in which the normal sexual aim seems unattainable or its fulfillment prevented' (*The Freud Reader*, 250). Insofar as it seeks to concretize the desire for intimacy in a particular thing, the fetish is curious but not necessarily perverse or pathological, since it is often a manifestation of a quite ordinary drive for love.

4 Frank Schallow also makes the important point that fetishes require a double layer of meaning, so that a stocking, for instance, becomes not just a leg covering but an erotic enticement ('Fantasies and Fetishes', 73). For Schallow, this double meaning opens a 'play-space' that allows eroticism room to develop freely (74). Here, though, I am concerned with the development of fetishes in tandem with a partner and thus would like to emphasize the intimate potential of fetishes rather than their implications for psychic health.

5 I thus want to avoid any connection with the simplified version of Freud that treats the fetish always as a substitution for something, particularly the penis or phallus. In my usage, what matters most about the fetish is the fixation it inspires, and it may or may not be a substitution for something else. Connections of my usage of the term 'fetish' to Kant and Marx, on the other hand, are encouraged.

6 Marx, *Capital*, vol. 1, 165.

7 This relatively trivial example risks obscuring a somewhat confounding loop in the dialectic of recognition. While it is easy enough to analyse the Gaga-lovers' respective aesthetic judgements solely as interests, many times we place value on an object not just to pursue intimacy, but because we believe it is valuable. As I hinted in the introduction, I take the dialectic of value to follow the dialectic of intimacy in the dialectic of recognition, which means that many of the bonds we form by valuing works of art, other people, abstractions like nationalism, and so on, cannot be considered here. There thus may be good reasons to reject a partner for valuing the wrong objects that fall outside of a dialectic of intimacy.

8 There is thus a playful insincerity in Leonard Cohen's line: 'I loved you for your beauty / That doesn't make a fool of me / You were in it for your beauty, too.' We are given no context for this one-sided argument in 'Closing Time', but we can presume that the complaint lies not in the speaker's fetishization of his partner's beauty itself, but in their divergent expectations of the implications of this fetishization. The next line reveals the speaker's ironic attitude to this divergence: 'I loved you for your body / There's a voice that sounds like God to me / Declaring that your body's really you.' The consequences of this fetishization are excusable, the speaker suggests tongue-half-in-cheek, because the fetish had overwhelmed the totality from which it had been abstracted.

9 I include Perniola in this discussion of the fetish even though he uses the term differently, arguing that 'the fetish is a caricature of the sex appeal of the inorganic' (53). I noted at the beginning of this chapter the dismissive and limiting connotations that 'fetish' still carries today, but given Perniola's

approval of what he calls 'fetishist love' (64) and the increasing breadth of significations encompassed by the modern use of 'fetish', it seems appropriate to include Perniola's work under this heading.

10 Benjamin, *Reflections*, 153.

11 It is beyond the scope of this book to determine whether this form of sexual experience really is new in modern times, or for that matter whether it has actually been emerging at all. Regardless of the prevailing social scene, Perniola's book introduces a unique dimension of intimacy that deserves to be considered.

12 To be fair to Perniola, he never argues that treating oneself as a 'feeling thing' promises greater capacities for intimacy. Much of his language appeals to immediacy in interpersonal relations, but the primary direction of his argumentation is largely tangent to the dialectic of intimacy.

13 At times this seems to be Perniola's true intention, since he repeatedly emphasizes both the compulsion to transgress the philosophical tradition that treats the owner of the body as a subject and the pleasure to be found in doing so (Perniola, 13).

14 Kant, *Metaphysics of Morals*, Ak. 6: 277. Kant, no doubt, would object to this contract's classification as a fetish, since his reason for treating marriage as such a contract is to avoid the unregulated use of one another's bodies for the purpose of enjoyment, which would constitute an immoral reduction of one's partner to a mere thing (6: 278). With a marriage contract, in contrast, such enjoyment is (at least from a legal perspective) freely bestowed, and thus the spouses recognize one another's freedom. Nevertheless, there is no reason why a contractual sharing of one's body would not constitute fetishism, and indeed, we will see later that promises (of which contracts are a species) can themselves be fetishes.

15 Perhaps sensing this failure of intimacy, Kant cements the marriage relation with a double fetish. Not only is marriage an agreement to use one another's bodies, but it is a *contract* to this effect. Contracts are promises, which (as we will see below) constitute their own form of fetish.

16 Given this affirmation of independent subjectivity, I take Kant's conception of marriage to be destructive not only of intimacy, but of the neutral sexuality to which Perniola takes Kant to be an ambivalent ally (Perniola, 18–20).

17 In an unconventional example of attempting to relate to a partner entirely through her body, Bronwyn Parry tells of 'meeting' Iris Murdoch's brain after it had been donated to the UK Institute of Public Health for scientific research ('Inventing Iris'). While she admits to being put at great unease at the sudden and unexpected intimacy of encountering something that was once an actual piece of Murdoch, she observes that 'my relationship to the scientific object of her archived brain was constructed almost entirely through my relationship with the artifacts, books, films, etc., that were a product of her brain'. In this case, as in so many, physical proximity constitutes one of the least intimate aspects of the relationship. Her relation to Murdoch has thus left the realm of body fetishism and taken on the structure of mourning, which we will address in Chapter 10.

18 This distinction in presentation, I should note, does not reflect the dialectical necessity of each form of fetish's collapse. Neither gets any closer to a 'true' form of intimacy, since the latter does not exist.

19 Seana Shiffrin argues that promises are essential for intimate relations. While I follow her in thinking of promises in terms of intimacy, I would not go so far as to maintain that intimacy is impossible without promises.

20 While he does not use the term 'fetish', Daniel Markovits presents an argument parallel to this one in 'Promise as an Arm's-length Relation'. I agree with Markovits that promises limit intimacy, but I disagree with his assessment that promises and intimacy are two different types of recognition. Formalized promises like contracts inject the dimension of value into a transaction that may otherwise strive to be intimate, but the fact that promises fail to achieve complete intimacy does not separate them from any other moment of the dialectic of intimacy.

21 Kant, *Groundwork*, Ak. 4:403.

22 *Genealogy of Morals,* Essay 2, Section 3; Nietzsche, KSA 5: 295.

23 In many cases, as when a new citizen promises to uphold the laws of her adopted country, promises involve forms of recognition quite different from intimacy, but promises are never exclusively a relation of a self-identical self to a self.

24 This makes a broken promise a special kind of what I will call the dismissal in Chapter 7.

25 Daniel Markovits provides an illuminating discussion of the restrictions that wedding vows place on intimacy (313).

26 Daniel Friedrich and Nicholas Southwood ('Promises and Trust') have argued that the moral obligation of keeping one's promises can be explained entirely in terms of trust, but it would not follow even from this ambitious claim that trust is reducible to any set of promises. A partner can rigidly adhere to every explicit promise she makes and still prove untrustworthy if she is unreliable in other ways.

27 For a reflection on this problematic assumption, see Giddens, 138.

Chapter Six

1 I do not mean to imply by naming these partners with variables that this impossibility is a logical or mathematical impossibility. There is no logical contradiction, for instance, in the claim that a father could at the same time grow closer to his wife because of their relationship to their daughter and closer to his daughter because of their relationship to the wife/mother. Rather, Montaigne's principle of incongruity holds because of how embedding conceives of intimacy. So long as intimacy is understood as an enveloping of the rest of the world, instances of reciprocal embedding are impossible.

2 Deleuze, *The Fold*, 5.

3 Giddens, *The Transformation of Intimacy*, 139.

4 As Levinas explains in *Totality and Infinity*, it is precisely the exclusion of others that makes the erotic relationship so intimate. The sharing of a part of oneself with a single partner marks an active distinction between lovers and the universal community. Because this relationship 'excludes the third party, it remains intimacy, dual solitude, closed society, the supremely non-public '(265). Thus while the intimacy of the erotic relation trades on a secret, the secret only matters because it is a way of breaking the unity of the community as a whole.

5 From the very beginning of this discussion I would like to disavow any resonnances with Lacan's account of the resolution of the Oedipus complex in the figure of the phallus as third term. I am not offering a genetic account of the capacity for intersubjectivity, but exploring the consequences of a decision by two partners who are able to form bonds with others but choose to bond with each other to incorporate another into their relationship. Any Levinasian resonances are also likely to prove shallow.

6 On the book's final page, Françoise (or perhaps the narrator) judges of Xavière: 'everything that she was, she drew from within herself, she barred all dominance over her, she was absolute separateness' (403).

7 Elsewhere, Xavière explains this aversion to attachment as a preference for a gift economy over an exchange economy. When she notes that observing all the work that goes into a play makes it less beautiful to her and Pierre's sister answers that all great works of art require work, she grumbles: '"The things I call precious ... are those that fall like manna from heaven ... If they have to be bought, they're merchandise just like anything else"' (52–3). Here she reveals her preference for the pure possibility of the gift to the intimacy of exchange.

8 Merleau-Ponty, *The Visible and the Invisible*, 81.

9 *The Visible and the Invisible*, 81.

10 See Chapter 1.

11 This is the position Kierkegaard names 'pure irony' in opposition to the 'mastered irony' of a Goethe or Shakespeare. For a reconstruction of Kierkegaard's critique of pure irony, see Brad Frazier, 'Kierkegaard on the Problems of Pure Irony'.

12 Jill Gordon argues that one of the reasons for the character Socrates' special appeal, both to his interlocutors and to readers of Plato, is his ability to make the boundary between insiders and outsiders permeable (*Turning Toward Philosophy*, 128). In the language of embedding I am employing here, Socrates' gift lies in allowing those who have been embedded in the more intimate relationship to join this very process of embedding. As we will see, however, this acknowledgement of irony's permeability is an admission that it can only fail on its own terms.

13 This doubling of meaning does not require the ironist to be abstruse or cryptic, and it often does not require language at all. The public display of affection, for instance, is an ironic gesture that requires no language at all. Whereas the hidden meaning in an ironic statement could potentially be shared by a third party and its surface meaning shared by all competent speakers of the language, the public display of affection announces that it is intended for one person only. The surface meaning makes no gesture toward the immediate situation but announces only its withdrawal from it.

14 Menand, 73. Various references to the date can be found in Joyce's *Letters*.

15 If he simply reminded her of the significance, the act would lose the force of irony, since would no longer be a message delivered in a way only she could understand, but would be a simple secret.

16 Cf. Aristotle, *Nicomachean Ethics*, 1100a.

17 Kierkegaard, *The Concept of Irony*, 152.

18 Barthes, *A Lover's Discourse*, 1

19 This line of escape is one that Wallace anticipates in the story but closes off for metaphysical reasons. In the third part of the next chapter I explore how debate seeks intimacy in the search for mutually agreeable reasons. Wallace's narrator (or rather, both narrators, since a stand-in for Wallace himself turns out to be a hidden narrator) chooses not to pursue the course, since natural language inevitably fails to express thoughts completely. (The preferability of the language of formal logic is suggested off-hand, and it is difficult to know how seriously to take it.) I will discuss the implications of the inevitable incompleteness of reason-giving in the next chapter.

Chapter Seven

1 This is the mirror image of what I am calling the dismissal. Instead of pretending to dismiss you knowing that you'll know I'm really accepting you, in this case I am pretending to fail to come to intimate terms with you knowing you'll know that I know that the failure is necessary. Since this case involves a complex combination of embedding and conflict, it straddles the preceding and present chapters.

2 See Roberts, 'From Bickering to Battering' for a review of the psychological literature on conflict and intimacy. Roberts's foundational distinction between destructive and constructive conflict would be out of place in the present dialectical study, since it assumes that relationships can be assessed according to their relative success in measuring up to a given *telos*.

3 It should go without saying that I do not intend to endorse any therapeutic consequences of the observation that intimacy can be pursued through conflict.

4 Hegel, *Phenomenology of Spirit*, ¶178. Hegel, *Vorlesungen* 13: 175.

5 Hegel, *Phänomenologie*, 96, ¶157. See Gadamer, *Hegel's Dialectic*, 35–53 for a discussion of the role of the inverted world in Hegel's system.

6 'For all forms of [friendship] that are forged and nourished by pleasure or profit, by public or private necessity, are so much the less beautiful and noble – and so much the less friendships – in that they bring in some purpose, end or fruition other than friendship itself' (*On Friendship*, 3).

7 Consider also *Rameau's Nephew*: 'Virtue makes itself respected, and respect is uncomfortable.'

8 See Lauer, 'Kierkegaard and Aristophanes on the Suspension of Irony' for an argument defending this claim.

9 See, e.g. Gordon, *Turning Toward Philosophy*, 131.

10 A scene on a lobster trawler reveals that fishermen call lobster cages 'bedrooms' and that storing three lobsters in the same bedroom frequently causes fights.

11 The dispute is thus distinct from what Jessica Benjamin has called 'anti-play': that moment in the interaction between mother and baby in which frustration with the other's inability to respond adequately results in a mutual failure of recognition (*Bonds of Love*, 28). The dispute is not a withdrawal from the partner for her differences, but an active attempt to bring these differences to the fore.

12 Here I will reemphasize that the sequence I am describing is dialectical, not psychological. I am not making an empirical claim about the psychological causes of violence (which I suspect are manifold), but explaining how the very concept of intimacy implies the possibility of violence.

13 Bowlby gives some particularly heartbreaking examples of withdrawal (which he calls 'detachment behavior') in young children who, having been left in residential nurseries, resisted reuniting with their mothers to the detriment of both (*Loss*, 20).

14 Barthes describes the longing built into the withdrawal: 'the hiding must be seen: *I want you to know that I am hiding something from you*, that is the active paradox I must resolve' (*A Lover's Discourse*, 42).

15 See Baracchi, 23 for an explanation of how philosophical friendship transcends mere engagement with common interests. Baracchi contends that for Aristotle friendship is never merely an engagement with common concerns, but always exceeds the limits of individuality.

16 In my choice of examples I do not mean to imply that scientific discussion in general does not take on the dialectical structure of what I am calling 'debate'. Honest, some of my best friends are scientists!

17 Since philosophers have concerned themselves with the process of debate at least since Xenophanes, it might seem flippant to treat it here so cursorily. The second half of the twentieth century in particular saw a wealth of theories like Habermas's and Grice's that sought to analyse the various social assumptions and imperatives that structure even the simplest debates, and the present account cannot hope to add any depth to them. Instead, it aims to show which parts of these theories help inform a dialectic of intimacy and which must be accounted for through other approaches.

18 While disagreement is generally the most salient feature of debate, James Crosswhite notes that we generally pay 'quite remarkable deference' to one another's initial claims (*Rhetoric of Reason*, 62). While debate requires a good faith search for grounds of disagreement, it also involves a great deal of agreeing to common assumptions.

19 Crosswhite, 115.

20 The present dialectic says nothing about the desirability of ideal speech situations in general, since they would frame a public debate whose object is something other than intimacy.

21 Generally the debaters will not be able to specify in advance what makes a reasons belong to one category rather than another, but if every possible reason is acceptable to both parties, then there is no debate.

Chapter Eight

1 While war and sex tend to serve the imagination as paradigmatic examples of the intimacy of the *mêlée*, Nancy notes that their modern forms for the most part have lost the form of the *mêlée*: 'modern war begins by exterminating hand-to-hand combat; it aims to crush and suppress combat, rather than attempting to set it aside … Today, war is an unlimited and *pure mélange. It is not the mêlée.* With regard to orgies and porn films, the same can be said of the *mêlée* of Aphrodite' (BSP 150). For Nancy, the most visible manifestations of modern sexuality have lost the *mêlée*'s taste for recognizing individuality as it undermines it. The empirical side of Nancy's claim is beyond the scope of the present investigation, but it does show that the *mêlée*'s conception of intimacy is not easily won.

2 The Greek ὀργιασμός would have been a pretty decent translation of what I mean by *mêlée*. As Schelling notes in his late lectures on the *Philosophy of Mythology*, the Greek ὀργή carried senses of anger and wrath as well as sexual connotations (11: 351–2; see also Krell, *Tragic Absolute*, 203). Yet in contemporary English 'orgiastic' has been so overwhelmed by a sense that takes bodies as commodities that it is hard to hear anything besides such commoditization.

3 As Nancy uses the term, '*mêlée*' is primarily a political term that refers to the nonidentity of people who nevertheless find themselves together. In this chapter I examine the development of non-identical togetherness in more localized relationships, but since the togetherness of the *mêlée* is dialectically prior to political differentiation, our divergence in how we use the term is not as great as it initially seems. Our larger divergence lies instead in my resistance to Nancy's ontological approach to the *mêlée*, which analyses it as a condition for all possible culture and community.

4 We have already addressed versions of the *mêlée* in the rupture, Perniola's neutral sexuality, and the dispute, but none of these explores the full radicality of the conjunction of the *mêlée*.

5 Thus Nancy notes that every event is a 'surprise' (BSP 159).

6 As someone who has been both a teenager and underemployed, the latter more recently than the former, I can attest that when a party's participants have less experience balancing the books in their professional lives, there is a concordant lack of scruples at pure consumption.

7 It would make no difference if we were actually working together in our destructive activity. Even in working together to overturn a car, delinquents still must fixate on the objects they are destroying, and their activity reduces to their private contributions of force and anger. Bataille, in contrast, takes the suspended fetishization involved in destruction and waste as an explanation of its intimacy: 'Sacrifice particularly, is in essence, as we have seen, the ritual violation of a taboo; the whole process of religion entails the paradox of a rule regularly broken in certain circumstances' (*Erotism*, 109). For Bataille, what I am calling alienation is actually a form of *ritual*. But while the establishment and perpetuation of such rituals does indeed involve communal action, neither the transgression of taboos nor the activity of destruction is shared in any real way among the group members.

8 There is, of course, much more that could be said about destruction and waste in the dialectic of intimacy. While they are dead ends as contributors to the intimacy of a *mêlée*, they appear at so many other moments that they constitute a kind of rhyme in the dialectic. Gifts, for instance, can gain a sense of purity if they are distanced from utilitarian concerns, but as Bataille observes, this purity is only intelligible as a reaction against the very fetishism they reenact. Jewels, for instance, are suitable gifts because they are useless, but this uselessness only becomes glorious because it reflects the relative insignificance of the partners: 'jewels, like excrement, are cursed matter that flows from a wound: they are a part of oneself destined for open sacrifice (they serve, in fact, as sumptuous gifts charged with sexual love). The functional character of jewels requires their immense material value and alone explains the inconsequence of the most beautiful imitations, which are very nearly useless' (Bataille, *Visions of Excess* 119). We should thus be careful to avoid treating any stage of the dialectic of intimacy as superseded by another. While the *mêlée* must be understood by the way it contrasts itself with previous stages, the case of extravagant gifts of jewellery shows that the very movement of fetishism and futility of gift-giving can enhance the breakdown sought in the *mêlée*.

9 Working from some of the studies from Panksepp et al. that I cited in Chapter 2, Gervais and Wilson argue that laughter developed in early hominids as 'a medium for playful emotional contagion' (306). The metaphor of an emotional contagion is an appealing one in that it evokes laughter's communicability, but it also implies that emotions are just sitting dormant in each of us waiting for a vector in which they may be shared. Insofar as tickling brings intimacy to both the tickling and tickled partners, it is never simply a sharing of emotions, but a demonstration of the vulnerability of one partner. We like to tickle and be tickled because touching by itself is never enough to establish an intimacy between two partners. Humour, likewise, fosters a kind of playful contagion, but there are plenty of kinds of emotional contagion that do not make us laugh. Since Duchenne laughter is mostly confined to cases of tickling, irony and humour, I suspect that Gervais and Wilson are generally correct that signalling a lack of seriousness plays a key role in laughter, but there is undoubtedly more work to be done.

10 *Critique of Judgment*, Ak. 5: 332.

11 Provine and Fischer 293; Gervais and Wilson, 399. Phenomenologically, the claim that we never laugh alone seems vastly overblown. Even if I exclude

all those cases when I am laughing with an imagined or virtual human being on TV or in a book, I can still easily recall instances of bubbly private laughter.

12 Hurley et al., 109.

13 See Colebrook, 220.

14 In 'The Festive Character of Theater', Gadamer also finds that the common thread in contemporary festivals and their Dionysian roots is their disruption of ordinary temporality (*Relevance of the Beautiful*, 61; see also *Truth and Method*, 122–3). The festival is neither a simple recollection of some historical event nor a repetition of it nor a forgetting of it. While there are some resemblances between Gadamer's analysis and the one I am presenting here, he is describing primarily the role of festivals in cultivating solidarity rather than intimacy. Seen from the standpoint of solidarity, the festival suspends the insistence on the group's eternity found in many other religious rites, and its appeal thus lies in the group's narrative of self-becoming rather than the promise of intimacy.

15 A key exception to this trend in rave music is dubstep music, which emphasizes its playfulness with time signatures by oscillating between melodies and breakdowns in melodies. This oscillation reinstitutes traditional pop music's regular movements between verse, chorus and bridge and thus strives more for a perversion of time than the anti-time of trance music.

16 Thus while I share Bataille's sense for the close relation among orgies, death cults and festivals, I think he is being one-sided when he claims that in each of these forms 'Erotic activity, by dissolving the separate beings that participate in it, reveals their fundamental continuity, like the waves of a stormy sea' (*Erotism*, 22). While the frenzy seeks to restore the continuity that underlies all differentiation, it never succeeds in 'revealing' any such continuity, but strives to find a way to posit it without losing the conditions under which intimacy might be established. If anything is revealed in this process, it is the vast amount of energy that goes into both the establishing and the suspending of the distinctions of individual identity.

17 Bataille covers over this distinction in his statement that laughter sums up the very meaning of the festival (*Accursed Share*, II: 90). For Bataille, the orgiastic festival restores a lost intimacy not by breaking its participants down to their animal essences, but by renouncing this essence as transcended by the community. I would argue, however, that the ecstasy of the festival (frenzy) is distinct from the ecstasy of laughter. While each involves a renunciation of essences, the frenzy offers no time or space in which to share this renunciation.

18 For a reflection on the role of transgression in the cultivation of intimacy, see David Allison, 83–98.

19 The same applies if we seek the intimacy of the *mêlée* in a purely sexual realm. While simultaneous orgasm is nothing to sneeze at by itself, it only takes on its mythic value in combination with some ideal (a future together, an elevation of pleasure as a principle, etc.).

Chapter Nine

1 *Works of Love*, 48.

2 Note in this example that a commitment does not necessarily require reciprocation. While it would not be a commitment if both I and my students did not understand what it means for me to be committed to them as their teacher, this requirement does not require them to make any reciprocal commitment to me. The practical activity of education of course requires them to put work in to learn, but my commitment to them could exist regardless of this work.

3 *Sein und Zeit*, 122. While the intimacy of planning requires the kind of care involved in Heidegger's 'leaping ahead', it is not identical with it. While Heidegger is doubtlessly right that purporting to know what is best for one's partner closes of the possibility of openness to her future, leaping ahead of her as he conceives it is also an isolating activity insofar as it serves to highlight the *Jemeinigkeit* and constitutive guilt of Dasein. Heidegger of course saw this and maintained that because it is always founded on a being-toward-death that recognizes death is always my own, authenticity itself involves a withdrawal from others (though not from the existential structure of *Mitsein*). While this calls attention to the essential rupture of intimacy as was discussed above in Chapter 4, it does not yield any resources for thinking of intimacy as a comparative concept – that a given relationship can be more or less intimate than others.

4 I tried to show in Chapter 7's discussion of the debate that debate cannot be understood as common activity toward a common end because it continually defers the grounds of commonality to more distant reasons. Even when both partners treat the adversarial structure of a debate as a mutually agreeable one oriented to the common ends of mutual understanding and greater knowledge, this adversarial structure cannot be entirely suspended.

5 Another possible interpretation of the complaint is that in order for the action to count as a genuine gift, it must be offered without a preceding negotiation or shared inquiry into propriety; it has to come purely from the giver and straightforwardly to the receiver. In this case the complaint would obviously fall under the dialectic of the gift.

6 There is plenty of evidence that close identification of two partners allows feelings to pass from one partner to the other more easily (see, e.g., Iacobini), but *qua* individual experiences they are private no matter how widely shared.

7 Helm makes a similar point about identification being possible even when partners approach an activity with different goals (271), but to resolve the problem he introduces elements of value and community that I consider out of place in a dialectical account of intimacy.

8 Cynthia Willett makes the related point that the creation of a future equally requires the creation of a past. She observes that friendships and marriages require 'creating a sense of a past together' just as much as multicultural democracies do (100).

9 This is not to say that there is no intimacy at all in such identification, but merely that it is better understood according to the hypothesis of a commitment than the hypothesis of identification. The child could recognize the parent's commitment to her future without attempting to accommodate that future to the parent's.

10 Hegel, *Vorlesungen*, 171–2.

11 In such a scenario, the only thing that could differentiate one relationship into which the possibility of walking away has been built from the beginning from others would be if it were designated by an expression of commitment, which would reintroduce the dilemma shown above.

12 I realize that this argument from dilemma has an air of sophistry about it and that dividing up decisions into positive and negative possibilities introduces a distinction in word that may not actually be present in fact. When partners identify with a common future, do they *really* open up an entire realm of unchosen lives? This question has lost sight of the dialectical role of identification. I am not trying to determine the metaphysical status of a relationship that seeks intimacy in identification with the future, but to show that this very search supposes an incoherent sense of being together. Identification must posit *some* sense in which the future is shared, and whatever sense it chooses gives rise to contradictions.

13 In the context of mourning her mother's loss even before she has died, Meghan O'Rourke cites the Bashō haiku:

Even in Kyoto –

Hearing the cuckoo's cry –

I long for Kyoto. (O'Rourke, 112)

14 *Beyond the Pleasure Principle*, 8–10.

Chapter Ten

1 What follows is not exactly a phenomenology of mourning, or if it is, it is the sort of phenomenology that Hegel practises – one informed and mediated by reading and not intending to memorialize any individual experience. Subjective reports of mourning often highlight its privacy and ineffability and thus straddle the boundary between irony and a dismissal of the reader. The following chapter grew out of an attempt to reestablish intimacy with (a few) mourners and thus develops a kind of dialectical approach that direct phenomenology of mourning generally rejects.

2 Augustine, *Confessions* IV.vi.11, 59. See Cassidy, '*Le phénomène érotique*', 213.

3 While the possibility of a very brief or unobserved period in which one partner survives the other still points to a structural flaw in the conception of intimacy we saw in the last chapter, it also shows, as we will see below, that mourning is not a necessary constituent of any relationship – even very close ones.

4 Bataille, *Erotism*, 101.

5 Bataille, *Erotism*, 20.

6 Though he uses the term 'intimacy' differently than I do, Bataille generally agrees that the goals of eroticism are antithetical to closeness and togetherness. When he states that his 'starting point is that eroticism is a solitary activity' (*Erotism*, 252), he means not only that pairs of lovers tend to isolate themselves from others, but that erotic drives tend to isolate lovers from each other.

7 If mourning provides any kind of ethical education, this is even less relevant to intimacy. Kierkegaard's ideal of mourning, for instance, envisions the truest of all loving relationships as only an indirect relationship to the dead. He asks us to practise loving the dead because doing so shows the absoluteness necessary to any love: 'One who uses this criterion will with ease abbreviate the prolixity of the most complicated relationship, and he will learn to loathe the mass of excuses which actual life usually has right at hand to explain that it is the other person who is selfish, the other person who is guilty of being forgotten because he does not bring himself into remembrance, the other person who is faithless' (*Works of Love*, 328). This call to 'practise' is likely to strike the mourner as mordantly funny: 'How desperately they try to pretend that the world hasn't been ripped in two.' Kierkegaard's earnestness in reminding the reader that 'our duty toward the dead cannot separate our contemporaries from us so that they do not remain objects of our love' (329) seems to miss the rivenness of the mourner's world entirely.

8 Nancy, *Birth to Presence*, 3–4

9 It is, to be sure, possible to think dialectically and express oneself differently. For instance, one can follow a dialectic without seeking to thematize it philosophically, but this requires poetic gesturing in place of the more traditional type of philosophical explication I am presenting here.

10 Kristeva, *Black Sun*, 6.

11 Parkes (1987) seeks to explain such behaviour in terms of a 'searching' instinct that humans share with the greylag goose, among other species (61). Because we are social animals, we seek to restore contact with those who are missing and thus circle around looking for them, even if we know consciously that we will never find them. While this hypothesis has significant explanatory potential, it treats intimacy as the goal of the searching rather than the activity of searching itself.

12 Meghan O'Rourke writes that her grief shared many characteristics with depression, with the crucial exception that 'the world appeared to me in heightened, shimmering outlines, like a mirage. At times it seemed excruciatingly beautiful, a place I never wanted to leave' (140).

13 Augustine offers another memorable account of the jealousy sparked by frustrated gathering: 'My eyes looked for him everywhere, and he was not there. I hated everything because they did not have him, nor could they now tell me "look, he is on the way", as used to be the case when he was alive and absent to me' (Augustine, *Confessions* IV.iv.9, 57).

14 Since Carson herself uses the term it seems the only appropriate descriptor, though the various notes and reproductions stretch the sense of the term.

15 Barthes, 'A Cruel Country', 27.

16 Ibid. It feels small and pedantic for me even to mention this in light of the evident beauty of Barthes's reflection on his own mortality in light of his mother's, but enough commentators have called attention to Barthes's reference in *Camera Lucida* to his 'total, undialectical death' (72) that I think I should explain why I think it is misleading in the context of mourning. By 'undialectical death' I (and Derrida in his own reflection on Barthes [*The Work of Mourning*, 50]) take Barthes to mean that, like his mother's, his own death presents no higher truth, but only the annihilation of truth. This presumes that to view a phenomenon dialectically is always to be looking for what greater abstract truth it reveals. But this is not how my own models of dialectical thinking (primarily Hegel and Beauvoir, but also, more distantly, Plato, Schelling and Marx) actually proceed. For Hegel in particular, there are quite a few dialectical moments (including death itself) that produce no higher truth than their own lack of fulfilment. As we saw in Chapter 6, even irony's effort to suspend the dialectic is not falsified simply by being considered dialectically.

17 Levinas, *Otherwise than Being*, 3.

18 See especially Joan Didion and C. S. Lewis's accounts of their respective spouses' deaths.

19 Barthes provides a memorable account of the sheer boredom of mourning in *Camera Lucida*.

20 *The Freud Reader*, 501, 507.

21 Thus while my approach in this chapter is not at all 'Freudian' or psychoanalytic, I do not think my reading of Freud is an especially unfaithful one. While I take Freud's aim in the essay to be working through some thorny issues on the way to a more developed psychoanalytic theory, his consideration of various explanations is hypothetical – that is to say, dialectical.

22 Linking mourning to melancholia, Kristeva frames this as the central question of the despairing soul: 'Where does this black sun come from? Out of what eerie galaxy do its invisible, lethargic rays reach me, pinning me down to the ground, to my bed, compelling me to silence, to renunciation?' (*Black Sun*, 3).

23 In 'On Transience', written the same year (1915) as 'Mourning and Melancholia', Freud displays similar sympathy and expresses similar doubts about psychology's ability to understand the process of mourning: 'Mourning over the loss of something we have loved or admired seems so natural to the layman that he regards it as self-evident. But to psychologists mourning is a great riddle, one of those phenomena which cannot themselves be explained but to which other obscurities can be traced back' (14: 306).

24 In a similar vein, but for vastly different systematic reasons, Bataille writes: 'If it sees its fellow-being die, a living being can only subsist *outside* itself' (Bataille, *Oeuvres Complètes*, vol. 7: 245). Like Marion, Bataille finds an educational role not just for the knowledge that one's partner is mortal, but for experiencing the moment of her death. Yet this announces more the access to the other through rupture (a modification of the between) than genuine mourning.

25 For Heidegger in *Being and Time*, because I cannot appropriate another's death, no matter how much care is evinced in commemorating the dead, this commemoration is always a relation to something with the mode of being of objective presence (*Vorhandenheit*) rather than Dasein (*Being and* Time, 230; *Sein und* Zeit, 238). Heidegger makes an important point in criticizing the observation that, even as others die, life goes on as an obfuscation of the possibility of my own impossibility (cf. Marion, *Being Given*, 58). But this does not imply that the only way I can encounter another Dasein who has died is as something objectively present. We do not need to be acute ontologists to recognize the absencing in the appearance of our dead partner or to wish to commemorate their singularity.

26 On the other hand, mourning tends to disrupt intimacy with the outside world because it produces a secret that cannot be shared. Meghan O'Rourke remarks that while Americans 'have become more open about everything from incest to sex addiction, grief remains strangely taboo' (13), but this is not so strange. When we talk about these other things, we share a secret, and, according to the logic of the secret, the farther from mainstream experiences they are, the more intimate their discussion is. With mourning, however, distance from the empathizer is built into the very act of 'sharing'. The mourner in effect says: 'I am bereaved; I am riven. For the time being, at least, I am incapable of connecting with anyone but the one I have lost' – including, presumably, the one with whom the mourner is speaking.

27 Brault and Naas in Derrida, *The Work of Mourning*, 16.

28 Derrida, *The Work of Mourning*, 225. I should probably pause to note here that the present dialectical account is not troubled by these scruples, especially in light of how deeply informed this account is by Derrida's own writings on mourning, which clearly were troubled by them. Dialectical thinking wants to explore every moment of a dialectic as it appears, but this does not mean that it wants to be intimate with it, much less to mourn it. While I am not reappropriating the experience of mourning for any *particular aim*, dialectics is nevertheless a kind of reappropriation in the sense that it cannot help but treat history hypothetically – that is, as structured by a logic other than its singularity. On the other hand, it should also be noted that this dialectical approach sidesteps Derrida's entire set of worries about the 'success' or 'failure' of an act or expression of mourning (*Memoires*, 35). For while one might feel a sense of ethical responsibility to express the meaning of a dead friend's life, both in some 'objective' sense and in terms that the friend herself would understand and appreciate, this sense of responsibility is not entailed by a drive for intimacy. Since every moment of the dialectic of intimacy after the fetish assumes that it is never possible for partners to achieve unanimity, and at least the last four require a willingness to suspend respect for what one's partner values, it is not necessarily a failure of intimacy to reflect on one's partner in one's own terms.

29 See, e.g., *The Work of Mourning*, 107.

30 Blanchot, *Unavowable Community*, 5.

31 Butler, *Precarious Life*, 30. I suspect that there are significant limitations to a politics of mourning that I intend to pursue in a future book, but for now I will just note that Butler's more ambitious claim that possibility of grief unites us all as humans (*Precarious Life*, 20) concerns solidarity, a form of recognition outside of a dialectic of intimacy.

32 Jameson, *Valences of the Dialectic*, 279.

33 While I have been treating Hegel's dialectical approach, especially his comments on the spatialization of the dialectic at the end of the *Phenomenology of Spirit*, as a model for my own approach, Hegel himself was not always so liberal and at times suggests that every dialectical transition he describes is necessary. Stephen Houlgate (*Introduction to Hegel*) gives the strongest reading of Hegel in this direction I have seen. But in addition to the comments in 'Absolute Knowing' that I have already referenced, Hegel also presents some powerful examples showing that the successor of a dialectical stage is not necessarily its destiny. Jean-Luc Nancy usefully distinguishes between Hegel's account of the end of art in philosophy and a tendency in the 1980s to view the sublime as the destiny of art (*A Finite Thinking*, 214). Whereas the latter thinkers and artists claimed to find something essential in art that guides it toward self-effacing sublimity, Hegel claimed instead to show that art does not meet its own aims of transparent self-presentation. Given the density of Hegel's various accounts of absolute spirit, this is easy to miss, but he never claims that philosophy is the *destiny* of art, but merely its successor. Similarly, my project cannot pretend to find a destiny for intimacy, but can only hope to expose its structural limitations. While my tight focus will prevent me from addressing the interesting and important question of how the drive for intimacy derives from the structure of self-consciousness, and in particular the drive for recognition, it at least prevents any attempt to overreach the phenomenon and find an *essence* of intimacy.

Afterword

1 Indeed, deconstructionists like Derrida and Nancy have been much more consistent on this count than dialecticians, who only intermittently recognized the imperative of modesty in assessing his philosophical accomplishments (*Phenomenology of Spirit*, §807; *Phänomenologie des Geistes*, 433).

2 Derrida in particular was frequently vexed by this shallow interpretation of his work. See *Limited Inc*, 46 for a sample response.

3 See my *Suspension of Reason*, 102–3 for my take on this hoary term. Gabriel and Žižek offer a useful summary of the relation of the role of subjective self-alienation in Schelling's positive philosophy (6–7).

4 In acknowledging this haunting, I am sympathetic to Derrida and Jameson's claim that there is something perversely nostalgic about Western ontology's longing to eliminate all ghosts. Marx's mistake, Derrida asserts and Jameson reiterates, is that 'he wants to get rid of ghosts, he thinks he can do so, and he also thinks it is desirable to do so. But a world cleansed of spectrality is precisely ontology itself; a world of pure presence, of immediate density, of things without a past' (Jameson, *Valences of the Dialectic,* 173; cf. Derrida, *Specters of Marx*, 83). As we saw in Chapter 9, the past need not appear in a ghost-like form, but its appearance in mourning shows that it is also not simply a matter of choice whether to see these ghosts.

Bibliography

Abramson, K. and A. Leite. 'Love as a Reactive Emotion', *Philosophical Quarterly* 61 (245) (2011): 673–99.

Allison, D. 'Transgression and the Community of the Sacred'. In A. Mitchell and J. Winfree, eds., *The Obsessions of Georges Bataille: Community and Communication*, 83–98. Albany, NY: SUNY Press, 2009.

Aristotle. *On the Soul*, trans. J. Sachs. Santa Fe: Green Lion Press, 2001.

Aristotle. *Nicomachean Ethics*, trans. J. Sachs. Newburyport, MA: Focus Publishing, 2002.

Augustine. *Confessions*, trans. H. Chadwick. New York: Oxford University Press, 1991.

Baracchi, C. 'Politics and the Perfection of Friendship: Aristotelian Reflections'. *Universitas Philosophica* 53 (26) (2009): 15–36.

Barthes, R. 'A Cruel Country: Notes on Mourning', trans. R. Howard, *The New Yorker*. 13 September 2010.

Barthes, R. *Camera Lucida: Reflections on Photography*, trans. R. Howard. New York: Hill and Wang, 2010.

Barthes, R. *A Lover's Discourse: Fragments*, trans. R. Howard. New York: Hill and Wang, 2010.

Bataille, G. *Visions of Excess*, trans. A. Stoekl. Minneapolis: University of Minnesota Press, 1985.

Bataille, G. *Erotism: Death and Sensuality*, trans. M. Dalwood. San Francisco: City Lights Books, 1986.

Bataille, G. *The Accursed Share, Volume 1*, trans. R. Hurley. New York: Zone Books, 2001.

Beauvoir, S. de. *L'invitée*. Paris: Gallimard, 1943.

Beauvoir, S. de. *The Ethics of Ambiguity*, trans. B. Frechtman. New York: Kensington Publishing, 1976.

Beauvoir, S. de. *She Came to Stay*, unsigned translation. London: W. W. Norton, 1999.

Beauvoir, S. de. *The Second Sex*, trans. C. Borde and S. Malovany-Chevallier. New York: Alfred A. Knopf, 2010.

Benjamin, J. *The Bonds of Love: Psychoanalysis, Feminism, and the Problem of Domination*. New York: Pantheon Books, 1988.

Benjamin, J. *Like Subjects, Love Objects*. New Haven: Yale University Press, 1995.

Benjamin, J. 'Response to Commentaries by Mitchell and Butler', *Studies in Gender and Sexuality* 1 (3) (2000).

Benjamin, W. *Reflections: Essays, Aphorisms, Autobiographical Writings*, ed. P. Demetz. New York: Harcourt Brace Jovanovich, 1978.

Bergson, H. *Laughter: An Essay on the Meaning of the Comic*, trans.
C. Brereton and F. Rothwell. New York: Richard West, 1977.

Blanchot, M. *The Unavowable Community*, trans. P. Joris. Barrytown, NY: Station Hill Press, 1988.

Bourdieu, P. *The Logic of Practice*, trans. R. Nice. Stanford, CA: Stanford University Press, 1990.

Bourdieu, P. 'Marginalia—Some Additional Notes on the Gift', trans. R. Nice. In A. D. Schrift, ed., *The Logic of the Gift: Toward an Ethic of Generosity*. New York: Routledge, 1997.

Bourdieu, P. *Outline of a Theory of Practice*, trans. R. Nice. Cambridge: Cambridge University Press, 1977.

Bowlby, J. *Loss: Sadness and Depression*. New York: Basic Books, 1980.

Bowlby, J. *Attachment*. New York: Basic Books, 1983.

Braun, J. 'Modernity and Intimacy', *Culture and Society* 47 (2010): 257.

Butler, J. 'Longing for Recognition: Studies on the Work of Jessica Benjamin', *Studies in Gender and Sexuality* 1 (3) (2000): 271–90.

Butler, J. *Precarious Life: The Powers of Mourning and Violence*. London: Verso, 2004.

Caputo, J. D. and M. J. Scanlon, eds. *God, The Gift, and Postmodernism*. Bloomington: Indiana University Press, 1999.

Cassidy, E. '*Le phénomène érotique*: Augustinian Resonances in Marion's Phenomenology of Love'. in I. Leask and E. Cassidy, eds. *Givenness and God: Questions of Jean-Luc Marion*, 201–19. New York: Fordham University Press, 2005.

Ciavatta, D. 'The Unreflective Bonds of Intimacy: Hegel on Familial Ties and the Modern Person', *The Philosophical Forum* 37 (2) (2006): 153–81.

Clark, M. S. and J. K. Monin. 'Giving and Receiving Communal Responsiveness as Love'. In R. J. Sternberg and K. Weis, eds., *The New Psychology of Love*, 200–24. New Haven, CT: Yale University Press, 2006.

Colebrook, C. *Irony in the Work of Philosophy*. Lincoln: University of Nebraska Press, 2002.

Crosswhite, J. *The Rhetoric of Reason: Writing and the Attractions of Argument*. Madison: University of Wisconsin Press, 1996.

Darwin, C. *The Expression of the Emotions in Man and Animals*. New York: D. Appleton & Company, 1872.

Deleuze, G. and F. Guattari. *Anti-Oedipus: Capitalism and Schizophrenia*, trans. R. Hurley et al. Minneapolis: University of Minnesota Press, 1983.

Derrida, J. *Limited Inc*, trans. Samuel Weber. Evanston: Northwestern University Press, 1988.

Derrida, J. *Memoires for Paul de Man*. New York: Columbia University Press, 1989.

Derrida, J. *Given Time I: Counterfeit Money*, trans. P. Kamuf. Chicago: University of Chicago Press, 1992.

Derrida, J. *The Work of Mourning*, eds. P.-A. Brault and M. Naas. Chicago: University of Chicago Press, 2001.

Derrida, J. *On Touching – Jean-Luc Nancy*, trans. C. Irizarry. Stanford: Stanford University Press, 2005.

Descartes, R. *The Passions of the Soul*, trans. S. H. Voss. Indianapolis: Hackett, 1989.

Didion, J. *The Year of Magical Thinking*. New York: Vintage, 2007.

Eppel, A. B. *Sweet Sorrow: Love, Loss and Attachment in Human Life*. London: Karnac Books, 2009.

Feuerbach, L. 'Towards a Critique of Hegel's Philosophy'. In L. Stepelevich, ed., *The Young Hegelians*, 95–128. Amherst, NY: Humanity Books, 1997.

Fichte, J. G. *Grundlage des Naturrechts nach Principien der Wissenschaftslehre*. Werke 3. Berlin: Walter de Gruyter, 1971.

Fisher, H. *Why We Love: The Nature and Chemistry of Romantic Love*. New York: Holt Publishing, 2004.

Frazier, B. 'Kierkegaard on the Problems of Pure Irony', *Journal of Religious Ethics* 32 (3): 417–47.

Freud, S. 'Mourning and Melancholia', trans. J. Strachey. *Standard Edition of Complete Psychological Works of Sigmund Freud*, vol. 14, 239–60. London: Hogarth Press, 1957.

Freud, S. *Beyond the Pleasure Principle*, trans. J. Strachey. New York: W. W. Norton, 1961.

Freud, S. *The Freud Reader*, ed. P. Gay. New York: W. W. Norton, 1985.

Friedrich, D. and N. Southwood. 'Promises and Trust'. In H. Sheinman, ed., *Promises and Agreements: Philosophical Essays*, 277–94. Oxford: Oxford University Press, 2011.

Friend, T. 'First Banana: Steve Carell and the Meticulous Art of Spontaneity', *The New Yorker*, 5 July 2010, 50–9.

Gabriel, M. and S. Žižek. *Mythology, Madness and Laughter: Subjectivity in German Idealism*. London: Continuum, 2009.

Gadamer, H. G. *Hegel's Dialectic: Five Hermeneutical Studies*, trans. P. C. Smith. New Haven: Yale University Press, 1976.

Gadamer, H. G. 'Dialectic and Sophism in Plato's *Seventh Letter*'. In *Dialogue and Dialectic: Eight Hermeneutical Studies on Plato*, trans. P. C. Smith. New Haven: Yale University Press, 1980.

Gadamer, H. G. *The Relevance of the Beautiful and Other Essays*, ed. R. Bernasconi. Cambridge: Cambridge University Press, 1986.

Gadamer, H. G. *Truth and Method*, trans. J. Wensheimer and D. G. Marshall. New York: Continuum, 2003.

Galchen, R. *Atmospheric Disturbances*. New York: Picador Press, 2008.

Gervais, M. and David S. Wilson. 'The Evolution of Laughter and Humor: A Synthetic Approach', *The Quarterly Review of Biology* 80 (4) (2005): 395–429.

Giddens, A. *The Transformation of Intimacy: Sexuality, Love and Eroticism in Modern Societies*. Stanford: Stanford University Press, 1992.

Godelier, M. 'Some Things You Give, Some Things You Sell, but Some Things You Must Keep for Yourselves: What Mauss Did Not Say about Sacred Objects'. In E. Wyschgrod et al., eds., *The Enigma of the Gift*, 19–37. New York: Fordham University Press, 2002.

Gordon, J. *Turning Toward Philosophy: Literary Device and Dramatic Structure in Plato's Dialogues*. University Park, Pennsylvania: Penn State Press, 1999.

Gordon, J. *Plato's Erotic World: From Cosmic Origins to Human Death*. Cambridge: Cambridge University Press, 2012.

Halling, S. *Intimacy, Transcendence, and Psychology*. New York: Palgrave Macmillan, 2008.

Hegel, G. W. F. *Phänomenologie des Geistes. Gesammelte Werke, Bd. 9*, eds. Nordrhein-Westfälischen Akademie der Wissenschaften. Hamburg: Felix MeinerVerlag, 1980.

Hegel, G. W. F. *Phenomenology of Spirit*, trans. A. V. Miller. Oxford: Oxford University Press, 1977.

Hegel, G. W. F. *Philosophy of Right*, trans. A. White. Newburyport, MA: Focus Publishing, 2002.

Hegel, G. W. F. *Vorlesungen Bd. 13: Vorlesungen* über die Philosophie des Geistes Berlin 1827/1828. Hamburg: Felix Meiner Verlag, 1994.

Heidegger, M. *Sein und Zeit*. Tübingen: Max Niemeier Verlag, 2001.

Heidegger, M. *Being and Time*, trans. J. Stambaugh. Albany, NY: SUNY Press, 2010.

Helm, B. W. *Love, Friendship, and the Self: Intimacy, Identification, and the Social Nature of Persons*. Oxford: Oxford University Press, 2010.

Honneth, A. *The Struggle for Recognition: The Moral Grammar of Social Conflicts*, trans. Joel Anderson. Cambridge, MA: MIT Press, 1995.

Houlgate, S. *An Introduction to Hegel: Freedom, Truth, and History*. London: Wiley-Blackwell, 2005.

Hurley, M. M., D. Dennett and R. Adams. *Inside Jokes: Using Humor to Reverse-Engineer the Mind*. Cambridge, MA: MIT Press, 2011.

Hyde, L. *The Gift: How the Creative Spirit Transforms the World*. Edinburgh: Canongate, 2007.

Iacobini, M. *Mirroring People: The Science of Empathy and How We Connect with Others*. New York: Picador, 2009.

Irigaray, L. *An Ethics of Sexual Difference*, trans. C. Burke and G. C. Gill. Ithaca, NY: Cornell University Press, 1993.

Irigaray, L. *This Sex Which is Not One*, trans. Catherine Porter. Ithaca, NY: Cornell University Press, 1985.

Irigaray, L. *The Way of Love*, trans. H. Bostic and S. Pluháček. London: Continuum, 2002.

Irigaray, L. *Sharing the World*. London: Continuum Press, 2008.

Jameson, F. *Valences of the Dialectic*. New York: Verso, 2009.

Joyce, J. *Selected Letters*, ed. R. Ellman. London: Faber and Faber, 1975.

Kant, I. *Kritik der reinen Vernunft*. Hamburg: Felix Meiner Verlag, 1998.

Kant, I. *Schriften*. Ausgabe der königlich preussischen Akademie der Wissenschaften. Berlin: Walter de Gruyter, 1902–.

Kierkegaard, S. *Either/Or*, trans. H. Hong and E. Hong. Princeton: Princeton University Press, 1987.

Kierkegaard, S. *The Concept of Irony. With Continual Reference to Socrates*, trans. H. Hong and E. Hong. Princeton: Princeton University Press, 1989.

Kierkegaard, S. *Works of Love*, trans. H. Hong and E. Hong. New York: Harper Perennial, 2009.

King, A. 'Thinking Bourdieu Against Bourdieu: A "Practical" Critique of the Habitus', *Sociological Theory* 18 (3) (2000): 417–33.

Krell, D. F. *The Tragic Absolute: German Idealism and the Languishing of God*. Bloomington: Indiana University Press, 2005.

Kristeva, J. *Black Sun: Depression and Melancholia*, trans. L. S. Roundiez. New York: Columbia University Press, 1989.

Kristeva, J. *Tales of Love*, trans. L. S. Roundiez. New York: Columbia University Press, 1987.

Lauer, C. *The Suspension of Reason in Hegel and Schelling*. London: Continuum, 2010.

Lauer, C. 'Kierkegaard and Aristophanes on the Suspension of Irony', *Idealistic Studies* 39 (1–3) (2010): 125–36.

Lauer, C. 'Reason at Play: "The Place of Schellingian Childishness in the *Phenomenology*'s Dialectic of Reason"', *The Owl of Minerva* 38 (1–2) (2006–7): 57–76.

Lauer, C. 'Sovereign Gratitude: Hegel on Religion and the Gift', *Research in Phenomenology* 41 (3) (2011): 374–95.

Lauer, C. 'Multivalent Recognition: The Place of Hegel in the Fraser-Honneth Debate', *Contemporary Political Theory* 11 (1) (2012): 23-40.

Lauer, C. 'States of Peace: Ricoeur and Fichte on Gestures of Recognition'. In T. Mei and T. Lewin, eds., *From Ricoeur to Action*. London: Continuum, 2012.

Lefort, C. 'Flesh and Otherness'.In G. A. Johnson and M. B. Smith, eds., *Ontology and Alterity in Merleau-Ponty*, 3–13. Evanston: Northwestern University Press, 1990.

Levinas, E. *Totality and Infinity: An Essay on Exteriority*, trans. A. Lingis. Pittsburgh: Duquesne University Press, 1969.

Levinas, E. *Time and the Other*, trans. R. A. Cohen. Pittsburgh: Duquesne University Press, 1987.

Levinas, E. *Otherwise than Being: Or Beyond Essence*, trans. A. Lingis. Pittsburgh: Duquesne University Press, 1998.

Lewis, C. S. *A Grief Observed*. London: Bantam, 1960.

Lucretius. *On the Nature of Things*, trans. W. Englert. Newburyport, MA: Focus Publishing, 2003.

Macke, F. J. 'Sexuality and *Parrhesia* in the Phenomenology of Psychological Development: The Flesh of Human Communicative Embodiment and the Game of Intimacy', *Journal of Phenomenological Psychology* 38 (2007): 157–80.

MacKendrick, K. 'Sharing God's Wounds: Laceration, Communication, and Stigmata'. In A. Mitchell and J. Winfree, eds. *The Obsessions of Georges Bataille: Community and Communication*, 133–46. Albany, NY: SUNY Press, 2009.

Mauss, M. *The Gift: The Form and Reason for Exchange in Archaic Societies*, trans. W. D. Halls. New York: W. W. Norton, 1990.

Marion, J.-L. *God Without Being*, trans. T. A. Carlson. Chicago: University of Chicago Press, 1995.

Marion, J.-L. *Being Given*, trans. J. L. Kosky. Stanford: Stanford University Press, 2002.

Marion, J.-L. *In Excess: Studies of Saturated Phenomena*, trans. R. Horner and V. Berraud. New York: Fordham University Press, 2002.

Marion, J.-L. 'The Reason of the Gift', trans. S. Mackinlay and N. de Warren. In I. Leask and E. Cassidy, eds., *Givenness and God: Questions of Jean-Luc Marion*, 101–34. New York: Fordham University Press, 2005.

Marion, J.-L. *The Erotic Phenomenon*, trans. S. E. Lewis. Chicago: University of Chicago Press, 2007.

Markell, P. *Bound by Recognition*. Princeton: Princeton University Press, 2003.

Markovits, D. 'Promise as an Arm's-length Relation'. In H. Sheinman, ed., *Promises and Agreements: Philosophical Essays*, 295-326. Oxford: Oxford University Press, 2011.

Marx, K. *Capital, Volume 1*, trans. B. Fowkes. London: Penguin, 1990.

Mashek, D. and A. Aron, eds. *Handbook of Closeness and Intimacy*. Mahwah, NJ: Lawrence Erlbaum, 2004

McAdams, D. P. 'Human Motives and Personal Relationships'. In V. J. Derlega, ed., *Communication, Intimacy and Close Relationships*, 41–70. Orlando: Academic Press, 1984.

McGrath, S. J. *The Dark Ground of Spirit: Schelling and the Unconscious*. New York: Routledge, 2012.

Merleau-Ponty, M. *The Visible and the Invisible*, trans. A. Lingis. Evanston: Northwestern University Press, 1968.

Menand, L. 'Silence, Exile, Punning: James Joyce's Chance Encounters', *The New Yorker*, 2 July 2012, 71–5.

Meyer, M., S. Baumen, D. Wildgruber and K. Alter. 'How the Brain Laughs: Comparative Evidence from Behavioral, Electrophysiological, and Neurorimaging Studies in Human and Monkey', *Behavioral Brain Research* 182 (2) (2007): 245–60.

Milbank, J. 'Can a Gift be Given? Prolegomena to a Future Trinitarian Metaphysic', *Modern Theology* 11 (1) (1995).

Montaigne, M. de. *On Friendship*, trans. M. A. Screech. New York: Penguin, 1991.

Nancy, J.-L. *The Birth to Presence*, trans. B. Holmes et al. Stanford, CA: Stanford University Press, 1993.

Nancy, J.-L. *The Experience of Freedom*, trans. B. McDonald. Stanford, CA: Stanford University Press, 1988.

Nancy, J.-L. *The Inoperative Community*, trans. P. Connor et al. Minneapolis: University of Minnesota Press, 1991.

Nancy, J.-L. *Being Singular Plural*, trans. R. D. Richardson and Anne E. O'Byrne. Stanford, CA: Stanford University Press, 2000.

Nancy, J.-L. *Hegel: The Restlessness of the Negative*, trans. J. E. Smith and S. Miller. Minneapolis: Minnesota University Press, 2002.

Nancy, J.-L. *A Finite Thinking*, trans. S. Sparks. Stanford, CA: Stanford University Press, 2003.

Nancy, J.-L. *Corpus*, trans. R. A. Rand. New York: Fordham University Press, 2008.

Nancy, J.-L. *Noli me Tangere: On the Raising of the Body*, trans. S. Clift et al. New York: Fordham University Press, 2008.

Nietzsche, F. *Kritische Studienausgabe* (15 vols.), eds. G. Colli and M. Montinari. Munich: Deutscher Taschenbuch Verlag, 1967–77.

Nietzsche, F. *Beyond Good and Evil*, trans. W. Kaufmann. New York: Vintage, 1989.

Nietzsche, F. *On the Genealogy of Morals*, trans. W. Kaufmann. New York: Vintage, 1989.

O'Learey, J. 'The Gift: A Trojan Horse in the Citadel of Phenomenology?' In I. Leask and E. Cassidy, eds., *Givenness and God: Questions of Jean-Luc Marion*, 135–66. New York: Fordham University Press, 2005.

O'Rourke, M. *The Long Goodbye: A Memoir*. New York: Riverhead Books, 2011.

Panksepp, J. 'Neuroevolutionary Sources of Laughter and Social Joy: Modeling Primal Human Laughter in Laboratory Rats', *Behavioral Brain Research* 182 (2007): 231–44.

Panksepp, J. and J. Burgdorf. '"Laughing" Rats and the Evolutionary Antecedents of Human Joy?' *Physiology and Behavior* 79 (3) (2003): 533–47.

Parkes, C. M. *Bereavement: Studies of Grief in Adult Life*. Madison, CT: International Universities Press, 1987.

Parry, B. C. 'Inventing Iris: Negotiating the Unexpected Spatialities of Intimacy', *History of the Human Sciences* 21 (4) (2008): 34–48.

Perniola, M. *The Sex Appeal of the Inorganic: Philosophies of Desire in the Modern World*, trans. M. Verdicchio. London: Continuum, 2004.

Plato. *Symposium*, trans. A. Sharon. Newburyport, MA: Focus Publishing, 1998.

Plato. *Phaedo*, trans. E. Brann et al. Newburyport, MA: Focus Publishing, 1998.

Plato. *Phaedrus*, trans. S. Scully. Newburyport, MA: Focus Publishing, 2003.

Plato. *Republic*, trans. J. Sachs. Newburyport, MA: Focus Publishing, 2007.

Popper, K. *Popper Selections*, ed. D. Miller. Princeton, NJ: Princeton University Press, 1985.

Prager, K. J. *The Psychology of Intimacy*. New York: Guilford, 1995.

Provine, R. R. and K. R. Fischer. 'Laughing, Smiling, and Talking: Relation to Sleeping and Social Context in Humans', *Ethology* 95: 291–98.

Putnam, R. D. *Bowling Alone: The Collapse and Revival of American Community*. New York: Touchtone Books, 2000.

Ramachandran, V. S. *A Brief Tour of Human Consciousness: From Impostor Poodles to Purple Numbers*. New York: Pi Press, 2004.

Roberts, L. J. 'From Bickering to Battering: Destructive Conflict Processes in Intimate Relationships'. In P. Noller and J. A. Feeney, eds., *Close Relationships: Functions, Forms and Processes*, 325–51. New York: Psychology Press, 2006.

Sallis, J. *Logic of Imagination: The Expanse of the Elemental*. Bloomington, IN: Indiana University Press, 2012.

Scarry, E. *The Body in Pain: The Making and Unmaking of the World*. Oxford: Oxford University Press, 1985.

Schallow, F. 'Fantasies and Fetishes: The Erotic Imagination and the Problem of Embodiment', *The Journal of the British Society for Phenomenology* 40 (1) (2009): 66–82.

Schelling, F. W. J. *Die Weltalter*, ed. M. Schröter. Munich: C. H. Beck, 1966.

Schelling, F. W. J. *The Ages of the World*, trans. J. M. Wirth. Albany, NY: SUNY Press, 2000.

Schelling, F. W. J. *First Outline of a System of the Philosophy of Nature*, trans. K. R. Peterson. Abany, NY: SUNY Press, 2004.

Schelling, F. W. J. *Schellings sämmtliche Werke*, ed. K. Friedrich August Schelling, 156–61. Stuttgart-Augsburg: J. G. Cotta.

Scott, C. *The Lives of Things*. Bloomington, IN: Indiana University Press, 2002.

Shiffrin, S. 'Promising, Intimate Relationships, and Conventionalism', *Philosophical Review* 117 (4) (2008): 481–524.

Shipton, P. *The Nature of Entrustment: Intimacy, Exchange, and the Sacred in Africa*. New Haven: Yale University Press, 2007.

Turkle, S. *Alone Together: Why We Expect More from Technology and Less from Each Other*. New York: Basic Books, 2011.

Vlastos, G. *Platonic Studies*. Princeton: Princeton University Press, 1981.

Wallace, D. F. *Oblivion: Stories*, 141–81. New York: Little, Brown, and Company, 2004.

Wendling, A. *Karl Marx on Technology and Alienation*. New York: Palgrave Macmillan, 2009.

Wiman, C. *My Bright Abyss: Meditation of a Modern Believer*. New York: Farrar, Straus and Giroux, 2013.

Willett, C. 'Engage the Enemy: Cavell, Comedies of Remarriage, and the Politics of Friendship'. In S. Sullivan and D. Schmidt, eds., *Difficulties of Ethical Life*, 88–111. New York: Fordham University Press, 2008.

Winfree, J. 'The Contestation of Community'. In A. Mitchell and J. Winfree, eds., *The Obsessions of Georges Bataille: Community and Communication*, 31–45. Albany, NY: SUNY Press, 2009.

Williams, R. R. *Recognition: Fichte and Hegel on the Other*. Albany, NY: SUNY Press, 1992.

Žižek, S. *Tarrying with the Negative: Kant, Hegel, and the Critique of Ideology*. Durham, NC: Duke University Press, 1993.

Žižek, S. *The Indivisible Remainder: An Essay on Schelling and Related Matters*. London: Verso, 1996.

Index

absence 19, 23, 25–8, 64, 65, 88,
    108, 110, 135–6, 143, 148, 178
accessibility 37, 41, 50, 69–70, 101,
    119, 132, 143, 149, 150, 174
Allen, Woody 47, 126–7
anthropology 23, 38–9, 155, 169
    between, the 57–70, 71, 73, 74,
        76, 82, 84, 110, 116, 119, 124,
        126, 135, 142, 149, 179
    beyond, the 61, 63, 66, 74, 82,
        126
Aristotle
    on dialectics 165
    on friendship 1, 22–5
    on touching 36–7, 43, 77
    see also familiarity (συνήθεια)
Augustine of Hippo 13, 117, 124, 139,
    193

Bashō Matsuo 192
Bataille, Georges 116, 139, 152, 174,
    175, 189, 190, 193, 194
Beauvoir, Simone de
    dialectical thought 44, 155, 174,
        194
    Ethics of Ambiguity, The 13
    L'invitee (She Came to Stay) 85–8,
        92
    myth and sexuality 38–40, 42, 44,
        174
    Second Sex, The 38–40, 44, 174
Benjamin, Jessica 11, 58, 72, 76
Bergson, Henri 119
Blanchot, Maurice 152, 180
boundary 26, 142, 185
Bourdieu, Pierre 22–3, 25, 28, 30, 74,
    168–70
Bowlby, John 13, 166, 187
Butler, Judith 152, 180, 196

Carson, Anne 142–4, 146
commitment 82, 108–9, 127–9, 133,
    134, 156, 191
consummation 18, 46, 54, 60–2, 64,
    66, 75, 84, 100, 101, 123, 165,
    172, 174

Darwin, Charles 41, 180
death 8, 51, 53, 64, 90, 93, 108, 124,
    135–6, 139–54, 181, 190, 191,
    194, 195
deconstruction 7–9, 155–6, 164, 173, 196
Deleuze, Gilles 84, 165
Derrida, Jacques
    deconstruction 7, 196
    gifts 20–4, 167, 168, 169–70
    heartbeat 178
    mourning 150–1, 156, 194, 195
    touching 35, 36, 172
Descartes, René 10, 55, 61
Doubting Thomas 41–2

Eucharist 40, 173

familiarity (συνήθεια) 3, 23, 24, 47, 56,
    74, 88, 114, 117, 120, 124, 128,
    129
feelings 3–4, 35, 36, 38, 55, 56, 72,
    77–8, 82, 93–5, 108, 117, 135,
    140–1, 144, 161, 162, 183
festival 117, 121–3, 190
fetish
    and the between 70, 83
    definition of 71–2, 181–2
    dialectic of 71–82, 83, 133, 173,
        181–4, 195
    dissolved by mêlée 116–18, 122,
        189
    faith as 60, 86

opposed to commitment 125–30, 132
opposed to debate 111–13
opposed to embedding 88, 89, 94
opposed to humor 120
secret as 84–5
virginity 38–40
Fichte, J. G. 19–22, 28, 31, 112, 168, 171
Fraser, Nancy 3
fraudulence 95–7, 149
Freud, Sigmund 71, 136, 145–7, 153, 156, 181–2, 194

Gadamer, Hans-Georg 162–3, 190
ghosts 33, 158, 197
Gordon, Jill 161, 185

Habermas, Jürgen 11, 153
Hegel, G. W. F.
    dialectics 5–7, 10, 49, 155, 163, 181, 196
    intimacy in the family 162, 179
    inverted world 102
    neuter 61
    phenomenology 9, 142, 166, 192
    recognition 2, 100, 133, 161
    science 157
Heidegger
    death 150, 195
    on dialectics 4
    leaping in 130, 191
Honneth, Axel 2, 11, 166
humour 118–21, 153, 189
Husserl, Edmund 7, 9, 167
Hyde, Lewis 167–8, 170

identification 132–5, 191, 192
immortality 140
interests 20, 23, 66, 69–70, 71–5, 79–80, 82, 101, 112, 131, 132, 181, 182
intimacy
    contrasted with *Innigkeit* 48
    contrasted with love 2, 59
    etymology of 4, 8, 33, 36, 67, 70
Irigaray, Luce
    the between 57–8, 59, 60–7, 70, 136

chiasm 35
longing for meaning 14
neuter 61, 86, 104, 179
on touching 176
irony
    contrasted with gifts 27
    contrasted with humour 119–20, 189
    dialectic of 89–94, 125
    in mourning 150, 151, 192
    perfect instance of 92
    pure versus mastered 185
    role in fraudulence 95–7
    Socratic 90, 91, 185
    threat to dialectic of intimacy 93
    transition to conflict 100–4, 109, 116

Jameson, Frederic 153, 164
Jesus 38, 41, 42
jokes 92, 119–20, 153
Joyce, James 92

Kant, Immanuel
    disparagement of dialectics 4
    laughter 118
    marriage 78, 183
    promises 80
    transcendental conditions 158, 164
Kierkegaard, Søren
    the "between" 57, 58
    gifts 180
    humour 120
    the interesting 181
    irony 89–91, 93, 102–3, 185
    love 1, 59, 62–6, 126
    mourning 193
    typologies 13
Kristeva, Julia 161, 194

laughter 118–21, 123, 152, 175, 189, 190
law of the excluded middle 136
Levinas, Emanuel
    the caress 175
    the Other 14, 67, 144
    on virginity 42, 175
    play 7
    the third 185

Lucretius 42, 71

Marion, Jean-Luc
  event 58–9
  gifts and absence 25–6, 170–1
  mourning 142, 148
  touching 172, 174
  see also saturated phenomena
Mark, Gospel of 38
Markell, Patchen 3, 161
Marx, Karl 5, 6, 74, 155, 162, 182, 197
Mauss, Marcel 20, 22, 167, 169
mêlée 110, 115–24, 140, 151
Merleau-Ponty, Maurice
  on Beauvoir's She Came to Stay
    87
  seeing as if for the first time 46–7,
    55
  touching 34–6, 77, 172
millenarianism 123–4, 125
Montaigne, Michel de 1, 58, 70, 83,
    84, 85, 102, 166, 184
moods 85, 163
mosh pits 118, 120

Nancy, Jean-Luc
  Being Singular Plural 36, 67, 115,
    164, 181
  Catholic Eucharist 40, 173–44
  dialectics 196
  gifts 26, 181
  mêlée 115, 122–3, 188
  mourning 141
  rupture 57–9, 67–8, 180
  touching 34–6,175–6
Nietzsche, Friedrich 13, 27, 80, 102

orgasm 172, 188, 190
O'Rourke, Meghan 192, 193, 195

Panksepp, Jaak 41, 189
peekaboo 72, 104
Perniola, Mario 76–8, 182, 183
Plato
  dialectics 4–5, 155, 163
  love for Socrates 91, 185
  Phaedrus 28–31
play 7–8, 73, 79, 83, 86, 101, 104,
    118, 128, 136, 164, 165, 169

Popper, Karl 5
Prager, Karen 6, 166
progressive aspect 33–4, 39, 40, 45,
    49, 52, 54–6, 77, 115, 144, 176
promises
  dialectic of 80–2, 155–6, 183, 184
  gifts as 18, 19, 24, 27–30
  opposed to commitment 127–9, 134
proportion 36–8, 46, 173
psychoanalysis 12, 95, 157, 165, 194
public displays of affection 91–2, 94,
    185–6

race 75
Ramachandran, V. S. 3
 reverse-dispute 131
Ricoeur, Paul 17, 25, 30, 161

Sartre, Jean-Paul 14, 174
saturated phenomena 10, 54, 142
Scarry, Elaine 34, 175
Schallow, Frank 182
Schelling, F. W. J.
  dialectics 10, 155, 164
  heartbeat 45, 48–54, 177
  identity philosophy 93, 165, 178
  indifference 55, 56
  on ὀργιασμός 188
Scott, Charles 55–6
secret 3, 26, 84–5, 90, 100, 122, 185,
    186, 195
seriousness 7, 104, 189
sight/vision 17, 34, 36, 45, 63, 121,
    167, 172, 173

Taylor, Charles 1, 2
tickling 41–2, 118–19, 175, 189
Tully, James 3

virtual 130, 135

Wallace, David Foster 52, 95–6, 186
Wiman, Christian 59–60
wound 41–4, 73, 109–10, 118, 123,
    167, 172, 174, 175, 176, 180,
    189

Žižek, Slavoj 130
Zurn, Christopher 3

www.ingramcontent.com/pod-product-compliance
Lightning Source LLC
Chambersburg PA
CBHW062024270326
41929CB00014B/2305